A LONELY KIND OF WAR

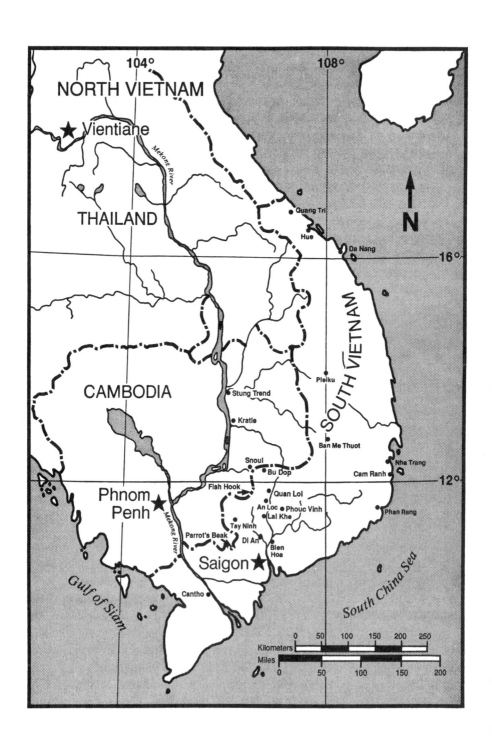

A LONELY KIND OF WAR
Forward Air Controller, Vietnam

Marshall Harrison

PRESIDIO

All of the names in this book have been changed to protect the anonymity of the people involved. In addition, an astute reader may recognize that I have played loose with the geography of South Vietnam and the location of American units in several instances to further protect the identies of those about whom the story is written. Nevertheless, the characters and events described in this book are real.

Published by Presidio Press
505 B San Marin Drive, Suite 300
Novato, CA 94945-1340

This edition printed 1997

Library of Congress Cataloging-in-Publication Data

Harrison, Marshall, 1933–
    A lonely kind of war : forward air controller, Vietnam / by Marshall Harrison.
        p. cm./
    ISBN 0-89141-352-9 (hardcover)
    ISBN 0-89141-638-2 (paperback)
    1. Vietnam Conflict, 1961–1975—Personal narratives, American. 2. Vietnam Conflict, 1961–1975—Artillery operations, American. 3. Harrison, Marshall, 1933–   . I. Title.
    DS559.5H37 1989
    959.704'348—dc20   89-32055
                                                                            CIP

Printed in the United States of America

Contents

This book is dedicated to my brother and best friend, Chief Warrant Officer Richard Harrison, a Vietnam gunship pilot who survived the hell of Tet, 1968, only to lose his life in a helicopter crash at Fort Sill, Oklahoma. A gallant warrior and a gentle man.

Prologue

Forward air controllers, FACs, as they were called, were a small group of dedicated ex-jet pilots flying lightly armed and slow-moving aircraft in South Vietnam. Their job was to find, fix, and direct airstrikes against an elusive enemy, concealed for the most part by the heavy rainforest and jungles. It was a near-impossible proposition to precisely locate the targets hidden beneath the heavy tree growth, then direct the bombs dropped by their fighter pilot brethren, often against an enemy engaged in close contact with friendly troops. For the FAC, the question always foremost in his mind was how close dare he bring in the bombs without injury to the friendlies and still thwart an enemy attack.

These forward air controllers were proud of the job they did and the respect it earned them from friend and foe alike. These "bringers of death," as their enemy called them, roamed the battlefields and were seldom far from any action on the ground. They lived with the troops in the field and flew from unimproved airstrips, and virtually controlled the aerial battlefields of South Vietnam. Their losses were staggering and they usually died alone. They were brave men and I am proud to have been one of them.

Glossary

AAA   Antiaircraft artillery. Rapid-firing cannon or machine guns, often with interlocking fields of fire.

ALO   Air liaison officer.

AO   Area of operation.

APU   Auxiliary power unit. A mobile power cart used for starting aircraft, particularly jet aircraft.

Arc Light   Code name for B-52 bomb strikes in South Vietnam, Laos, and Cambodia.

Arty   Artillery.

BDA   Bomb damage assessment.

Bingo   A minimum fuel state for safe return to base. Not an emergency situation but could develop into one if not carefully watched.

Call sign   The identifying words assigned to an aircraft for the purpose of radio communications.

C and C   Command and control. Sometimes called Charley-Charley.

CAP   Combat air patrol. Fighter aircraft which provide cover for strike or rescue aircraft.

CBU   Cluster bomb unit.

CCS   Command and Control South. A field command established by MACSOG to control unconventional warfare in southern Indochina.

DASC   Direct Air Support Center.

DEROS   Date of estimated return overseas. The magical date when one was supposed to leave Vietnam.

Didi   Vietnamese for move quickly or run.

DZ   Drop zone. The place of intended landing for parachutists or parachute-dropped supplies.

FAC   Forward air controller. The pilot who controls attacking strike aircraft engaged in close air support of friendly troops or against other targets.

FO   Forward observer. A soldier who coordinates and directs artillery against enemy locations. May be done from the ground or air.

FOL   Forward operating location. The forwardmost base where USAF deployed its forward air control aircraft and personnel.

HE   High explosive.

KBA   Killed by air. By either fixed-wing aircraft or helicopter.

KIA   Killed in action.

Klick   Kilometer.

LOH   Light observation helicopter. Pronounced "loach."

LRRP   Long range reconnaissance patrol. Pronounced "lurp."

MACSOG/SOG   Military Assistance Command Vietnam, Studies and Observations Group. Responsibilities included the unconventional warfare and cross-border operations in Laos, Cambodia, and North Vietnam.

Napalm/Nape   An incendiary, usually air delivered as an anti-personnel weapon.

NVA   North Vietnamese Army.

Over the fence   Military operations, normally covert, carried out against targets in Laos, Cambodia, or North Vietnam by U.S. or U.S.-backed forces.

PSP   Pierced steel planking. Interlocking metal planks which can be used to quickly construct a runway.

R and R   Rest and recreation.

RP   Rendezvous point. An easily identifiable point on the ground over which the FAC can meet his attack aircraft.

RTU   Replacement training unit. An organization charged with training replacement pilots for the various combat commands during the Vietnamese war.

SAM   Surface-to-air missiles.

SAR   Search and recovery.

SCU   Special commando units.

SF   United States Army Special Forces. The Green Berets.

Slicks   Lift helicopters.

Snake-eye   Bomb designed so that after release fins pop open to act as air brakes which allow the bomb to fall far behind the attacking aircraft. This decreases the risk of damage to the aircraft from the bomb blast.

SOI   Special operating instructions. A booklet issued to all participants on a radio net. It carried daily codes, call signs, and frequencies.

TACP   Tactical Air Control Party. All USAF personnel located at the FOL to support the forward air control mission.

TIC   Troops-in-contact. A situation in which ground troops have made sustained contact with an enemy force. From a FAC's point of view it implies that the enemy and friendly troops are in a close proximity.

TOC   Tactical Operations Center. The operations center for an army unit.

VC   The communists of South Vietnam. A contraction of Vietnam Cong San. VC could be fulltime (hardcore) or sometime soldiers. Distinguishable from the fulltime soldiers of the NVA.

VNAF   Vietnamese Air Force.

VR   Visual reconnaissance. The USAF forward air controller spent most of his time engaged in airborne VR, attempting to confirm or to locate new targets in his AO.

WIA   Wounded in action.

Willie Pete   A white phosphorous warhead installed on a rocket or artillery round. Used to mark a target with a large ball of white smoke easily identified by an observer.

PART 1

Binh Duong Province

The radio came alive with the flight leader's voice just as I saw them.

"Blade Flight, check in."

"Two."

"Three."

"Sidewinder Two-one, this is Blade Lead. Are you up this frequency?"

"Blade Lead, this is Sidewinder Two-one," I replied. "I've got you loud and clear. Go ahead with your lineup."

"Rog, Sidewinder; Blade Flight is three F-100s, all loaded with snake and nape, plus a full load of twenty mike-mike."

With a grease pencil I copied this onto the Plexiglas of my canopy for reference during the strike. There weren't any surprises here; it was a standard load for preplanned strikes in-country. Snakes were retarded bombs and napes were napalm. Each plane also had a full load of 20mm cannon ammunition on board.

"Blade Flight, this is Sidewinder Two-one. The targets today are reported bunkers, although I haven't been able to pick them up. The elevation is about 650 feet. I've seen no ground fire, so I'd like you to run in on an east-west heading, with a left break off target. I'll be orbiting over the target at about 1,500 feet. The best bailout area is back toward home plate and I'll clear each pass. I want you to call the target and the FAC in sight before each pass. Any questions?" I wanted them to be particularly sure that they had the forward air controller (FAC) in sight. That was me.

"Blade Lead, negative. OK Blade Flight, take your positions; let's arm 'em up."

"Two."

"Three."

"Blade Lead, this is Sidewinder. I want 'em dropped in pairs with the snake first."

"Rog. Blade has you visually over the Testicles."

"OK, I also have you. The target is about five klicks north. I'm turning toward it now."

I watched over my shoulder as they dropped down to their perch altitude from which they would be rolling in to deliver the bombs. They moved into trail position as they descended over the rendezvous point, a prominent double oxbow in a slow-moving, dirty-looking river, charmingly nicknamed the Testicles. From 2,000 feet the countryside was a brilliant, verdant green that almost hurt the eyes. A true triple-canopy jungle with the tallest emergents thrusting out more than 200 feet in their search for sunlight. The green was broken only by several old bomb craters showing the nutrient-poor laterite beneath the luxuriant growth. From the air the green was deceptive. It looked so solid that you would have thought it impossible to move through it; however, the bomb craters gave away its secret. Looking diagonally down at the green, it was apparent that beneath the solid treetops was an almost parklike growth. The lack of sunlight beneath the branches discouraged any forest floor growth except for a few of the hardiest, shade-loving plants. Accurate map reading was impossible from the air or the ground, and some friendly long-range reconnaissance patrol (LRRP) unit could be lurking down there in the bushes despite the fact that I had checked all known friendly locations before takeoff.

I glanced again at my map where I had marked the target on one of the one-kilometer grids, and I thought I was as close as I'd be able to get to it. I double-checked the area but still didn't see anything moving. I could only hope that if the friendlies were down there they'd have enough sense to try to contact someone when the bombs began falling around them. Except for a few dry streambeds, the map showed only solid green squares in every direction, indicating solid tree growth. One streambed to the west meandered toward the sluggish river, its bed now cracking into geometric patterns as the dry season became firmly entrenched in the countryside. The shape of the streambed didn't correspond to the bright blue line on my map. It probably changed courses several times a season, staying one step ahead of the mapmakers. I had only the roughest idea of where the target was supposed to be. I had tried to triangulate on any features I could find, but with the solid tree growth I wouldn't have bet on my accuracy. If there were indeed bunkers down there, they weren't visible from the air. For that matter they may have been ten years old and only recently resurrected from a moldy file by an intelligence officer hunting for some sort of target. Almost certainly, there would be no enemy troops in them. Their intelligence was normally better than that.

"OK, Blade Flight. Sidewinder is in for the marking pass." I put the stick over and rolled into a forty-degree dive. The lighted sight in the windscreen drifted over and settled near a prominent tree that I could use as a reference point during the air strike. With all the twisting and turning I'd be doing trying to keep track of the fighters, I'd need a good reference point. Since I didn't really know where the target was anyway, this tree was as good as any other. We were probably going to be making toothpicks out of perfectly good trees anyway. I armed one rocket pod and punched the firing button on the stick, then watched the rocket down to the ground. It wasn't bad—about twenty meters south of the trees. The smoke blossomed as the white phosphorous warhead detonated, the small white cloud standing out vividly against the wild green backdrop. It made a perfect target, although its usefulness would be short-lived as the smoke from the exploding bombs and their shock waves blended and mixed. No problem there though: my Bronco carried twenty-seven more marking rockets.

"Blade Lead, put your first bombs about twenty meters north of my smoke."

"Roger, Sidewinder. Twenty north of the smoke. Lead is in from the east with the FAC and target in sight."

"Blade Lead, this is Sidewinder. You're cleared in hot."

The first pair of bombs detonated about thirty meters south of the white ball of smoke.

"Pretty good, Lead," I said as I hauled the aircraft around in a tight, sixty-degree banked turn to face the number two aircraft already starting his dive. The marking smoke was already being blown away from the target, but now there were two bomb craters to use as a reference. I banked the Bronco quickly upon each wing, eyeballing the area exposed by the first pair of blasts. No bunkers were visible.

"Blade Two is in hot from the east, FAC and target in sight."

"Blade Lead is off left." His voice was fuzzy over the radio from the heavy g-force he was pulling.

"Blade Two, you're cleared in hot," I said. "Put 'em about thirty meters long on Lead's craters."

"Roger."

I flew directly at him until I was sure his run-in angle was good, and as he passed beneath me in his dive, I started a tight diving left turn to keep him in sight. Both bombs were good but they didn't uncover anything that looked promising.

"Blade Two is off to the left."

"Blade Three is in from the east with the FAC and target in sight." This one sounded nervous. Probably new in-country, which wasn't a crime. We all started there not too long ago. I'd have to watch him pretty closely though, for most new guys tried to press things a little beyond their capabilities. If he was a newbie he'd be all thumbs and elbows in the cockpit right about now, afraid he'd screw up.

"You're cleared in hot, Blade Three." Jesus Christ! As I spoke the words clearing him to start his bomb run, I saw two snake-eye bombs separate from his aircraft, at least 400 meters short of the target area. The explosions were more than a quarter mile on the far side of the dry streambed.

"Blade Flight, hold high and dry," I said as I banked my aircraft to stay out of his way. Well, no real damage done, since there were not supposed to be friendly troops anywhere in the area. It would probably be best not to make too big a deal out of it. But if there had been friendlies, I'd have fried his ass, new guy or not.

I tried to keep my voice light. "Blade Three, you were just a tad short there. Any problems?"

"Negative," he stammered, sounding very young.

"OK, Blade Three," I said. "No damage done. Let's see if we can't do some good bombing." We might as well let him practice a bit, I thought. Today's environment was hardly hostile, but his next flight might involve a troops-in-contact situation where a short bomb like he'd just delivered would be a disaster. We all had plenty of fuel and I had no pressing engagements for the next nine months.

"OK Lead, this is Sidewinder. Let's drop singles from now on. If you have me in sight you're cleared in hot." Maybe they'll buy me a drink the next time I'm at Bien Hoa, if I'm nice to them. We FACs are great at cadging drinks at the fighter clubs when we have the opportunity. Some blackmail is implied but unspoken in this, for we call in the results of their bombing, which, in turn, determines the scores of their fitness reports.

"Good idea, Sidewinder. Are you going to re-mark?" the lead pilot asked.

"Yeah, I'm in for the new mark now." I was almost directly over the target, so I rolled inverted and pulled through the horizon until I was headed down in an almost vertical dive. I had too many g's on the aircraft to shoot accurately, but what the hell? I didn't know what I was shooting at anyway. I punched off another rocket and watched the white smoke erupt from the tree canopy.

"Hit my smoke, Lead. If you have the target and the FAC, you're cleared in hot."

"Lead is in from the east, FAC and target in sight."

We played stateside gunnery range for the next few passes. The Lead pilot got into the spirit of things and began coaching his new wingman between his own runs. I took the part of the range officer, calling errors for number three by azimuth and distance. We'd all come to the same conclusion: There wasn't jackshit beneath those trees.

Blade Three pulled up sharply on his next pass; I didn't see any explosions.

"Three, this is Sidewinder. You must have had a dud. I didn't see anything go off."

"Negative, Sidewinder. I didn't release. I think somebody was shooting at me."

His voice was uncertain but it got everyone's attention. You could almost feel the tension increase over the radio. I slammed over into a vertical turn, pulling the stick back as hard as I dared.

"Blade Flight, hold high and dry. Three, where did it look like it was coming from?" Damn! I was supposed to be the one to see any ground fire, not some rookie pilot on his first in-country mission.

"It looked like tracers coming from those trees," he said, "just south of where I dropped those short bombs."

He was new and wouldn't know a lot about ground fire yet, but surely he'd know a tracer coming up at him if he saw it. Sometimes, though, they can be hard to see during the daylight on a 400-knot bombing run. Perhaps he'd seen the sun glint off a stream beneath the tree line; that sometimes looked like ground fire. Maybe he'd seen some debris from one of the other bomb blasts, which had been flung skyward. And maybe one day I'd be chief of staff. Actually I had already accepted the fact that he'd uncovered something with his wild-assed bombing. Maybe we'd never been in the right place to begin with. I sure wasn't that positive of having found the exact coordinates on my map. I checked to see that the fighters were holding in a racetrack pattern well above me and out of my way, then pushed the throttles forward and turned toward the craters marking Blade Three's first bombing effort.

"Break, Sidewinder. They're hosing you down!"

I had already figured that. The left side panel of my canopy starred crazily from a small-caliber bullet. That concerned me but not as much as the two streams of green tracers drifting toward me. Without thinking, I again rolled inverted and dove for the treetops, which seemed to be the safest haven at the moment, since heavy-caliber weapon fire was sweeping the sky. It could be either a .50 caliber or a 12.7mm, either of which could be disastrous to an OV-10 Bronco doing 180 knots. Ten feet over the treetops I turned north and looked back at the tracers falling away. There was also the flash of small automatic weapons winking at me from beneath the tree line surrounding the bomb craters. I found I had instinctively hunched my shoulders and tightened my sphincter the way I always did when being fired upon. It doesn't do any good, but you feel like you're doing something.

Pulling the stick back sharply, I traded airspeed for altitude. At 5,000 feet, I leveled off and took stock. First, I had to admit to myself that I had made a serious mistake in judgment. No way should I have flown over that area without knowing a little something about what was going on. The round through the canopy was the only damage I could see. Some little man with an AK-47 had almost put my eye out for me. I had gotten away luckier than I deserved. I became conscious of Blade Lead trying to reach me over the radio.

"Lead, this is Sidewinder. Just got a little careless and took one through the Plexiglas. No damage done. Blade Three was right though— they're down there. I don't know in what strength, but they're shooting mad. There are at least two heavy automatic weapons and I saw several AKs but didn't stick around to count them. What kind of ordnance do you have left?"

"We should each have one bomb and two napes left, plus the twenty mike-mike."

That wasn't very much to be going against those people. I berated myself for not keeping track of the remaining weapon load for that was part of my job. I had allowed myself to be lulled by what I thought was going to be a cakewalk. Carelessness got a lot of people killed over here.

"OK, Blade Flight. I'm going to come in from the north at 2,000 and mark from there. Since there are no friendlies around, you'll be cleared in on a heading of your choice. Break off the target is also your option, just let me know which way you're going so I can stay out of your way."

I swore at myself for having squandered the bombs. The napalm would be almost useless with this tree cover, since it would have to be delivered in a high-angle dive to get any sort of penetration through the trees. The normal flattened delivery allowed for a great deal of spread, but released from a more vertical dive the greatest danger was probably getting conked on the head by the canister. The 20mm cannons ran into the same problem. The heavy tree canopy would deflect or destroy most of the rounds before they could penetrate to the ground. I'd better get some help lined up in case this turned out to be more than an isolated group of Indians.

"Blade Lead, Sidewinder is going off freq for one to see if there are any alert birds available."

"Roger that. We still have more than thirty minutes of loiter left."

"OK, I'll see you back on in one."

To enhance the OV-10 Bronco's role as a forward air control aircraft, its designers had put in a marvelous communications system. Using a simple row of toggle switches and a round wafer-selector switch, the pilot could simultaneously monitor two UHF radios, two FM radios, a VHF radio, an HF radio, a secure scrambler system, an FM homer, a Guard channel radio for use in emergencies, and assorted navigational gear. However, only one radio at a time could be used for transmissions. Unfortunately, no one else on any of the nets could do the same and therefore had no idea who else was trying to talk to the FAC. This jumble of voices breaking in on each other, each call more strident than the last as they competed for the FAC's attention, often became an audio nightmare. I turned my switches to talk to my control room on UHF.

"Sidewinder Control, this is Sidewinder Two-one. Call Division and see if they've got any spare fighters in the AO. I may be needing some more real soon. If they've got 'em, have them rendezvous with me over the Testicles. Keep 'em high and have them monitor my frequency in case I don't have time to do much briefing. You may have to do their briefing yourself, so stay alert to the situation and make sure you've got the big picture. Monitor me at all times and alert Brigade that we may have uncovered something sizable. You might also get the Duty FAC cranked up in case we need him."

"Yes sir, I've already done all of that except call for more fighters. I've been listening."

"Thanks, I'll get back to you. Out."

I switched back to the fighter frequency. If Bos said it was taken care of, it was. That rotund figure was as sharp as any two-striper I had ever seen.

"Blade Flight," I called, "I'm back with you and in for another marking round."

"Rog. Watch your ass."

He could bet money on it. This time I knew there were automatic weapons down there. I chose a high-angle dive to shoot the rocket, figuring they'd have less of my profile to aim at, and also I'd be in and out of the danger zone that much quicker. Luckily, I'd used only a few of my marking rockets while we'd been assing around before. Counting backward in my memory I figured I should have at least fifteen or so left.

I eased the stick back and let the nose rise as far above the horizon as it could without beginning to shudder with an approaching stall. I tried to keep the impact point I wanted fixed in my sight. Fortunately, the airplane was designed with a canopy that provided optimum viewing angles. Thanks to the bulbous, dragonfly-eye design, you could even see directly beneath the aircraft in level flight. As the stick began shaking, indicating the approaching stall, I eased it to one side of the cockpit, holding the rudder depressed to bring the nose almost straight down toward the target. The lighted sight pipper settled just under the target. I nudged the stick back slightly, adjusting the sight until it nestled over the point I wanted. Making sure that I had no pressure on any of the controls, I punched off another rocket. Without waiting to see its impact, I put the aircraft into a maximum-rate climb turn. The g-forces pulled my lower lip down toward my navel. Releasing some of the back pressure on the stick, and consequently some of the g-forces, I was again able to talk.

"Blade Lead, this is Sidewinder. All of you drop your snakes on this pass. Lead, you hit my smoke. Blade Two, if Lead uncovers anything, be ready to go with both your napes. If he doesn't find anything, we'll go with your bomb."

"Lead, rog."

"Two, rog."

"Blade Lead is in hot with the FAC and the target in sight."

The exploding bomb came from immediately under the slowly rising remnants of my smoke rocket.

"Good bomb, Lead. Blade Two, go through dry one time while I check it out."

I had been slowly turning the aircraft to keep the lead ship on my nose as he made his pass. As his bomb exploded, I let the plane drop rapidly, building up all the airspeed I could. OK, so even at top speed it wasn't all that much. Even so, the jokes were unnecessarily cruel about an OV-10 needing radar in its tail to prevent it from being overtaken by thunderstorms.

Leveling at 500 feet, I pointed myself at the impact area. Things very quickly became interesting. Rapidly moving my eyes about the area, I picked up the blinking of automatic weapon fire from the tree line surrounding the bomb blasts. I felt several rounds strike the aircraft and fancied that I could hear the firing of the larger guns, an obvious impossibility wearing my tight-fitting ballistic helmet. The helmet was guaranteed to either stop or deflect a .30-caliber round. I didn't know if the claim was true, but like other FACs and helicopter pilots, I wanted to believe with the fervor of a disciple. Of course, if it didn't work, who would be able to complain about it?

The craters were shallow because we had been using instantaneous fusing on the bombs to blow down trees and open up the jungle. The giant hardwoods had been leveled in a large circle around each impact point. Around the lip of the shallow craters, several bodies were flung about in the uniquely grotesque postures achieved only by violent death. The movies have never been able to do justice to the position.

I bored straight ahead, shoving the nose down until I was just missing the tops of the taller trees. Clear of the hottest area, I pulled into a steep climbing turn to 1,500 feet.

"Blade Flight, it looks like we've gotten into an ants' nest down there. You've got some of them but there's still lots of automatic weapon fire. Blade Two, give me your bomb fifty meters into the tree line on any side of Lead's crater. You're cleared in hot if you have the FAC and target in sight."

"Roger, Blade Two is in hot from the east and I have the FAC and target in sight."

His bomb landed among the trees. Three strings of green tracers followed him from his dive. One stream was very close.

"Blade Two, Sidewinder. Are you OK?"

"Yeah, I think so. I felt something hit the aircraft, but I don't see any damage. They must have plinked me in the aft part of the fuselage.''

"OK, Lead, do you want to take him out of the orbit and look him over while I finish up with Blade Three?''

"Rog. Come on Two, let's head over toward the river and I'll check you out.''

Blade Three was too new for this. I was afraid we'd end up getting him hurt without anything to show for it. I had to let him go through for one last pass though, just so he wouldn't lose face with his flight.

"Blade Three, I want you to clear your racks on this pass. Call me and the target in sight and you'll be cleared in hot. Watch yourself on pullout because those guns are awfully active down there. Put everything just to the west of Two's smoke.''

"Roger. In from the east, FAC and target in sight.''

He bottomed out of his dive a little higher than normal, but it wasn't a bad bomb. The tracers had reached out again, trying to tickle his belly. I half-listened to Blade Lead checking over his wingman while I tried to decide whether or not to do another BDA (bomb damage assessment). There didn't appear to be any substantial damage to Blade Two. I decided against making another assessment.

The two F-100 pilots finished their caucus and announced they were ready to enter the fray once again. I directed them to clear all their remaining external stores on one last pass, scattering everything around the area.

"Before you leave me, Blade Flight, I'd like you each to give me a good long burst with your twenty mike-mike. I'm in for the mark now.''

I'd been cruising at 1,500 feet, out of the range of the small arms fire from below. Letting the nose slip down below the horizon, I fired another marking round without losing much altitude. They wouldn't be aiming their cannon fire at a specific target anyway, so an accurate smoke rocket was unneeded. I watched each aircraft make a single firing pass, sloshing their fire around the jungle before they regrouped and headed south toward their home base.

"Good work, Blade Flight,'' I called. "I'm giving you 100 percent of your ordnance in the target area. You're going to have to wait a bit until I can get a BDA to you. I'll pass it back to your squadron just as soon as I can. I know for sure that you got some of them though.''

What the hell? Blade Three couldn't hit a bull in the ass with a bass fiddle, but it was his short bomb that had uncovered Mister Charley.

I watched them join into a tight formation and depart. Well, back to work.

"Sidewinder Control, this is Two-one. Do you have any more fighters inbound to me?"

"Sidewinder Two-one, this is Control. Affirmative. There's a flight of F-4s, call sign Fever, parked at 18,000 over the Testicles, and a flight of F-100s, call sign Blinky, coming up shortly to the same spot at 12,000."

"Good boy. Have they been briefed?"

"Affirmative, both flights have been briefed."

"You'll go far, lad. Fever Flight, are you up this freq?"

"That's correct, Sidewinder Two-one. We're up and briefed and we've been monitoring your festivities with Blade Flight, but you boys were having so much fun we didn't want to interrupt."

"Thank you, Fever. You're a charmer, you are. If you're ready to go to work, you can go ahead with your lineup."

"Roger, Fever Flight is three Fox-Fours. We've each got a full load of snake-eyes aboard. Negative guns."

"Way to go, Fever! The bombs are what we need for that crap down there. Stand by one while I check on another flight that's inbound. Blinky Flight, are you in the neighborhood yet?"

"Blinky reads you Sidewinder and we're coming on station now with three F-100s. All aircraft have a standard load."

Shit! More napalm. I needed bombs. Better than nothing though. The problem was that any fighters we got coming off the alert pads had to be configured to work in any part of the country. Napalm and guns were good for working down in the flat and almost treeless delta. In triple-canopy rain forest, they didn't work as well.

"This is Sidewinder Two-one. I'm going to use Fever Flight first. I want you to use three passes each for your external stores. You can run in from any heading, but call FAC and target in sight on each pass and call break off target with direction. You can expect ground fire any time on the run-in. Best bailout area looks as if it's going to be back toward the south. If you get hit or have any kind of a problem, try to let me know as soon as possible. I'll put the necessary wheels into motion. If I'm badly hit, call Sidewinder Control on this frequency and pass the word. We can have another FAC here within fifteen minutes. Any questions?"

"Fever Lead. Nope."

"Blinky Lead. Negative."

Announcing that I was in for the mark, I pushed the throttles on the Garrett engines to 100 percent power, rolled inverted, picked my spot, and rolled upright again but in a seventy-degree dive. The lighted sight in the windscreen drifted onto the target and I punched the button on the stick that fired the smoke rockets. From among the trees surrounding the blast areas, I saw the sparkle of automatic weapon fire begin once more. Tracers drifted toward me, then fell away rapidly, curving well behind the aircraft. An optical illusion. Unconsciously, I had scrunched into as small a ball as possible, my ass trying to bite chunks out of the seat cushion. Which way to turn? Most of us thought it was best to just plow straight ahead and not give the gunners any more belly than necessary. Everyone except headquarters agreed that treetop flying was about the safest place to be when taking ground fire. This reduced the gunner's tracking time tremendously. You couldn't be a pussy about it though; you really had to get down to where you were just clearing the trees or you had set yourself up to be blown from the sky.

As I was literally lifting over the taller trees, another small hole appeared in my lower left canopy. I wouldn't have noticed it except for the new stream of fresh air. It also erased forever some of the data I had written on the canopy in grease pencil. Things were happening quickly. I still had no clear idea of how many we were running against or how many larger weapons they had. The ground fire seemed to be coming from everywhere. Mentally, I revised my first estimate on the number of people down there. A VC company wouldn't have the kind of firepower I was seeing. There were a lot of AK-47 muzzle blasts, but there was also a growing number of larger-caliber tracers beginning to flow again. It was puzzling that the force didn't try to break away the way they normally did, unless they were a larger unit that was prepared to stand and fight. Maybe we'd already killed the decision-makers. Highly unlikely that communist forces wouldn't have a disengagement plan, even if they lost their commanders. One thing for sure, the large-caliber weapons made them NVA. But, how many? At least a company, probably larger.

Seeking the path of least resistance, I shoved the rudders from one limit to another, skidding the aircraft away from the areas of most intense ground fire. Finally reaching calm waters again, I pulled the stick back into my belly, trying to gain all the altitude that I could, as quickly as possible. Level at 4,000 feet. That should put me well above the AK fire. The larger guns would have no problem reaching me here, but I had a pretty good idea where they were and they couldn't get the angle on me in my present position. Fever Lead was shouting at me over the radio.

"Sidewinder, are you OK? There was crap all over the place down there. Do you want me to look you over?"

"Negative. I took a few hits I think, but I don't see anything dripping out. Let's get some." Nothing noble about it. We could have horsed around all day with him trying to slow down enough to formate on me.

"Fever Lead, hit anywhere within thirty meters of my smoke."

"Rog, Lead is in hot from the north with the FAC and target in sight."

"Fever Two, Sidewinder. Start your pass immediately from that position. Aim at Lead's explosions and let's get 'em as close together as we can. You're cleared in hot." There was little chance of him hitting exactly where the lead ship's bombs had gone. Some dispersion would happen, but we should still get a good concentration. Another voice broke in on the net.

"Sidewinder Two-one, this is Sidewinder Control."

"Go ahead Bos, this is Two-one."

"Roger, Big Boy wants you to come up TOC frequency."

Great. The army brigade I was attached to wanted to talk on their Tactical Operation Center radio. As I switched frequencies, I watched Fever Two's bombs impact. They looked good. Just about where I wanted them. The smoke from all the explosions was starting to rise and drift around the area, obscuring the visibility. It was those kinds of little things that they never told you about in FAC school. Or having to talk on three radios at a time. I made the call to the army.

"Big Boy Three, this is Sidewinder Two-one."

The response was immediate. They had obviously been waiting for my call. My radio operator in the control room sat only about ten feet from his army counterpart in the TOC. Between the two of them they generally knew what was happening around the brigade's area of operations (AO). This time, however, the call was returned by the brigade ops officer, a lieutenant colonel with whom I didn't get along too well. For that matter, no one got along with him too well, perhaps because of his job, which was a real ass-kicker. Or maybe he'd always been an asshole.

"Sidewinder, this is Big Boy Three. Can you adjust some arty on that position you're working?"

"I can try to do some adjusting between air strikes. Where will they be shooting from?"

"The battery out of Poppa Victor. Also, can you give me an estimate on the number of people down there?"

"Negative, not really. I'd guess that it's more than a company from the amount of ground fire we've been receiving, but I really don't have anything to back that up."

"Roger. I understand you're unable to make a good estimate at this time. Be advised that we're launching a Blue Team to be inserted on the november side of the blue line to your sierra. We're going to have them work november-whiskey."

I tried to decipher this bit of intelligence. I'm sure that Charley, if he were listening in, didn't have nearly as much trouble with it as I did.

"You mean you're going to put some troops in on the north bank of the river and have 'em move northwest?"

Long pause.

"Affirmative."

"OK, have the choppers orbit at 2,500 feet right over the river. Sidewinder out."

I tuned my other FM radio to the artillery battery at Phouc Vinh while I tried to figure out where to put the next bombs. Glancing quickly at my map I decided to work the artillery along a north-south line about two kilometers west of the target area. That should provide sufficient blocking fire to keep the little people from disengaging in that direction and to still provide a clear area in which to work the aircraft. I scribbled these numbers onto my canopy with my trusty grease pencil. By now there were so many figures scrawled there they were starting to reduce my visibility. I switched my radio back to the fighters.

"Fever Flight, I hate to do this to you but I'm going to have to restrict your run-in heading to either north or south, with an east break off target. We're going to have arty working about two klicks west of us." We tried to avoid a constant run-in heading if at all possible. Otherwise, after the first couple of passes the gunners didn't have to be graduates of Uncle Ho's military academy to realize that the next passes would probably be down the same tube.

"OK, Sidewinder. If we gotta', we gotta'." His voice betrayed no emotion at the news, still the same drawl affected by pilots everywhere to show how cool we really are. I knew he hated the idea, particularly now that we knew there was going to be a lot of ground fire. Too bad. Let him be an accountant if he didn't like this business.

"Lead, put 'em about twenty left of the heaviest smoke down there."

"Rog. Lead is in hot from the north. FAC and target in sight."

"You're cleared in hot, Lead."

The characteristically heavy black smoke trail of the F-4 made it easy to pick up as he turned onto his final run-in heading. He was moving fast as the bombs released. Before they detonated I was in toward the target, following his path but doing about one-fourth his speed. My aircraft pitched as the shock waves from the bomb's blast hit me. As quickly as I had the plane under control again, I corrected to put the sight on a new target area, slightly north of the bomb craters. I watched my rocket impact before I pulled hard back on the stick, partially losing my vision due to the g-forces. I relaxed enough back pressure to allow me to speak.

"Fever Two and Three, you're both cleared in hot. Put your bombs right and left of my new smoke. I'm going to have to leave you for one to talk to arty. Continue to make your calls and be sure that you have me in sight before you start your runs. And Lead, you were taking ground fire through most of your run. I saw at least two heavy calibers going after you. You all watch your butts while I'm off frequency."

"Fever Lead, roger."

I listened to Fever Two make his inbound call and then quickly switched to the artillery frequency, while continuing to monitor the calls of the other fighters over the other radio.

"Logger, this is Sidewinder Two-one. Fire mission."

"Sidewinder, this is Logger. Understand you have a fire mission. Pass us the coordinates."

There was an elaborate ritual that an artillery observer used, according to the Fort Sill School for Wayward Boys and Artillery Adjustment. Forward air controllers had discovered that the tube crews were as willing to dispense with it as we were, should the situation warrant that. Paring it to the bone, we could establish contact with them, pass the target coordinates, and tell them to start shooting. Unless there was some compelling reason to do otherwise, they usually did it. I passed the target coordinates to them.

"Sidewinder Two-one, this is Logger. We're ready to shoot."

"Let her go," I said, ignoring the standard terminology. I was in a hurry to get back to the fighters' frequency.

"Sidewinder, this is Logger. Shot. Out."

"Roger, Logger. Shot," I repeated. Their white phosphorous marking round was in the air. I turned toward the dry streambed to wait for the round's impact. I rotated the wafer switch to put me back on the fighters' frequency.

"Fever Flight, a willie pete arty round will be impacting momentarily to the west of your run-in line. I'm talking to the battery, so don't worry about it."

"Fever copies. Listen, Sidewinder, we're getting the shit shot out of us."

"Rog, I know. Tell you what let's do. On the next pass everyone clean your racks on my marker. You're all cleared in hot if you have me in sight. Maintain your assigned run-in headings after release and until you're clear of the area. I'm off frequency again to give the arty a quick adjustment."

"Logger, that looks real good," I told the artillery controller. "Work it at that distance, right and left 200 meters of that point. Fire for effect."

Another frequency shift back to the fighters. In only moments I watched the 105s begin to tear up the jungle west of the bombing area. It looked pretty good and should be enough to discourage Charley from breaking in that direction.

Time to mark again. This time I used a different sort of approach. Never do the same thing twice and maybe you'd stay alive. So, I was down to the treetops and boring in toward the target at low level; a quick pop-up, thumbing the button, then back to the treetops once more. A hard right turn when the most dangerous area was passed and a quick climb back to altitude. The OV-10 looked so slow and ungainly that the NVA gunners frequently made the same mistake as a novice duck hunter. They both forgot to lead their prey sufficiently, and most shots fell somewhere behind both the aircraft and the duck. Either that or they were laughing themselves silly at the appearance of Uncle Sam's newest efforts in counterinsurgency aircraft. My turn completed, I looked at my last mark. An overshoot; a common error when trying to fire from a low angle.

"Fever Flight, put everything you have about seventy-five meters due south of my smoke. I overshot it quite a bit."

"Sidewinder, this is Fever Lead. Do you think we could get you to put in a new mark a little closer to the target? There's so much smoke down there I'm not really sure which one I'm supposed to aim at.''

Oh, sure. Why not? I'm going so slow that I have to map read across the target area, but I'll be glad to hang my bare ass out for you so that you can have your new mark. I'm tempted to tell the flight that I've changed my mind again and we'll have to drop their bombs in singles. That ought to increase his exposure time by about half an hour. Would you like that, Fever?

"Roger, Sidewinder in for the new mark."

I couldn't think of a real excuse not to do it, but I didn't want to. In fact, I would rather have done about anything else than stick my nose into that area again. At 2,500 feet I did a wingover down toward the target. It's generally acknowledged that in attacking a hot target it's all for the best to just try to ignore the ground fire coming at you. There's nothing the pilot can do about it anyway. You might as well just look straight ahead and think pure thoughts. One friend advocated shouting poetry into his oxygen mask while on the bomb run. He swore that it bored him so much he forgot to be frightened.

The forward air controller unfortunately cannot do this. He must see as much of the target area as he can in order to place the bombs with maximum effectiveness. During this process, he also gets to see many unfriendly faces. In the fifteen seconds it took to dive and launch a new marking rocket, my eyes flicked painfully from point to point, dreading the sight of the tracers coming from all quadrants. Automatic weapons were twinkling from the tree lines surrounding the blast areas. I punched the rocket release on the stick and kicked hard left rudder, then fired again. Leveling at the treetops I "egressed" the area, as they like to say in military briefings.

"Fever Lead, hit the easternmost smoke. Fever Two and Three hit the westernmost mark."

A bright orange sheet of flames sprouted from the aft part of Fever Two's fuselage as he pulled out of his run. He was on fire from just behind his cockpit to the end of his tail. Something must have gotten a fuel cell and let the jet fuel pour out into the slipstream where it enveloped his aircraft.

"Get out, Two. You're on fire!"

It sounded like the voice of Fever Three. The lead ship wasn't in position to see his flaming wingman when he was hit. Unconsciously, I glanced quickly at the target, automatically registering the explosions of their bombs before turning my eyes back to the stricken fighter. The bombs looked good.

"Roger," Two's voice was tight and tense but under control. "I'm going to try to get to the other side of the river."

Good thinking. Charley probably wouldn't be too happy with one of the pilots who had just been bombing him. The pilot would be real lucky to even reach the ground alive aboard the old nylon elevator. It didn't really matter, for Fever Two suddenly exploded. One moment he was in a flying aircraft; the next he was in a close formation of junk metal, rapidly decelerating toward the ground. Most of the debris continued toward the river, clearing it to the far side.

"Fever Three, this is Lead. Let's set up an orbit over him. Did anyone see any chutes?"

I hated to be the bad guy, but that was what they were paying me for.

"Fever Flight, this is Sidewinder. Get your butts back where they belong. I'll decide whether we need a CAP or not. What are you planning on using anyway? You're out of ordnance. I'll let you know if I need your help on the SAR. But I was looking at him and no one got out. I'm going to clear you both out of the area at this time. My control is listening in on this freq and I'm sure that he's already alerted the closest rescue birds. Isn't that right, Sidewinder Control?"

"Sidewinder Two-one, this is Sidewinder Control. That's affirmative, sir. We're in the process of diverting two Hueys right now. They ought to be at your location in about five." Good old Bos.

"We've got enough fuel to cap them until the choppers arrive," Fever Three cut in. He sounded combative. This thing had gone far enough.

"Negative, Fever Flight," I said. "No one got out. Now, rejoin your leader and clear the area to the north. We've still got a war going on here."

"Goddammit, Sidewinder. You don't know that no one's alive. It's possible that you missed it."

"Fever Flight, this is Sidewinder Two-one. Get your asses out of my AO immediately. We've got work to do here and your BDA will be passed to you. Out."

There would be no free drinks for me from that squadron. I switched to the artillery frequency, gave them a quick adjustment, and told them they were doing good work. Then, quickly, I switched to the chopper frequency.

"Rescue birds inbound to the Testicles, this is Sidewinder. What's your call sign?"

"This is Roach Four-eight and Roach Five-two. We're a slick and a Charley model. We've got the smoke from the air strike up ahead. Where did that fighter go in?"

"Most of it hit the south bank of the westernmost Testicle. Some of it may have gone into the river as well. I'm positive that no one got out but we ought to look the area over anyway. Be advised that I'll be working air strikes north of the river and arty is going in northwest of the crash site. I'd suggest that you stay as low as possible."

"You can count on it, Bro." I recognized the voice. It was a huge black warrant officer who flew the old model gunships. They were pretty lightly armed, but I hadn't seen any movement in the area of the crash, and if Charley was down there he'd more than likely didi out of the area after the burning fighter fell on him, knowing that rescue choppers would soon be overhead. It shouldn't take them long for I knew there were no living friendlies down there. I was sure the helicopter pilots would recognize that too as soon as they saw the wreckage.

"Sidewinder Two-one, this is Sidewinder Control. Got an update for you. You've got a flight of VNAF A-1s inbound to the Anthill [another nearby rendezvous point] and I told their controller to park them at 8,000. There's also a company-sized Blue Team just about airborne that ought to be in the insertion area in about ten. Two snake fire teams are en route to cover the insertion. I told all of them to head to the Anthill too, and that you'd get in touch with them as soon as you could. Nestor is the gunship call sign. Unknown on the VNAF."

"Unknown sounds about right. Did their controller have any idea what sort of ordnance they were carrying?"

"That's negative, Two-one. I had trouble understanding him at all."

"Not to worry, Bos. We'll figure something out. You're doing a good job. I may adopt you when I leave."

"Thank you, sir, but I'm already spoken for by a rich, elderly nymphomaniac back in Saginaw."

"Well, shit. Maybe you two could adopt me. Out."

"Blinky Lead, this is Sidewinder Two-one. Are you folks still with me?"

"Rog, Sidewinder, but I thought I was going to lose Two and Three when that Fox-Four went down. Those boys were ready to head back to the bar."

"Your ass," growled one of the wingmen.

Callous? Maybe. I found that everyone deals with tragedy in their own way. And you did have to learn how to deal with it.

I told the flight of F-100s to descend to orbit altitude and to stand by. Clamping my knees to the control stick to keep the wings level, I reached into the leg pocket of my flight suit and brought out a baby bottle of water. I had two more left. We used them because they would fit into the pocket and didn't leak. A canteen held more water, but we were upside down almost as much as we were straight and level, and didn't relish having a two-pound projectile loose in the cockpit. I drained the bottle in a single draught, then removed my helmet and gave my head a vigorous scratching, finishing up by toweling my face with the rolled sleeve of my flight suit. The suit was completely dark with sweat. The OV-10 was not air-conditioned, relying instead on two small ram-air vents by the leg and one overhead in the canopy. The temperature in the cockpit was roughly the same as it was on the ground, possibly higher due to the sun beating down on the large canopy. Of course, I had the new, improved version with the AK-47 holes for additional cooling. Replacing my helmet, I heard Blinky Lead calling.

"Sidewinder, Blinky Flight is down to fifteen minutes loiter before we have to leave you."

"No problem, Blinky. I've got you in sight and we won't be making that many passes. You've probably heard that I'm going to have to restrict your run-in heading to north or south with an east pull-off. I'll be directly over the target at 2,000 feet. I want all your bombs on the first pass. Next pass, all of the nape. If you've got any time left after that we may try some twenty mike-mike sloshed around the area. They're getting pretty touchy, so let's try to make it in and out as quickly as we can. Keep your patterns as tight as possible and keep alert to the artillery working to the west of us. We've also got two army choppers inbound to the crash site, but they'll be working real low. Before we get started, did any of your flight happen to pick up a beeper on that F-4 that went in?"

"Negative. I've already checked with the rest of the flight. No one heard anything. We'll run from south to north with a right break off target. Let's arm 'em up, Blinky Flight."

"Sidewinder Two-one is in for the mark," I called. Turning hard left I put the nose of the Bronco down into a thirty-degree dive, flying a parabolic curve to the target. We had to stop most of the antiaircraft fire if we didn't want to lose someone else. I let the sight pipper ride through the target area to compensate for the g-forces of the turn, then fired another rocket. Continuing the turn, I looked back over my shoulder and watched the rocket impact in the jungle. The ground fire from light automatic weapons looked like a child's sparklers against the darkness beneath the trees. Dirty gray puffs blossomed beneath my right wing. Not too accurate, but it put things into a different perspective. It was probably a .37mm tracking me. That meant that I could no longer stay over the target at 4,000 feet with immunity from the fire coming from below. That baby could be aimed accurately up to 15,000 feet. Obviously, there was no way I was going to be able to get over it and still work the target. I'd have to dazzle them with my low animal cunning by staying too low for them to be able to track me properly. I'd have to keep some trees between the .37mm and me. That thing had to go immediately, and I hoped they didn't have another one. The heavy machine guns were bad enough. Mentally, I marked its location, figuring an azimuth and distance from my last marker. I went back to the fighters.

"Blinky Lead, you've got some heavy stuff about fifty meters west of my smoke, just inside that tree line by the westernmost crater. I want your entire flight to scatter the snakes in that area. Keep 'em jinking because he was really after me that time. There's lots of AK fire down there too."

"Rog, we saw that. Blinky Lead is in hot. FAC and target in sight."

An unintelligible singsong of Vietnamese broke in on the radio. Obviously, the flight of VNAF A-1s that Bos had told me about had arrived. Unless a pilot's diction is good, it's very hard to understand him over the radio. In this instance it was impossible. I couldn't even tell if they were trying to speak English.

"Blinky Lead, you'd better hold your flight high and dry until we can get this sorted out. It seems our comrades from the VNAF have joined us. Try to stay out of their way and they'll probably be finished in a few minutes."

"Roger that," he replied with some feeling. A midair collision can ruin your whole day.

I went through the briefing spiel with them, not having a clue as to whether or not they understood any of it. I didn't even know where they were, for that matter.

That question was answered when a bomb suddenly erupted in the target area. None of the F-100s had even been close to it. As usual, the Vietnamese Air Force seemed to prefer the direct approach. They took off; they flew to what they thought might be the target area; they dropped their bombs on it; they went home. Life was really very simple for them, but it did cause some complications in ours. They knew how to bomb with those old A-1s, though. They flew over the target, rolled the nose nearly vertical into a dive, and came straight down with those huge dive brakes hanging out to slow them down. They usually dumped everything on one pass, and the effect, if they were on the correct target, could be devastating. Any of their old aircraft could carry its own weight in bombs. This time was no exception. All three loads hit within twenty meters of each other. It was still fifty meters away from my smoke, but it was in the right area and must have done some good. Smoke from their explosions completely obscured the target area for a few moments.

A new voice broke in on my helmet: "FAC working north of the Testicles, this is Big Boy Six. Over." Absolutely charming! The brigade commander had decided to join us. This made a perfect day. He was a prickly old fart who completely dominated a communications net once he got on it. He was ferried daily around the brigade's AO by whatever hapless Huey crew drew the black bean. I tried to sort my communications problem in my mind before I answered him. Let's see, I would have the brigade commander dominating one of the FM radios; the artillery would be on the other FM; the command-ship pilot would want to be in contact on the VHF radio, unheard by his passenger; the fighters and my control room would be on UHF; when the Blues arrived they'd be working VHF; and God knows where the VNAF would be.

"Big Boy Six, this is Sidewinder Two-one. What's your position, please? I've got artillery going in on a 400-meter line, fronting that dry streambed to the west, and a flight of VNAF fighters are now engaging in the target area with no control."

The colonel began his usual tirade over the airways, almost as if he were thinking aloud. The command-ship pilot spoke to me over the VHF radio, unknown to the colonel, who continued to voice his views ad nauseam.

"Where do you want us, Sidewinder?" He was wisely concerned about being pinched between the artillery on one side and the air strikes on the other.

Rotating the radio wafer switch to get on his channel, I suggested the safest area would probably be about a klick west of the smoke over the target. He would have to keep his turns tight and find some altitude that would keep him clear of the ground fire as well as the jets coming off target.

I was still talking when my windscreen was filled with the shiny, olive drab HU-1B that the army aviation battalion provided their VIP passengers. I pulled back the control stick as hard as I could and the earth rapidly rotated around me. While still inverted in the top half of a loop, I swiveled my head until I picked up the chopper, then nudged the rudder so that I could complete the maneuver away from him.

Still on the helicopter pilot's frequency, I said, "That was close. Another three feet and I'd have been wearing you." I was pretty steamed, but I couldn't blame the pilot too much. I knew that he was flying where the colonel directed, and it would have taken a lot of balls to tell him that he wouldn't.

"Roger that," he said. His voice was tight but calm. "We're going to try to get out of your way." The colonel continued to rave, unaware how close he had been to being a dead colonel.

Another burst of Vietnamese announced that they had either completed their bombing or were going to attack the helicopter. I'd seen no more bombs or rockets from them and assumed they were leaving. I tried to find them, but the rising smoke from the bombs and my smoke rockets had substantially reduced the visibility.

"Sidewinder, Blinky Lead here. It looks like our gallant allies are departing to the south. We're going to have to go to work pretty quick. We're all approaching bingo fuel."

"No problem, Blinky. We'll put you right in. Be advised that we've now got a C and C chopper orbiting between the target and that line of arty fire. I'll try to keep everyone clear, but try to keep an eye in that direction in case he strays. You'll be cleared in hot just as soon as you see my new mark."

After he started his run-in he'd be lucky to spare a glance in that direction, for the smoke was drifting badly and he'd be coming down the tube at about 500 knots.

Playing it safe, I lowered the nose and fired another smoke rocket from 1,500 feet. After this pass, I'd have to do another assessment run over the target. I was already dreading it.

"Hit anywhere in the vicinity of my smoke, Lead. Two and Three, I'm going to make a BDA after Lead's pass. Be ready for a quick change of targets. Also, acknowledge that you have the info about the chopper working west of the target."

They dutifully acknowledged and I watched the lead aircraft being tracked by long trails of green tracers and several puffs of gray flak. The bombs missed them, for they continued to track the jet as he broke off target. I decided to delay the BDA until we'd put away the gun.

"Blinky Two and Three. Change of plans. You're both cleared in hot, in sequence. Both of you put your bombs about fifty meters north of Lead's last explosions."

The colonel continued to natter on the FM radio. Screw him. I watched Two pull off the target, jinking wildly. Three was already halfway down his run. Both sets of bombs were good—about thirty meters or so from where I had wanted them, but good enough. Damned good under the circumstances.

"Where are you guys from? That was good stuff."

"Thanks, neighbor. We're out of Tuy Hoa," the leader replied in a corn-pone accent. "We thank you for the compliment, but I think I might have dumped something other than bombs on that pass. My flight suit sure does feel heavy."

"I know what you mean," I replied. "Now if I could get a pair of you to make simultaneous gun runs from the north, about a hundred meters east and west of the last target, I'll try to sneak in between you and go down to see if we've done anything. After that, I'll clear you from the area."

"You heard the man, Blinky Two. You take the east and I'll take the west. Three, you hold high and dry and keep your eye on Sidewinder while he dazzles us with his feats of daring and airmanship. Just let us know when you're ready, Sidewinder."

Very funny. "OK, let's go." My strategy was simple enough. I planned to fly directly at the attacking fighters but at a slightly higher altitude. Just before I reached their spread formation, I would roll the Bronco inverted and change directions completely, using the dive to increase my airspeed. If I timed it right I would complete the course reversal at low level, going in their direction, and be able to use the cover of their strafing run to survive should there be more heavy guns down there.

It almost worked. I relaxed the g-forces and leveled out above the trees, peering ahead in the smoke for the fighters. They were already by me though, bumping their rudders to disperse their cannon fire. I had misjudged the speed differential between their aircraft and mine. They simply had too much for me. They disappeared into the smoke; moments later I saw the sun glint on their wings as they made sharp pullouts from over the target. I was just getting into the target area.

Initially, there was little ground fire. The NVA were probably trying to get their brains back in gear after the cannon run. Either that or they couldn't believe what they were seeing. Here was the answer to the prayer of every frustrated Viet gunner who had been bombed, strafed, and generally harassed by aircraft every step of the way down the long Ho Chi Minh Trail. Here was meat on the hoof. A Yankee plane at low level, put-putting its way across the sky. I felt as naked as the day I was born. My eyes darted back and forth across the blast-cleared area. The jungle was mangled. The huge but shallow-rooted trees had been blown aside. Tiny human stick figures lay tumbled about the periphery of the blast zone. More of them were sprawled well up into the tree line as far as I could see into its darkness. There was nothing recognizable closer to the blasts except the remains of a crew-served antiaircraft gun, now on its side. Hopefully, this was the one that had been so active a little earlier. Maybe we really got them, I thought. Maybe I can just fly around here and count the pieces and this thing will be over.

Automatic weapon fire suddenly erupted from beneath the tree line and the now-familiar green tracers began to track me. They began flying at me from both sides and straight ahead. Good Christ, which way to go? I sawed at the rudders and ailerons in uncoordinated flight. The hair on my neck bristled and I tried to squeeze my shoulders into my crash helmet. Panic was only a breath away. I felt like a high-speed driver on an icy road just before he loses control. I stared straight ahead, slamming the stick from one side to the other, accomplishing nothing. My brain stem registered the impact of the rounds as they slammed into the aircraft, but the lobes were frozen. Suddenly, the bottom of the instrument panel blew into my lap. I could see the tops of the trees through the hole. At least two more holes were in the canopy; the one directly in front of me was long and jagged. Then as suddenly as it began, the ground fire stopped and there was nothing but unsullied rain forest in front of me again. I continued straight ahead until my brain took over from my reflexes, then made a slow climbing turn back to altitude. I forced my head left and then right to assess the damage. The air coming through the new hole in the instrument panel felt nice. Maybe I should petition the Air Force to install holes like that in all the OV-10s.

Ignoring the radio squawking at me, I took inventory. Aside from the instrument panel and the new holes in the canopy, there were several jagged holes visible in the wings and fuselage. The tanks were self-sealing up to a point. I didn't know if I had exceeded that point or not, but I didn't see anything flowing out. I took that as a good sign; I was more frightened of a fire in an aircraft than anything else that could happen. There also seemed to be a piece missing from the right wing tip, although I could see nothing dribbling out of the hole. The engines seemed to be running well, whining away with the normal screech of the turboprop. What engine instruments I had left on my instrument panel confirmed that they were pulling full power. Angling the mirror toward my face, I saw several deep scratches in my helmet's sun visor. As I ran my hand over the front of my helmet, I felt several small pieces of metal and glass embedded there, undoubtedly the result of the instrument panel's demise. Arms. Legs. Head. Torso. Everything seemed to be as good as it was before. I pushed the mike button and tried to talk, but couldn't. My mouth had dried so much that I could hardly part my lips. Pulling another baby bottle of water from my pocket, I gulped it down. Like an opera singer warming up, I experimentally warbled a few notes until my voice sounded almost normal.

"Blinky Lead, this is Sidewinder. We got a bunch of them, but there are plenty still full of fight. I'm going to clear you out of the area now 'cause we've got some gunships inbound. You guys did damned good work and I'll be sure to get a BDA up to you as soon as I can. I'll look you up sometime. So long."

"Roger, Sidewinder," the slow drawl came back. "It's been a pleasure doing business with you. We can stretch the fuel a bit more if you'd like. I'm sure we can stay until someone else gets into the area. You look like you were hit mighty hard on that last BDA."

"Naw, I think everything's OK. It kinda' shook me up for a minute but I'm all right now. Thanks for the offer, though. The choppers ought to be up here shortly."

"OK, Buddy. If you ever get up to Tuy Hoa, the drinks are on me."

"I'll take you up on that. Adios."

From my relatively safe perch I watched the three graceful aircraft join into a loose formation and turn northward, climbing quickly out of sight. To the south I could see the two army helicopters hovering around the wreckage of the downed F-4. They began to slowly quarter the area, apparently not finding anything to pick up. In that position they shouldn't be in anyone's way, although they could be in the way of the Blue Team's insertion. Let them figure it out. I was too tired. My hand that was holding the control stick seemed too heavy to keep in place. Some of my fatigue may be shock, I thought. Maybe some dehydration too. I'd drunk two of my baby bottles but had probably sweated twenty times that much. Using my left hand, I reached over and squeezed the right sleeve of my flight suit. Liquid dribbled out in a steady stream, as if it were being wrung from a wet dishcloth. Grabbing the stick with my knees, I raised my visor, unclipped my chin strap, and removed my helmet again. I leaned my head back against the ejection seat headrest and idly rubbed my gloved hand over the helmet, dislodging the shards of glass and metal that had been blown into it. I checked my face in the mirror; it was flaming red with heat and sweat but no cuts. Luck had been with me so far. I removed my last baby bottle and poured the water down my parched throat. It didn't come close to satisfying my thirst. I replaced and buckled my helmet just in time to hear the brigade commander swearing at me over the radio.

"Goddammit, Sidewinder Two-one. Do you read me? This is Big Boy Six."

"Go ahead Six, this is Sidewinder Two-one."

"What the hell is going on over there? Are there any dinks or are you people just pissing in the wind?"

I felt like telling him to get just a little closer and he'd find out for himself. But I didn't. Instead, I briefed him on the situation as I saw it. I explained that we had expended four flights of fighters in the area and that I could get more if he wanted. What I suggested, though, was that the artillery be adjusted onto the target. Additional alert birds would be standing by on the pads at Bien Hoa, only some fifteen minutes away and available for the Blue's insertion, should he want them.

Most of the ground commanders would accept the FAC's advice concerning aircraft employment, but they were mighty touchy if they thought you were straying from your area of expertise. Most of them knew that they didn't know any more about employing bombs than I did about running an infantry battalion. Some, like old numbnuts now circling the area, wanted to run the whole show. He also wanted to play platoon leader, recalling his glory years as a second lieutenant in the Ardennes. More times than I liked to remember, I had seen him circling above some hapless grunt platoon, giving directions to its harried young commander, who already had more than his share of problems humping in the bush.

He jumped at the opportunity to bring in the artillery. That way he could claim most of the KIAs (killed in action) as being done in by arty. He would have preferred that all of them be killed by his infantry, but this was difficult to achieve with bodies ripped asunder by high explosives. In his view, credit to the artillery would be better than letting the Air Force get away with destroying the enemy in his AO. He could claim them all as victims of his personal .45 for all I cared.

I watched the command helicopter ease cautiously toward the target area. The commander was an asshole, but not a fainthearted asshole. If any of those big guns were left in there, that Huey was going to die.

"Big Boy Six, Sidewinder. Best remain clear of that area. There still may be some big guns working down there." As I spoke, another string of tracers lifted toward the helicopter. It swiftly banked toward the west, clearing the hot area.

"Six, this is Sidewinder. If you can take over the arty adjustment, I'll see if there's anything airborne that we can put in quickly before the Blues get here."

"OK, Sidewinder. We'll take over the adjustment and we'll keep it clear of your area until you can get your damned planes in and out."

Gracious sod. I called Bos at the control room again. "Sidewinder Control, this is Two-one. I hope you've been monitoring. Is there anything we can use anywhere close to us?"

"Roger," he responded immediately. "Roscoe Flight; three F-4s inbound to you now. They've got a full load of iron bombs and they've already been briefed. They should be up this frequency now." Good old Bos!

"Thanks, Control. Roscoe Lead, are you up this freq?"

"Roger, Sidewinder. We're approaching the Testicles now. Can you give us some smoke?"

"Rog, Roscoe. Smoker is coming on now."

I put the Bronco into a shallow turn and pulled the toggle switch, which dumped oil into the hot exhaust ports, creating a dense white smoke like that used by skywriters. The smoke was very helpful in making a rendezvous with the fighters. Few know how difficult it is for one aircraft to see another aircraft in flight, despite Hollywood's insistence that an eagle-eyed hero can spot his prey miles away. In real life, aircraft routinely pass within yards of one another with no one being the wiser.

"OK, Sidewinder, Roscoe Flight has you in sight. We're at your eight o'clock, descending through 14,000 feet."

Peering over my left shoulder, I let go of the smoke switch. I saw the sun glinting off the F-4s' wings as the planes spread into attack formation.

"Roscoe Flight, Sidewinder. We'll make one pass and haul ass. OK? Dump it all because we're in a hurry here. Make your runs north to south with an east break off target. Call FAC and target in sight. I'm in for the mark now."

I handled the OV-10 very gently as I rolled in to shoot one of my few remaining rockets. I didn't know how much damage the aircraft had sustained, and I didn't want to take more chances than necessary. I watched the white smoke billow from the rocket, just about where I had last seen the tracers erupting. There was not nearly as much ground fire this time, and I saw nothing of the larger guns. Most of the stuff coming up was AK-47.

"Roscoe Lead, hit my smoke, and on pullout continue your easterly heading coming off target. Be advised we're still taking some small arms fire from the area. Roscoe Two, hit fifty meters west of my smoke. Roscoe Three, hit fifty meters east. If you have me in sight, you're all cleared in hot, in sequence. Watch yourself, everyone. We've already lost one F-4 in the area this morning."

"OK, Sidewinder. Understand one pass and haul ass. Lead's in hot."

Roscoe Two and Three called inbound shortly. The havoc created by a planeload of bombs dropped at once was impressive. All three runs looked good. I was already limping across the target at 500 feet before the smoke had cleared from the last explosion. The destruction to the rain forest had been awesome.

From one of the far blast areas, a lone AK-47 winked at me from the tree line. Quickly I flicked the arming switches to my four machine guns and, without using the sight, pulled the trigger on the control stick. I slewed the nose of the aircraft with the rudders toward the source of the fire. I wasn't trying to hit him. I just wanted to keep his head down until I was out of the area. Pulling gingerly on the stick, I crept back to safe altitude and made a last call to Roscoe Flight, now leaving the area. I promised to forward their BDA as soon as I could.

Nestor, the helicopter gunships inbound to cover the troop insertion, were calling on the VHF. I looked toward the Anthill and picked up the flight of six.

"Nestor, this is Sidewinder Two-one. I've got you in sight. Suggest you conserve your ordnance for the Blue Team's insertion. I've only got a couple of willie pete's left, but I'll put one in where we were taking most of the ground fire. I think we've pretty well taken care of it though, except for an isolated AK here and there. God knows how many are down there. You might try calling Big Boy Six, who's orbiting west of the area between that smoke and the dry streambed out there. I'm sure he'll be glad to mark the area he wants you to hit.''

"Sounds good, Sidewinder. I'm leaving freq to talk to Big Boy.''

I listened to the remainder of his flight acknowledge the frequency shift and then heard the gunship leader come up on the command frequency. As they discussed the planned insertion, I rolled in gently once more and fired my next-to-last rocket, then pointed the nose of the Bronco to the south. Over the river, I saw that the rescue attempt had been abandoned and the choppers had left unnoticed. Over the command net, the colonel sounded pleased to have a more active role. I waited for a break in the radio traffic to tell them I was leaving, carefully checking the one fuel gauge left on my instrument panel. The other one was in my lap. If the functional one was anywhere near accurate, it was going to be close on fuel. The youthful exuberance of the fire team leader was frightening. Most of the Cobra pilots seemed to be about eighteen years old, with all the fearlessness and the belief in their own immortality of that age group. Most of them had the judgment of a load of bricks. If the pilots could be controlled, they were great to have around. If left on their own, they were a hazard to every living thing in the area. I finally broke in for one last transmission.

"Big Boy Six, this is Sidewinder. I'm going to have to leave the area now. Another FAC will be up shortly in case you need any more fast movers. I'm departing to the south.''

"Sidewinder, this is Six. Thanks, that was a good job. I'd like you to pass along my compliments to the pilots.''

The old fart was actually being gracious.

One last chore. "Sidewinder Control, this is Two-one. Call the hootch and get the Duty FAC airborne. Have him take a good look at the situation map in the TOC before he takes off and then have him head to the Testicles and orbit. The Blues are inbound and the CO might change the insertion coordinates. Also, give Bien Hoa a call and tell them we're going to need another aircraft. This one is all used up until they can get it repaired. They'd better send a sheet-metal man too, so they can fix this one enough to fly back. They'll also need someone who can OK a one-time flight for it down there.''

"Roger, Two-one. Are you going to try to get in here or head on back to Bien Hoa?"

I knew what he was saying. Lai Khe had only a minimum of crash equipment for the airstrip, whereas Bien Hoa was like a stateside base, with big fire trucks and firemen in asbestos suits. Bien Hoa also had the capability to foam the runway if I couldn't get my landing gear down and had to belly it in. In that event, the foam went a long way in suppressing any fire caused by the friction of the aircraft skin against the hard surface of the runway. At Lai Khe they'd probably just walk over and try to beat out the flames with their entrenching tools.

"Negative, I'm coming back to home plate. I shouldn't have any trouble getting in. Besides, I don't think I've got enough fuel to go to Bien Hoa."

"Roger. Be advised that Sidewinder Two-five is airborne in your vicinity if you want him to look you over before landing."

"That's good, Bos. Tell him to come up this frequency and I'll be heading on slowly toward the house."

"Two-one, this is Two-five. I've been monitoring your frequency. Give me a shot of smoke, jefe."

My arms were so tired they felt numb. I could hardly reach the smoker switch. I glanced at the clock and saw that I had been airborne for almost four hours.

"Got you now, Two-one," Paco said. "Just keep her going toward home and I'll join up."

I looked behind me until I found the other OV-10 coming up on my left side, overtaking me rapidly. He brought his aircraft snugly in behind my left wing, then moved gently into a trail formation, then onto the right wing.

"You've got a lot of damage, but I can't see anything that would keep you from landing all right. Are you hurt?"

"Negative, I'm OK. And thanks, Paco, but you'd better head on in in case I tie up the runway."

"Naw. I got nothing better to do. I think I'll just practice some formation flying. I'm getting pretty rusty."

"Suit yourself." He was lying and we both knew it, but I was appreciative of the company. I heard the Duty FAC call airborne. He must have been primed and ready to go to get off that quickly. He called me.

"Sidewinder Two-one, this is Two-seven. I've been listening to your strikes in the control room with Bos. If we have to put in any more strikes, you got any idea where's the best place to put them?''

"The way they're shooting today, I'd suggest Des Moines," I said wearily. "If the dinks are smart, they'll be heading east because I think they're pretty well blocked in the other direction. Which means they'll probably do just the opposite of what I said. Whatever you do, watch your butt. They've got some gunners down there today."

"No sweat. I'll be the soul of discretion. See you later, boss." Yeah, the soul of discretion. If I knew him he'd be down in the treetops before the fighters ever got there, gunning with everything he had.

Lassitude crept over me like someone was pouring it from a bucket. I wiggled my toes vigorously in my jungle boots, trying to pump myself up for the landing. I leaned my face down toward the fresh air flowing through the shell hole in the instrument panel. It helped dry some of the sweat dribbling from under my close-fitting helmet. I loosened my shoulder straps and slid my pistol out of the position where it had been digging into my ribs. Suddenly, everything was uncomfortable. My mouth had dried out again, but I had nothing left to drink. I turned my helmet back and forth on my head, trying to find a comfortable position for my ears, which seemed to have grown in the last few hours.

Minutes later, the rubber plantation surrounding the Lai Khe airstrip came into view. The pockmarked runway wasn't visible until I was nearly upon it. The approach had to be made down a cleared lane through the rubber trees. I called the tower—a GI sitting on top of a sandbagged bunker—and announced my intentions to land straight in rather than flying the prescribed pattern. The landing gear came down just as advertised, and was verified by the green lights on the panel. I was delighted. At least the enemy rounds seemed to have missed my hydraulic system, which meant the brakes should also work. The landing was terrible, but I didn't care.

Between the holes in the canopy, the grease-pencil markings on my windscreen, and the deep scratches on my visor from the exploding instrument panel, I could hardly follow Butch's marshaling signals. I taxied slowly into the sandbagged revetment and shut down the engines. It was steaming in the cockpit, but I didn't have the strength to raise the canopy. Butch stood shirtless and scowling at me, red hair plastered to his head with sweat. He turned his head slowly as he looked at his aircraft, the scowl deepening at the sight. His eyes came back to me. I stared at him goggle-eyed, breathing like a derby loser. His features smoothed a little as he continued to watch me. Then he walked slowly to the side of the aircraft and opened the canopy with the external handle. I gasped at him as though I was giving birth to a whale.

He crawled up the steps and unlocked my parachute harness. Seeing that I hadn't safed my ejection seat, he reached into my leg pocket and pulled out the safety pins. Carefully, he installed them and then grasped my arm and gently urged me from the cockpit. I half-fell and half-crawled down to the pierced steel planking (PSP) ramp and sat heavily against one of the main tires. The rest of the ground crew stared at me, then at the aircraft. Butch walked to the Conex box that served as his maintenance storage area. Dixie, the black armorer, knelt and removed my helmet, then slid my parachute harness and survival vest from my torso. I think he thought I was wounded. Butch returned with two hot beers, opened them both with his sheath knife, and handed them to me silently. Two swallows and they were both gone.

"How was it, Major?" Butch finally spoke.

"Fine, just fine," I croaked.

As I felt the liquid giving life back to my body, I watched Butch walk slowly around the Bronco, shaking his head and muttering mechanical incantations. Dixie placed my gear in the duty jeep as I staggered over to it. Absentmindedly, I noticed that the Duty FAC, now airborne, had again forgotten to lock the chain around the steering wheel. If that continued unchecked, some grunt would more than likely steal the jeep from us. That would be discouraging considering all the trouble we had taken to steal it from them. I made a mental note to speak to the Duty FAC about it later.

I drove slowly back to the FAC hootch. The roads were covered with six inches of red dust, constantly being churned by the passing vehicles. I should have gone by the brigade TOC for debriefing, but I was too exhausted to even think straight. As I parked in front of the sandbagged hootch, one of the new guys burst through the door and ran toward me.

"Hey, Maj. They've got a real one going on up there where you were. I've been monitoring it over the radio. The Blues got the crap shot out of them on insertion, and we've already lost one slick and one gunship. Don took your place and has already put in three more sets of fighters. Shit hot, huh?"

"Yeah, shit hot," I replied. "How about calling up the TOC for me and telling them I'll be over later to debrief. I doubt if they've got time to talk to me now, anyway. Also, call the division TACP and let the air liaison officer know what's going on."

"No sweat. I was on my way to the TOC anyway. See you later, boss."

I walked to my bunk and placed my gear in my locker. The smell of mildew was strong as I opened the locker door. Wearily, I lay back on the bunk and shut my eyes. My brain was going too fast to turn off, though, and I could feel my eyes flickering wildly beneath the closed lids. Later, I heard some of the pilots gathering in what we laughingly called the "dayroom." Paco's voice, more strident than the others, hammered its way into my consciousness. We had, it seemed, been responsible for more than 300 KBAs—killed by air—so far in today's activities. The count was incomplete but still rising as the ground sweep continued. Not that different from many other days. It was my sixty-seventh day in the Republic of South Vietnam, and so far 1969 had been a hell of a year.

PART 2
Making of a FAC

The bright neon lights of the large briefing room accentuated the predawn darkness, and an occasional snow flurry beat against the windows, further reducing the visibility. There wasn't much to see anyway. The ancient buildings of the air base blended into the hardscrabble farm and ranch country of eastern New Mexico. On the parking ramp next to the long runway sat the jet training aircraft, old AT-33s, in which our initial forward air controller training would begin. They looked small and old-fashioned compared to the F-100s belonging to the fighter RTU (Replacement Training Unit).

Most of our little group of trainees weren't really sure what they were getting into. Our orders read only that the 3329th Combat Crew Training Squadron would provide preliminary training before we reported to Florida's Hurlburt Field for the primary forward air control school. We had already found out that there were several crosses we would have to bear because we were selected for such esoteric duty.

First, it was 100 percent certain that we would be in Vietnam within six months. Second, being attached to the Army and living with Army combat units in the war zone was not a particularly thrilling prospect for any air force pilot. Most of us had joined the Air Force to avoid being drafted into the Army. There was also the matter of the aircraft we would be flying in Southeast Asia. There were only three possible options, all bad from a jet pilot's point of view. One, the OV-10, was a new aircraft, but even it would have to strain to go over 200 knots. This limitation brought up the major problem with the job—the job itself. Flying low and slow, looking for targets for the jets to attack, didn't seem the most glamorous job in the world. We knew that the casualty rate among FACs was high, probably the highest in the Air Force.

Not many of the group had volunteered, but Vietnam was a way of life for military pilots in 1968. Many already had one combat tour, as

I did—a year in the Mekong Delta with an advisory team whose advice no one would take. The only reason the Vietnamese would listen to us was that we had control of the radio. And he who controls the radio, controls the allocation of aircraft. This was important to them.

That year in the southern delta, I had flown the O-1, one of the aircraft some of our group would be sent into. It looked like what the general public would call a "Piper Cub," a single-engine, high-winged aircraft. If there was any way possible, I did not plan to be in one of them for another year.

To myself I cursed the personnel officer who had taken my request for a transfer from staff duty back to the cockpit as an invitation to fill all his undesirable Vietnam slots. I had wanted Air Defense Command (ADC) fighters, but instead found myself with ten kindred souls force-fed into the funnel of a pipeline that would spit us out into South Vietnam in only six months.

The squadron ops officer, a portly major, grabbed the sides of the rostrum as if he had a personal grudge against it. Maybe he didn't like to get up this early either. The instructor pilots (IPs) lounged casually on the far side of the briefing room, bantering with each other and slurping coffee. The new students sat poker-faced on the other side. Everyone was an officer and a pilot, but we were the new guys. And we were transients. Three months and we'd be history, and the IPs would still be here. Besides, what kind of world would it be if fighter pilots went around speaking to everyone, for God's sake.

"Your attention please, gentlemen. Listen up for roll call." The major's high, shrill voice didn't go with his bulk. He began the roll and the assignment of students to instructors. I watched carefully as each man answered. Everyone else was doing the same. You can tell a lot about a military man by what he wears. In class-A uniforms, there are rank, awards, and badges. We were in flight suits, but there were shoulder patches, leather tags with embossed wings, and the color of the flight suit itself. Three of our group were wearing the distinctive international-orange flight suit issued only to Air Defense Command crew members. All three were wearing shoulder patches denoting varying degrees of skill as interceptor pilots. Two were majors, indicating fairly lengthy service. They'd probably been in ADC for most of their service, for that command was known to hold onto its pilots once they were trained. Only the Strategic Air Command (SAC) was better at it. Vietnam requirements were changing this to some extent though, as the war chewed up more and more pilots. You could bet that all three of the orange-suiters could fly an airplane, particularly in bad weather. Their stock-in-trade was the interceptor launch, initiated even when the rest of the world's aircraft were grounded due to bad weather. The star over their wings indicated that they all had the senior pilot rating. Consequently they all had more than 2,000 hours' flight time. That wasn't much to the captain of a Pan American 747, but to a pilot who averaged thirty minutes per sortie in all sorts of weather conditions, it meant a high-time interceptor pilot.

You could read the instructors' minds. They all wanted these guys because they'd have no problems. Teach 'em ground attack and you were in business. They probably knew more about formation and instrument flying than the IPs did.

Four of the remaining students were from the Military Airlift Command (MAC), which was a different kettle of fish indeed. The ranking officer of that lot was a captain with slick wings; that is, he was not a senior pilot, probably because he had less than seven years' service. That was no big deal except that he probably had been a copilot, because an aircraft commander would have worn a shoulder patch that shouted it to the world. The copilot's job in MAC had the reputation of being the least desirable in the Air Force. Deservedly or not, most pilots tried to stay away from the huge, lumbering beasts flown by MAC, and felt smug when they walked by them in transient ops. The only job of the pilots flying these was to go someplace, hauling a planeload of junk. They didn't really *do* anything. This group would have its work cut out. They'd have little recent hands-on experience in either formation or fighter-type flying in general. Secretly, most pilots thought that the only people who ended up flying for MAC were those who couldn't cut the aerobatics in flight school. Experience with this group would prove me dead wrong.

We also had two new second lieutenants in our group, obviously fresh out of flight school. I was surprised, for normally the Air Force didn't place newly winged pilots in the FAC program. A certain degree of judgment is called for when orchestrating an aerial ballet over a battlefield. Second lieutenants are not particularly noted for their maturity or experience. Maybe these were exceptions though. I was sure that the instructors had bitter discussions about who got these two in their group of students.

The student remaining other than me was a fugitive from SAC. God knows how they managed to pry away one of SAC's pilots. The Strategic Air Command was like a black hole; anyone who entered never came out. Watching this character during roll call, I began to get some idea why SAC released him. He was never still; his head was in constant motion, lips mumbling undetectable words to a neighbor, who was trying to ignore him. I caught the SAC pilot's gaze, his eyes those of a mischievous child. Fat little cheeks dimpled at me. He seemed ready to explode from excessive energy. Hardly the SAC stereotype, which ran to stolid family men who seldom stopped for a drink at the club, preferring to go home and mow the lawn.

My instructor had been eyeing me from across the room as I watched the chubby-cheeked captain. The patch on the left shoulder of my green flight suit indicated that I had arrived from Headquarters, USAF, and was probably from the Pentagon or its close environs. Except for that and my name tag, the suit was bare; no "Expert" badges, no "Aircraft Commander" patch, nothing but the bare green bag. His look cataloged me as a staff weenie caught up in the whirlwind of the Vietnam experience. I was obviously young enough to go back to the cockpit for a combat tour, but I was still an unknown quantity. Most staff pilots flew only their 100 hours minimum per year as required by the Air Force. Flying skills deteriorate rapidly under these conditions, particularly when they last for an extended period. The IP's eyes showed that he had already made his assessment of me; it wasn't one that I liked, but it was probably accurate. Until a few days ago, I had been on the intelligence staff at Headquarters, USAF. I came complete with a wife, three children, and a well-mortgaged home in the Virginia suburbs.

The staff work I had found incredibly dull and stultifying. The Air Force works on the assumption that staff duty is a broadening experience that potential chiefs of staff should undergo. To stay in the cockpit too long is considered the kiss of death for those seeking future high-ranking positions. Some cockpit time is, of course, required. We are a flying outfit, after all. *Twelve O'Clock High* proved it; I mean, Gregory Peck was a flying general. In reality, of course, this is bullshit. Future generals get just enough flying time for their advanced ratings, and with the war in its fourth year or so, combat experience also had to be obtained. There had to be the display of combat ribbons on the manly chest. None needed to be high awards, simply those presented for completing a tour of combat operations. Anything more smacked of damned foolishness and would probably be a handicap to those seeking higher positions in the corporate Air Force. After all, it's inappropriate to out-dazzle your boss, and few of them would appreciate subordinates with more decorations than they wore themselves.

I could hardly blame the instructor for the jaundiced look he'd been throwing in my direction. I'm sure he'd had his share of ticket-punchers come through before. But I wanted back into the cockpit with all my being. I'd decided there were plenty who wanted to compete for the eagles and the stars without my further participation. I'd always thought of myself as a pilot, and pilots fly airplanes. That's what I wanted to do. So if it meant Vietnam as a forward air controller, so be it.

During the roll call, one pattern quickly emerged. There were no student pilots in the Tactical Air Command, yet every FAC was supposed to be a qualified tactical fighter pilot. That was the air force rule. As I was to find out, it was a rule that applied only when the higher-ups wanted it to apply, along with the rest of the rules they hid behind.

There was a valid reason to have all FACs be qualified tactical fighter pilots. In Vietnam, almost every bomb dropped and every rocket fired from an aircraft had been cleared by a FAC. He ran the air war on the battlefield, coordinating all air strikes, the weapons to be used, and their employment. His was the responsibility to make sure that no friendly troops were hurt by the air strikes, and whenever possible he physically marked with a smoke rocket each target to be attacked. He was the focal point of the air-ground coordination, for the attack aircraft and the ground troops were unable to talk to each other because of incompatible radio equipment. He was the staff adviser to the battalion or division commander on the use of tactical aircraft. In short, you bombed where the FAC told you to, and if he said "no," then you didn't bomb. It was no wonder there were so few second lieutenants in the business.

Assignments made, we sat and waited for an appearance by the squadron commander. After only about five minutes, an amount of time designed to show us that he was not only a busy man but one powerful enough to keep thirty officers waiting, he strode briskly down the aisle.

"Gentlemen, the commander," the ops officer called. We rose and assumed the position of respectful "attention." It's hard to be at attention in a flight suit, which normally assumes "at ease" no matter what the body tries to do. As aviation cadets we had solved the problem by starching our flight suits. Now, we didn't bother. The compact lieutenant colonel pivoted neatly behind the podium to face us.

"Seats, gentlemen, please," as if he were surprised to find us standing for him. "As commander of the 3329th Combat Crew Training Squadron, I'd like to welcome you to Cannon Air Force Base and to this organization. You won't see much of me for the next three months unless you screw up." Mandatory chuckle from the audience.

"You'll find this to be a unique organization." Aren't they all.

"It's been in existence for only a few months and is made up of the 140th Tac Fighter Squadron of the recently activated New York National Guard, augmented by instructors from the F-100 RTU down the road.

"As you know, the AT-33 will be our primary training aircraft. It was the jet trainer for the air force's pilot training program for many years. Most of the older officers in the room probably trained in it." Christ, it was old when I was a flying cadet thirteen years ago.

"Let me explain the program to you in its most basic form. All forward air controllers are supposed to be qualified tactical fighter pilots. But, we're using up fighter pilots at a prodigious rate in Southeast Asia. Between the air war in-country—that is, inside South Vietnamese borders—and the fighters operating over Laos and North Vietnam, we're really having a difficult time keeping that pipeline filled. So, we're here to make you into instant Tac Fighter Pilots." He spoke in capitals.

"One or two of you may have some background, but for most of you, it will be completely new. We do not have the opportunity to qualify you in one of the first-line fighters, as would be desirable. All of those seats are filled by trainees scheduled for the operational units over there. So, you're going through initial gunnery in the AT-33, just the way a lot of us did back in the fifties. We've had bomb racks put back on them and two fifty-caliber machine guns replaced in the nose. It ain't elegant, but it works. Three months here and then it's to Hurlburt Field in Florida for your final training in either the O-1, the O-2, or the OV-10." Please God, not the O-2, I thought. It was an off-the-shelf buy by the Air Force of the civilian Cessna 337 model, favored by many doctors and accountants. I could live with the O-1 again if I had too. But I just couldn't see myself marking targets in an airplane flown by middle-class civilians.

"You'll get about sixty hours in the T-Bird," he continued, "about half of that being on the gunnery range." He rambled on describing the training for another ten minutes. Mine weren't the only eyes glazing over, I noticed.

"You will all be expected to qualify in dive-bombing, skip bombing, rockets, and guns. Don't ask me what we do with you if you don't.

Leave you here as an instructor, I guess." Low laughter from the IPs' side of the room. That eventuality had been thought out, I was sure. Any failures would probably mean a quick transfer to C-123 school and a year of Vietnam service hauling body bags and toilet paper for eight hours a day.

"The pace is going to be fast," he continued, "particularly for those of you who have never flown the T-Bird. For those of you who finish the training early, we have a special bonus. When the Guard unit that furnished the nucleus of instructors for the organization was activated, they brought their aircraft with them. I'm sure that most of you have seen the F-86Hs sitting on the flight line. Well, finish up our course in minimum time and you'll get to fly in those little beauties." Now there was an incentive. Those little swept-wing aircraft had been phased out of the air force inventory for some years, and now only a very few Air National Guard units and some of our allies still had them around. They had ruled the skies over Korea almost twenty years before and had the reputation of being one of the sweetest-flying aircraft ever made.

"Do any of you have any questions?" He looked slowly around the room. No one had any questions. He would have been shocked if anyone had. No one asks the commander a question. That was why he had an ops officer. We hastily came to our feet as he swept abruptly toward the door.

I caught the eye of Bill, the tall major in the orange flight suit.

"Ought to be fun," he said with a grin. We were to share an instructor.

"Yeah," I replied, "provided these old birds can hold together for another three months while we practice hurling our pink bodies at the ground. Just think about the abuse some of these old T-Birds have been through with twenty years of ham-fisted students wrapping 'em around."

"Knowing that ought to keep it exciting." Grinning still, he turned back to the podium as the ops officer concluded his briefing with the usual claptrap: Don't harass the natives downtown; as little blood and breakage in the O-Club as possible, or at least pay for it and mop it up if you're responsible; don't buzz the ranchers either in their homes or on horseback. He finally got bored with his speech and dismissed us to meet our instructors in the small flight briefing rooms.

The walls were covered with maps of the local area and photomosaics of the bombing ranges we would use. There was a table large enough for five people to scrunch around in reasonable comfort and a large scheduling board with our names already grease-penciled in on it. Each column showed an activity we were expected to accomplish satisfactorily while we were training.

We four students shook hands and chatted idly while we waited for our instructor, who wandered in shortly with a cup of coffee and a vague look on his face. His blond hair was cut so short he appeared to be bald until he was close enough that we could see the almost-white spikes sticking up about an eighth of an inch.

"My name is George," he said without putting down his coffee or offering to shake hands. "I'll be your instructor for the next three months. Things ought to go pretty smoothly, since I know that a couple of you have had quite a bit of T-Bird time. That will let me spend more time with the other two. The weather shouldn't really be much of a problem. We get crappy days like this, but they don't last very long. Wind is the biggest problem here, but you all should be gone before it really starts picking up in March and April. Your biggest problem is going to be freezing your butts off in the T-Bird, which has the lousiest heating and cooling system of any aircraft ever designed. There's no flying scheduled today; we'll just let you draw personal equipment and get squared away with any base clearance you've still got to do. Be sure you check the schedule before you leave every day, because the briefings and flying get started pretty early. If there are no questions, let's head down to PE."

In the PE (personal equipment) section, the specialist outfitted us with parachutes, g-suits, and helmets for those who hadn't brought one with them. The g-suits were chaplike garments worn over the flight suits; they had pneumatic bladders, positioned over the legs and abdomen, which would inflate if the pilot put his aircraft into a tight turning maneuver or pullout from a dive. This helped prevent blacking out or unconsciousness by keeping the blood from pooling in the extremities and denying it to the brain.

From the PE shop we wandered to the flight line, where George demonstrated a preflight inspection on one of the aircraft. I knew it pretty well but gave him my full attention when he was talking about the guns or bombs. The planes were old but appeared to be in good condition.

After being dismissed most of us spent the remainder of the day arguing with an airman second class over our pay records and advance per diem to live on. We made the grand tour of the base, leaving records at every stop with some bored enlisted clerk.

At the O-Club that evening I joined Bill for a predinner beer but found that he and another bachelor were then heading into town to lay waste the local female population. Entering the dining room alone I saw a familiar face sitting by himself at one of the tables. I had seen him around the BOQ several times and figured he was another trainee going through one of the programs. I walked to his table and asked if he minded company during the meal. A small smile came over his face.

"Major, you obviously don't know who I am, do you?"

"Not really," I said. "Are you something special? Do you mind if I pull up a chair? I'll be glad to listen to your war story if I can order a beer first. Can I buy you one?"

"Afraid not," he said. "But please sit down. It'll be nice to have the company."

We introduced ourselves. The waiter came and took my drink order. Dale asked for more coffee.

"Now then, tell me what you did. Did you try to cop a feel of the squadron commander's wife at a party? Do you have some strange social disease? Go ahead, I'm all a'twitter. Come on, it can't be all that bad."

"I'm afraid it is," he said, eyeing me over the rim of his coffee cup. "In fact, I'm quite sure that you'll get up and leave the table when I tell you what's going on. But remember, you did ask.

"I was in a staff job in the midwest when I got orders for F-100 RTU. As soon as we get out of training here it's off to Nam, as you know. I'd never really given the war much thought before I got my flying assignment. I know it's crazy, but I thought that my engineering AFSC would somehow exempt me from it. Well, it didn't. I was just starting the second year of what was supposed to be a four-year stabilized tour. I didn't think I'd even have to think about Nam for another three years when they dropped the assignment on me. I was so numb, I didn't know what to do. My wife was tearing around the house, crying all the time. I was trying to get everything together and figure out how I was going to support her in this house we'd just bought, or if I should send her to her folks, or whatever. I didn't really know what to do.

"I still didn't really start thinking about the war until I got down here and started flying. The more I thought about it, the more I began to realize that I didn't want to have anything to do with it. I decided that I'm not going to have any part in killing any Vietnamese, north or south, east or west."

He took another sip of coffee, staring at the tabletop.

"So, I just decided that I was going to have to take a stand," he continued. "I walked into the RTU commander's office and told him that I would complete the training, but I was not going to Vietnam. I'd fly against what I considered my country's enemies, but I didn't consider the Vietnamese as enemies.

"Well, he immediately grounded me and we began to have a few counseling sessions, as you might imagine. To make a long story short, I wouldn't give in and they wouldn't agree to let me out of my assignment unless I declared myself a conscientious objector, which I wouldn't do because I'm not one, unless they have a special category for somebody who refuses to fight Vietnamese."

"So, what's going to happen now?" I asked.

"A general court-martial," he said, staring into the distance. "They're going to convene one at their discretion, and hang my ass on the wall. In the meantime, I'm under house arrest and can only be in the BOQ or the dining room here at the club. I sit on my butt and read my daily mail from the peaceniks and the crazies from all over the country who think I'm just wonderful. The funny thing is that I'm not like them at all. I don't have any hang-ups about the military profession. My God, I've been an officer for six years and graduated from the Academy. It's just this particular war I don't believe in. They called me a coward and said I was just trying to save my own skin, but that's not it at all. I just think we're wrong about being in Vietnam."

"Well," I said. "You've taken a stand for sure. It's not one that I would have taken, but it's yours. It's just too bad that you didn't come to this decision before they cut orders sending you here. They'd probably have let you resign quietly rather than letting the world know about it in a court-martial. I'll be honest with you. I don't agree with what you've done, but you're the one who's going to have to live with the consequences. And I'm sure you've thought it all out pretty thoroughly, so I'm not going to start moralizing with you. Let's eat."

After dinner, Dale had to go back to his self-imposed exile, so I went to one of the quieter tables in the bar and thought about what I'd heard. I doubted I would have the courage to follow such a course of action. Was he really concerned about killing Vietnamese or about Vietnamese killing him? Only he knew that for sure, I suppose. I was glad not to be sitting on that court. I saw him around the BOQ frequently after that dinner and always tried to be friendly. But I never had dinner with him again. Maybe I was afraid his feelings would rub off on me.

Our initial rides in the aircraft began the next morning. For me, it was like being reacquainted with an old friend, since I had well over a thousand hours in the airplane. I strapped myself into the front cockpit while George, the IP, crawled into the rear seat. I signaled the ground crewman to plug in the APU (auxiliary power unit) and began the start sequence. My checklist was open in my lap, but I went through the procedures from memory. I closely watched the exhaust gas temperature peak, then settle back to the proper place on the gauge. My hands scurried around the cockpit like small animals with minds of their own, for they had done this procedure so often they were ahead of my brain. One final glance at the instruments and fuel panel settings and we were ready to taxi.

"Cannon Ground Control, this is Blue One. Taxi one T-Bird."

"Blue One, this is Cannon Ground. Taxi to runway two-six. Wind three-zero-zero at one-two. Altimeter is two-niner-niner-seven. Follow the flight of F-100s coming from your right."

I acknowledged his instructions and watched the fighter formation taxi past, then fell into sequence far enough behind them to allow me to avoid most of their exhaust. The T-Bird had no nose wheel steering, requiring the pilot to keep his taxi speed quite high and to tap a brake in the direction he wanted to turn, then tap the opposite brake to stop the turn. The plane was infamous for humbling pilots who attempted to make a sharp turn at low speed, the result almost always being a cocked nose gear. This required someone on the ground to either kick the gear straight or pry it straight with a crowbar. Either maneuver was usually accompanied by much mirth and grinning by the ground crew. I took care that this didn't happen to me.

The F-100 flight pulled into the arming area at the end of the runway, but since we had no weapons on board I bypassed the area and proceeded to the number one position by the runway.

"Cannon Tower, this is Blue One. Number one for takeoff at two-six. Request left turnout to the practice area please."

"Blue One, you're cleared for takeoff. Wind is two-niner-zero at one-five. Altimeter, two-niner-niner-eight. Left turnout approved. No other reported traffic."

We taxied and lined up on the center stripe of the runway. As I advanced the power to 100 percent, I checked all the instruments and then glanced quickly around the sky before I started the clock and released the brakes. As we gathered speed I could feel the controls come alive in my hands with the increased airflow over the control surfaces. Gently,

I lifted the nose and held the takeoff attitude until the aircraft started to fly, then moved the gear lever to "up" and let the aircraft accelerate. I moved the flap lever up; the airspeed began building rapidly, and I turned toward the practice area.

Yesterday's gloom had moved eastward and today's sky was a brilliant, startling blue broken only by the tiny balls of white cumulus clouds. Leveling at 20,000 feet, we immediately began the checkout routine: stalls done with gear and flaps up and down; accelerated stalls; low-speed flight; recovery from vertical climbs; loops and Immelmann turns; barrel and aileron rolls; chandelles and lazy-eights. We went from one maneuver to the next with scarcely a pause. I began to sweat with the exertion, for pulling g's was hard work and many of the aerobatic maneuvers required the pilot to sustain at least a four-g pull.

Returning to the field after we had completed the air work, I made several touch-and-go landings and taxied back to the parking area. The clock showed that the flight had lasted almost two hours. George cleared me for solo flight starting that afternoon.

The flying went smoothly and quickly after everyone in the flight had soloed. While we were waiting for those who were strangers to the T-Bird, Bill and I happily chased one another around the practice area as if it were our private flying club. There was minimal ground training associated with the course, so we often ended up sitting in the rear cockpit of someone else's flight when we weren't scheduled for an aircraft to fly. The boredom factor began to get us in a big way until we started formation flying and the gunnery range.

Most of us had some serious brushup work to do in the formation phase of the training. You can lose the knack for it very quickly. There is just no way you can fly "mechanically" in very close proximity to another aircraft. You simply must have the feel for it. From a distance, a formation of four close-flying aircraft looks as if the planes are locked together by an invisible wire. On closer inspection, the four aircraft can be seen to be constantly shifting and correcting their positions in small movements. Most of us were sweat soaked after an hour of formation flying, trying to regain lost skills.

Pilots who had flown larger aircraft had some problems finding their proficiency again; however, the orange-bagged ADC types acted as if they had been born to it. Most of us were somewhere in between the two.

The air-to-ground work started soon after the formation flying had commenced. Each flight would take off in formation and fly to the range to practice the four events in which we were expected to qualify—dive-bomb, skip bomb, rockets, and guns. Time after time, we rolled the aircraft and dove from the pattern to drop or fire at targets. It was great fun but exhausting work. Beers were wagered on the scores, the low man buying for the flight. Flights wagered against other flights and even, on occasion, squadron wagered against squadron. It would have taken a full-time bookie to keep track of all the bets on all the events. By the time most of us had finished and received the promised checkouts in the F-86, the betting results had become so hopelessly confused that most of them were wiped out by mutu   consent of the parties involved.

The end of the training in New Mexico lacked the dramatic. We simply packed our sparse belongings in our cars, waved a casual farewell to the others still finishing up, and pointed the cars toward Florida. We'd all be meeting there in less than two weeks.

Everyone had their families in Florida, whether they could afford it or not. This was the last stop before Southeast Asia, and everyone was going to take advantage of three months on the beach. Living conditions varied, ranging from five in a single-bedroom apartment, in my case, to large houses on isolated beaches. Everyone, particularly the children, turned brown enough to be used in swimsuit ads.

The initial introduction to the OV-10 training squadron went quite differently than we had expected. The commander, a trim-looking lieutenant colonel, was very brief:

"Gentlemen," he said. "Let's have no misunderstanding. Everyone here knows exactly where you're going in three months. I've just returned from Vietnam myself. There are, of course, certain things we're going to have to teach you here in order for you to do your job properly over there. But, I know that most of you brought your families down here to be with you for this last three months. For some of you it's going to be the last time on this earth that you'll be with those families. It's an unpleasant thought, but there it is. What I intend to do is to make this as pleasant a time period for you as I can. You will be expected to meet any scheduled ground school class, but we're going to hold those to a minimum. Also, you will be present for briefing one hour before any scheduled flight. Other than that, you are free to come and go as you please. Spend as much time as you can with your families. For those of you who do not have your families along, see the ops officer and we'll try to arrange schedules that will allow you some leave. The wing commander has gone along with me on the idea that we'll probably need to run some courier flights to the air force base nearest your family's domicile. That'll give you a chance for a free flight on an aircraft on a space-available basis. If you can't get space-A coming back, call me personally and I'll have your schedule rearranged so that you don't end up AWOL. Any questions?''

We were stunned. Was this really the Air Force? Then, spontaneous clapping filled the room. Max, the pudgy SAC escapee, yelled: "I want to have your baby, Colonel." He grinned, waved, and sauntered out of the briefing room.

True to the commander's word, ground school was cut to the barest requirements, and most of our studying was done on the beach under the warm springtime Florida sun. There were class parties at least twice a week, fostering a growing closeness among the pilots and the wives. The only thing to mar the happiness was the dwindling number of days before we had to leave. The wives were wonderful, bright and perky in their new tans and swimsuits. But if you looked closely, unobserved, behind some of that gaiety the looks would turn pensive when they thought no one was watching. There was a magnetism pulling everyone together, as if we could draw strength from one another.

We had to get accustomed to the appearance of the OV-10 Bronco. We'd never seen anything quite like it. The plane looked as if the manufacturer had gone out of his way to make it ugly. In aviation circles there is a truism that says a good airplane looks its role. That is, a fast jet fighter looks like a fast jet fighter. A bomber naturally looks big and tough. This thing had us stumped. As Bill put it, "The damned thing looks like it was put together using spare parts."

There were two sizable turboprop engines, which provided a good fuel burn, as well as twin-engine reliability. Extending behind each engine nacelle were twin booms, reminiscent of the World War II P-38 fighter. Two tandem cockpits provided the seating arrangement, although the one in the rear had only minimum instrumentation, being designed more to haul a spare body. Behind the rearmost ejection seat was a huge cargo bay, which supposedly could be used to carry three jumpers. Sponsons stuck out of the sides of the fuselage like little fish fins, providing weapon stations and housing for the four 7.62-caliber machine guns and ammunition bays. Additional weapon stations were provided on the wings and belly, where it was also possible to sling a large auxiliary fuel tank.

Housing the ejection seats was a huge, bulbous canopy, which allowed almost unrestricted visibility; it was constructed so that the pilot could lean outboard to its limit and see directly beneath the aircraft. The internal systems were simple but sturdy, with a minimum of frills. The landing gear was designed to take the shock of an unflared landing, the type we called "carrier approaches," where you just slammed into the ground. You pointed the nose of the plane at the place you wanted to land and kept it there. Most aircraft would have snapped off their landing gear if this were attempted, but with the OV-10, the maneuver helped reduce the ground roll, always a factor when flying off the unimproved strips we would be using in Vietnam. Once the plane was on the ground, the turbopropped engines could be moved into the reverse range, providing additional braking.

In flight, the OV-10 was the most agile aircraft I had ever flown. It was designed to withstand over eight g-forces, reducing the likelihood of its wings being torn off in a hard pullout. The only people who had trouble doing aerobatics in the little bird were those who didn't like the maneuvers to start with. But, the Bronco was not fast. To go over 200 knots you had to have the nose pointed straight down.

The aircraft was a joy to work on the gunnery range. On my first trip carrying ordnance, Bill and his instructor were leading the flight and I was flying number two position on their right wing. Two other aircraft made up the second element on their left wing.

"Wolf Flight, check in."

"Two."

"Three."

"Four."

A flight's ability is judged partially on the brevity of their radio transmissions. For a wingman to say anything more than an acknowledgment using his flight position is a sign of poor training. If a pilot has anything to question, he normally does it with a series of hand signals or, even better, after he's on the ground.

"Hurlburt Ground Control," Bill called, "Wolf Lead with a flight of four Broncos, ready to taxi."

"Wolf Flight, this is Hurlburt Ground. You're cleared to taxi to runway two-two. Altimeter is two-niner-niner-eight. Wind is two-four-zero at zero-eight."

Without further ado, we began to taxi in sequence, following the leader, pulling up into the arming area with the noses pointed away from the most populated portion of the flight line in the event a rocket or gun should inadvertently be fired. We set the parking brakes, and everyone aboard in each cockpit conspicuously raised their hands so they were visible to the ground crewmen, waiting in front of the aircraft. This signaled them to come forward and remove the safing pins from all the weapons. As they did so they continued to glance warily at the pilots, insuring that their hands were in sight and away from the firing buttons. Should one of the hands forgetfully stray to scratch an itch, the armorers would explode like frightened quail from the front of the aircraft and have to be conjoled into returning. They have good reason for distrusting the pilots, for once the pins are removed any inadvertent pressure on one of the myriad firing buttons or triggers garnishing the control stick can launch a rocket or fire the guns.

"Wolf Flight, go tower," Bill called. The ground crew had scurried away and were now standing twenty yards in front of each aircraft, displaying the arming pins like hunting trophies. Each pilot after counting the pins being held for his inspection responded by removing his ejection seat safing pin and holding it up for inspection by the crew chief. Everyone assured, we changed frequency and checked in with the lead ship.

Cleared for takeoff, we taxied onto the runway in pairs. I snuggled up as close as possible to Bill's right wing. He looked over at me and made a twirling motion with one finger of his hand. It was my signal to run up the engines and check all of my instruments, my last chance for a while, since I would be devoting all of my attention to maintaining the proper position on his wing. Everything looked good and I turned my head back to the lead ship, holding the brakes against the takeoff power on the engines. My legs were quivering with the strain. Bill stared at me until I nodded my readiness to go.

I watched his head come back against the headrest of the ejection seat in an exaggerated movement, then snap forward, simultaneously releasing his brakes just as I did so that we both moved forward together. I manipulated my throttle to maintain my position, knowing that he had a little less than normal takeoff power set, which gave me a little latitude to catch up should I start falling behind. We broke ground together and again I saw his chin come up and snap forward, the signal for us both to raise our landing gear. Another few hundred feet of altitude and he repeated the motion, this time for flap retraction.

We started a lazy, climbing turn to allow the other element to join us, then he rolled out on a heading for the gunnery range. This route took us along the beach, where we were signaled to spread out the formation so we could dip our wings to our wives, sunbathing on the beach below. After we passed over the beach we were signaled back into a tight formation for the short flight to the range. While we were spread, we took the opportunity to look over our instruments and fuel settings and quantities.

Bombing and shooting in the Bronco was pure fun. We were going slow enough to be very accurate, and the little aircraft could be maneuvered in an unbelievable fashion. I watched Bill make astounding scores in his usual way. He was better than any of the instructors in the squadron. The rest of us were coming on strong as well, particularly those with a background in the big birds. We were already acting like old fighter pilots.

The flight back was enlivened by some aerobatics in which we dutifully followed Bill, maintaining our position in relation to his aircraft whether he was inverted or not. We spread to wiggle once more at our wives on the beach before letting down for the landing, which was accomplished out of the echelon formation. Flying straight down the runway, I watched the lead ship pilot wave "bye-bye" at me and peel off to the left for landing. I counted five seconds to myself, then wheeled off in a hard left turn, picking up the lead ship now turning base leg. I followed him around for the landing.

At the debriefing, the instructor who rode in the rear cockpit of the lead ship conducted the critique.

"Everybody looked sharp today, except that the echelon on landing was strung out so much we looked like a bomber flight. Get it in there close. Bill, that was damned good bombing. Your rockets and guns were good too, but the bombs were the best I've seen in a long time. Too bad you're not going over in an attack aircraft. The rest of you did OK too. It's all coming together. Any questions? If not, see you tomorrow."

As the others left, I mentioned to the IP that the radio discipline was very good today.

"Yeah," he said. "But I don't give out compliments on that after having seen it in Vietnam. Sometimes over there it gets to the point where you can't get a word in edgewise. There are so many reasons for it; for instance, just the plain excitement of being in combat makes some people talk more. Being scared does the same thing for a lot of people; it gives them assurance from somebody they can't even see. Besides, just the sheer volumn of radio traffic over there means there's going to be a lot of frequency spillover. When you have the jets operating at 40,000 feet and they're working close to your frequency, it can get to be a damned nightmare. Hell, their transmissions at that altitude can carry 200 miles or more. Then, you get all the assholes flying everything from helicopters to gooney birds who are just plain bored and want to chat with somebody. You can forget Guard channel. The army pilots have taken that over as their personal interplane frequency.''

"That must be great if you've got an emergency and are trying to get in touch with somebody."

"I ain't saying it's right," he said, "just the way it is."

The training progressed, and the commander, true to his word, never burdened us with unnecessary work or classes. Primarily, the ground school consisted of explaining just what a forward air controller was supposed to do when attached to the U.S. Army. We knew, of course, that we were to find and mark targets for the jets. Few of us had realized, however, how extensive some of our other jobs might be.

Every line battalion was assigned a FAC to advise its commander on air matters, the senior FAC in the brigade being called the air liaison officer, or ALO, who advised the brigade commander and his staff in the same manner as the battalion FACs. Simply put, their job was to coordinate all of the USAF air activity for their assigned army unit insofar as it involved close air support for the troops and any other bombing within the AO.

In addition to advising the army staff on air matters, FACs were responsible for physically marking all targets or describing them in such a manner to all attacking air force aircraft that there could be no mistaking them. In addition to that primary duty, a FAC was expected to perform daily reconnaissance in his area of operations and find or confirm targets from other sources. We normally flew only in our AO, giving us the opportunity to know it like the backs of our hands. The exception to this would occur when the brigade's AO changed; then, so would ours.

Most of the instructors for the ground and flight courses were recent returnees from Southeast Asia, and we listened to them with rapt attention. For the first time, we were meeting the types of people we would be expected to replace over there. The comparison was not comforting, for they seemed very self-assured in everything they did, and they each handled the airplane as though it was an extension of their own bodies.

I was having an after-flight beer on the veranda of the officers' club with my instructor, Jim, who had been back only a few months.

"I'll say this," he began. "A FAC is the loneliest pilot in the world. You know, with every other kind of flying that you can think of, the pilot has somebody he can shoot the shit with. A wingman, or another crew member, or somebody. Except the FAC. On lots of your flights you'll never hear another human voice except for takeoff and landings or if you find something. Half the time you're out of range of your own control room, particularly in the mountains. You could have been shot down for four hours and nobody would even know where to start looking for you when you don't come home. You start thinking about it and it'll really screw up your mind. It's a real satisfying job when everything goes right. But things have a way of turning to do-do in a hurry in Nam, and everybody is tickled pink to have a FAC to blame for a short round or a fighter pilot who screws up. Don't give 'em any slack is the best advice I can give you because they'll just turn around and break it off in your ass if they get a chance. You'll find those poor simple VC are the least of your worries over there. The biggest problem is protecting your butt from every asshole with a chicken on his shoulder who wants to take all the chances for his own personal gain and leave you on the hind tit when responsibility is assigned for the screwup. Drink up, it's my round."

The date of departure grew closer and closer, and we made more of an effort to pretend it really didn't exist. There would be no leave for any student after completing the training. We were given minimum time to get to California for an Orient-bound flight.

After the children were asleep, Mary Ann and I would spend quiet evenings on the beach with a bottle of cheap wine. We seldom spoke of my departure, but it was always foremost in our minds. Those quiet times were interspersed with loud weekend pool and beach parties at someone's house. Our bachelors' activities among the north Florida belles were so strenuous that I actually feared for their health.

One final squadron party and suddenly the day was here. We would all make our ways separately to California for debarkation, but we would go to Vietnam as a group. Along the way there would be a one-week layover in the Philippines for jungle survival school.

I'd said my good-byes to the children, who were being watched by a neighbor, and Mary Ann drove me to the airport. They would be leaving to go back to Washington soon after I left. My last sight of my

seven-year-old was of him sharing his ice cream cone with one of the
local dogs. A year was going to be a mighty long time in the life of a
young family. As I watched my wife's big green eyes fill with tears at
the departure gate, I wondered how anyone could do this more than
once in a lifetime.

The best thing that can be said for flying across the Pacific is that it
has to end sooner or later. There were only five of our original group
on the civilian airliner when we departed Oakland—Larry, Joe, Max,
Willie, and me. The others had been delayed due to lack of student
slots in the jungle survival school we were to attend in the Philippines.
Those who had been delayed were given some leave time, but in talking
to them I could tell they were like football players pumped up to go in
the game. Not being allowed to play was depressing.

The survival course would take six days and be some respite from
Vietnam, albeit a short one. We didn't know much about the school, it
being a new requirement for all aircrews bound for Vietnam. We did
know about survival schools in general, though, for most of us had
just finished the USAF Survival School in the mountains of Washington.
There, among other things, we learned to build snowshoes and snow
houses, certainly a must for survival in Southeast Asia.

Landing at Clark Air Force Base in the blazing midmorning sun, we
were delighted to learn that nothing was scheduled for us until the next
morning. Exhaustion claimed us all after a quick dip in the O-Club
pool and a couple of beers. We slept the rest of the afternoon and
through the night.

Walking to the ground school the next morning, we had a chance to
look over the air base again. I had seen it only once before, though the
MAC types in our group had frequently landed there and staged through
to the rest of the Orient. It was an old base, having been built back in
the 1930s; it had the look of one of the old-time army posts, with
broad, tree-lined avenues and banyan-covered houses. The houses, we
noticed, were reserved for full colonels and up. I guess the lower ranks
had to live in the squalid town outside the gate.

The ground school consisted, for the most part, of war stories by
Vietnam returnees and so-called jungle experts who kept insisting that
"the jungle is your friend." We remained unconvinced. The only thing
of real interest was their assurance that we would not need to secrete
food on our persons when we departed for field training, since ample

chow would be provided. Remembering the starvation course provided by the stateside survival school, most students remained skeptical, taking emergency packets with them. In this case, however, the authorities would prove to be correct. We never needed the additional food supplies. Before we broke for the day we were assigned an instructor for each six-man crew. He was assisted by a small Negrito, less than five feet tall, to show us the mysteries of the jungle.

Early the next morning we were flown to the school's field location on another island. We formed into our crews and walked into the rain forest, our sergeant instructor telling us again that the jungle was our friend. It was starting to sound like a Madison Avenue campaign: "Now see here men, here's the new, improved jungle containing additional snakes, larger spiders, and assorted varmints not seen before." OK, Sarge. We believe you. It really does look friendly. Bullshit, it looked like it would swallow you up in a minute and never let you out. I couldn't think of a more horrible place to be alone.

You don't often think of a jungle as having mountains, or mountains having jungles. Ours did. We were also fortunate enough to time our entry into the school with the beginnings of the monsoon. Within a couple of weeks, this area right on through to northern South Vietnam would be subjected to ever-increasing thunderstorms and deteriorating weather.

Ramon, our Negrito guide, lived in a remote village not too far from our training area. He spoke no English and carried a wicked-looking bolo, a long, curved knife that he used for everything from building hootches to cutting his toenails. He was a marvel in the woods, seeming to blend into the verdant surroundings. He was also a great cook, using the foods growing wild in the area. He showed us how to find these edible foods, which plants to avoid, how to make hammocks from our parachutes, and how to find water—surprisingly difficult in the jungle. He did all these things without one word of English and with a gentle smile on his face, which turned to a broad grin when one of his clumsy charges did something approximately correct. As one of us would fall over a log or down the side of a muddy mountain, or reach for a piece of bamboo not noticing the viper resting upon it, I'm sure Ramon wondered at our innocence and at what sort of world we must have come from that we could survive with all our ineptness. We marveled at his ability to go without water as the rest of us sweated it out at a prodigious rate. In the unbelievable heat and humidity, with no air stirring beneath the gigantic trees, Ramon glided along as if he were on a Sunday stroll, whereas the rest of us felt as if our lungs were a cider press, trying to squeeze the moisture out of the air.

At night, the little Negrito would cook tasty dishes out of the wild rice and other free-growing items he'd found on our day's wanderings, using sections of bamboo as a steamer. During our breaks, as the rest of the crew lay floundering in the heat, he would be busy making little drinking or eating vessels out of more bamboo sections. On several occasions, he would step from the trail, his bolo would flash, and he would proudly hold up some sort of snake or lizard for our admiration. He always kept his booty and we refrained from asking what he planned to do with it, afraid he might tell us.

The field course was completed with a twenty-four-hour escape-and-evasion problem, giving the students a two-hour head start in an area in which we could run and hide anywhere. After the two hours, Ramon would be allowed to try to find us. Being a major and therefore much smarter than Ramon, I went only about a half mile into the rain forest until I found an extremely dense bamboo grove. Moving carefully so as to not disturb the growth, I worked my way into the bowels of the grove, an increment at a time. After each movement I turned to readjust the bamboo I had moved aside by my passage, making the grove look pristine once again. Judging that I had squirmed into the approximate center of the grove, I removed my mosquito net and snugged it around a cleared area that I thought would be my home for the next twenty-two hours. I really hated the idea that Ramon would be deprived of the two kilos of rice he would be rewarded for finding me, the standard for each student he found hiding.

Closing my eyes, I cursed the rain that had begun falling again. I was thoroughly wet with rain and sweat. Maybe I should have brought a book to help pass the time. But the sleep would feel good; we hadn't been getting that much of it.

Something gently shook my arm. I opened my eyes in panic to find myself staring at Ramon's smiling black face. He made hushing motions with his hand and squatted beside me. He pointed outside the mosquito net and grinned delightedly, glancing at me to see if I was enjoying his fun. There were two green bamboo vipers intertwined about chest high just outside the net. Instinctively, I flinched away. My movement startled the snakes, who quickly writhed out of sight. Ramon looked disappointed, his broad grin replaced once again by the sad, gentle smile. He motioned for me to follow him and began to slither from the cane thicket. I followed more clumsily.

As I stumbled back to camp while Ramon pursued more rice, I mulled over the thoughts of my recent capture and how it would have been different should it have been the real thing. Maybe that was the point of the whole school—to make you think about the real situation. If I were to be shot down, I thought, it would more than likely be over someone else's turf, which he would probably know much better than I would. On the ground, I would be in his element, and I sure as hell wouldn't be able to fool anyone with my woodcraft. The most sensible course of action would seem to be to get away from your downed airplane and move as carefully as possible to some hidey-hole. Then, stay still as a fawn until someone came to help you.

I trudged into camp, finding almost my entire crew already there. Ramon had been a very active little man in the last hour. Most of the crew had stories similar to mine. Long before the time for the exercise had expired, the Negrito had found everyone. It was fortunate he had found Larry, who had gone some distance from camp to hide. Larry found what he thought looked like a good spot—a small clearing surrounded by extremely thick undergrowth—and decided to set up housekeeping. Relaxing in his parachute hammock beneath a canopy of broad leaves to keep off the tropical downpour, he opened a can of C-ration biscuits and lay in his jungle bower nibbling on them until he dropped off to an exhausted sleep.

A huge jungle rat, probably attracted by the smell of the food, shimmied up one of the trees anchoring the hammock, crept across the nylon risers that tied the parachute to the tree, and began to eat the biscuit crumbs from Larry's chest. Finishing those and evidently still hungry, the rat finished the crumbs remaining on Larry's lip. Larry came awake at the additional weight on his chest and raised his head as the rodent was reaching for another choice morsel. Two sets of beady eyes locked onto one another, and Larry understandably jerked his head away. The rat, either in a pique at being denied the food or operating out of the survival mode, immediately clamped down on the nearest thing he could find—Larry's lip. Larry sprang from his jungle bed with the two-pound rodent hanging onto his lip for dear life. Only their collision with a huge jungle emergent dislodged the rat and brought Larry back to the world of the sane. He was shortly thereafter found by Ramon who, when told of the incident through sign language and much pointing, indicated his disappointment that Larry had not had the foresight to hang onto the critter just a little longer, for they were delicious eating.

At Clark Air Force Base that afternoon we found there would be only the remainder of the day and night before our departure to Saigon early the next morning. We cleaned and patched our various wounds and insect bites after agreeing to meet at the O-Club for a final steak before our departure. Our group had been augmented by Ed and Frank, both members of our Hurlburt class and placed on another airliner out of Oakland to replace the inevitable no-shows. During survival school they had been on another part of the jungle island.

Larry arrived late at the O-Club, having gone to the base dispensary for his first antirabies innoculation. There, he was told that he could either have his departure delayed to finish the series or he could carry an explanatory letter that required him to finish the innoculations wherever he was going. He opted to proceed with the group although not completely convinced by the medic's report that he would be able to find the needed serum all over Vietnam.

"What the hell happens if I get over there and they just don't happen to have the serum?" he asked us.

"Oh, stop your worrying," Max said. "They'll have your damned serum. Probably."

"Of course they will," Frank said, "but if they just happen to be out for the moment, could I have your watch?"

"Don't worry, Larry," I told him. "If anything happens we'll have the best wake your money can buy. Do you think you ought to cash a check before we go? You don't want to be caught short, you know."

"My only concern," said Ed, "is that we won't be able to tell if he has hydrophobia or not. You know, he usually foams at the mouth and howls like a dying dog whenever there's women around. I mean, what are we looking for?"

Having reassured Larry, we all went into the dining room. It was crowded with other crew members from the survival school as well as many of those here for other temporary duties. There were flight suits everywhere.

After dinner, the bar was crowded so the consensus was to head to one of the small bars outside the gate for one last drink in "civilization" before hitting the racks. Our group was soon firmly entrenched in the Great Pals Bar and Grill. Several of the bar's workers, as well as the patrons, were armed. We settled around the table and the San Miguel began to arrive. We felt dehydrated from our jungle vacation and the beer was ice cold. After a few more, our celebration seemed like a wonderful idea. Even the bar guard with his sawed-off Remington pump shotgun seemed benevolent. The near-exhaustion and the beers were having an early effect.

Before midnight more Americans arrived, several of them wearing the short-sleeved white naval uniform. Those in uniform had gold flight wings on their chests. Soon, they became as boisterous as our group.

It was obviously a source of irritation to Max that we had spent an entire evening without anyone even being superficially injured. Suddenly, he stood on his chair and bellowed at the top of his voice, "Let's say hello to our friends in the navy!"

Without thought, we all responded, "Hello, assholes!"

We were outmanned three to one and things suddenly became very quiet, if not sober. The navy fliers rose as one and very deliberately began to walk across the floor toward us. I glanced at the fat man with the shotgun at the bar. He moved so as to put a low counter between us and him, the barrel of the shotgun shifting ever so much in our direction but not focused on anyone specifically. It appeared that he was just going to insure that whatever damage was done was paid for before anyone departed. I didn't know whether to be happy with his noninvolvement or not. Do something, I thought, as the sailors steered in our direction. After all, you're the senior officer in your group.

Suddenly, Joe, our Chinese-American from Kansas, leapt into an Oriental fighting crouch and began a series of kung fu–type moves. He was obviously not very good at it; in addition, he was quite drunk. He flung himself about the floor screaming imprecations at the approaching naval tide. Perhaps his words sounded less fierce than they could have, since they were delivered in a flat midwestern drawl that was completely incongruous with his appearance. Then too, on his best day he weighed about 120 pounds and stood five-and-a-half feet.

Perhaps even this might not have detracted from his charge had he not caught his leg in one of the folding chairs while he was prancing around our table. The sight was astonishing, for he continued to shadow-box his imaginary opponent, dragging the chair behind him like an anchor. The approaching naval convoy looked stunned by his antics, stopping to stare in wonderment. Joe, apparently having difficulty in focusing on the real enemy, attacked Larry, who was still morosely thinking of the hydrophobic germs speeding through his bloodstream. He responded with a none-too-gentle shove to Joe's chest. I didn't blame Larry for being unhappy. The doctor had told him to abstain from alcohol for the duration of his treatment.

Still tangled in his chair, Joe fell and rolled under the table, then came up from the other side, still dragging the chair and spitting like a Chinese wildcat. Unfortunately, he came up on the side of the table closest to the wall, and immediately ran afoul of the heavy, brocaded drape covering the window. So enraged was he at being unfairly attacked by both the chair and Larry that he struck out in every direction, becoming entwined in the curtain. He finally succeeded in wrestling it to the floor, but in the process secured himself in it, along with the chair still clutching his leg as though it were alive.

Both groups of combatants became still, focusing their attention on Joe's performance. Eventually, his struggles became fainter and fainter, finally ceasing altogether. A blissful look came over his face and he began to breathe heavily and deeply. It was as if his body had needed only to get itself horizontal to purge itself of the unpleasant activity it had been involved with.

One of the sailors walked slowly over to the prostrate form, gently peeled an eyelid back, and peered in, as if he knew what he were looking for. With Larry's help the two unrolled Joe's body from the drapery and removed the killer chair from his leg. They grabbed him by the seat of the pants and the scruff of the neck and plopped him into a chair at our table.

"Gritty little fucker, ain't he?" the navy pilot said, and then grinned. We nodded solemnly.

Another round of San Miguels appeared, ordered by the navy group, accompanied by a friendly wave of the hand. We responded in kind, and soon the other group left, seeking greener pastures. Larry settled with the manager about the curtain, then herded everyone into a cab and directed us back to base. We had had about all the fun we could stand for one evening.

Fortunately, I had packed everything before we had left the base the evening before, for when the alarm went off at 0430 I didn't feel up to anything other than trying to get my heart started. My tongue was thick and my head felt as if it were several sizes too large for my body. I seemed to float to the communal shower.

Dressing and stumbling downstairs we found the bus waiting to take us to the flight line. Only Max seemed little the worse for wear. Joe was almost comatose and remembered virtually nothing of the prior evening, not even his three-round match with the window drapes. Larry was in a surly mood, not only due to the hour but already dreading his next shot in the stomach and not knowing where he would be able to get it. I think he'd already decided that he'd made a mistake and should have taken advantage of a few extra days in the Philippines rather than tag along with the group. Frank and Ed were not scheduled out until a later flight.

There was the inevitable four-hour wait before our aircraft was ready for loading; finding floor space to lie down was impossible, since most of it was already occupied by GIs in transit to the war zone. I remembered those great shots from World War II where entire units marched off together, then compared them to the khaki ghetto stretched out before me. It was obvious that few of the men knew each other, nor would they make friends until they had joined their unit. A lonely way for an eighteen-year-old to go to war.

The old Boeing 707 finally arrived, loaded to the gunnels with troops inbound to Vietnam. The only spaces available were those of aircrews who disembarked for the school we'd just attended. We took their seats. I stared at the company logo on the tail of the old aircraft. I'd never heard of the airline before. The logistics of the war were creating a new wave of entrepreneurs.

The flight to Saigon's Tan Son Nhut airport was relatively short. The young soldiers on board were exhausted from their long flight but were already stirring in anticipation of their arrival in the war zone. Most of them had that frightened yet curious expression on their faces I would come to know so well.

The seats in the troop-carrying airliners had been modified to accommodate the maximum number of people on board, so there was little room to do anything but sit bolt upright. Even so, most of us fell into quasi-unconsciousness as soon as the gear was up. It seemed a very short time before Larry, in the window seat beside me, nudged me gently and pointed outside. I leaned over him and saw Vietnam for the first time in more than two years. At 30,000 feet, it was beautiful. The green seemed greener than was possible, particularly in contrast to the red earth visible in places beneath the luxuriant growth. The paddy fields looked neat, and the small villages seemed doll-like nestled beneath the banana plants. Uniform squares of rubber trees marked the plantations north of Saigon, and myriad canals distinguished the Mekong Delta to the south. As we began a fast descent, the bomb and artillery craters began to show in the countryside. Here's home for the next year, I thought.

PART 3
In-Country

Our airliner touched down at Saigon's Tan Son Nhut airport just after 0900, and by noon it was apparent that no one from our assigned unit in Bien Hoa was going to meet us. The other occupants of the airplane had long since been collected by their units and departed. Gathering my stalwart but hung-over group about me, we made arrangements with an on-duty army sergeant to secure our baggage, and we began our search for lunch, or at least a beer. We found both in the air force officers' club only a few blocks from the airport terminal. I had been there once before on my initial Vietnam tour. We gawked like tourists as we walked to the club. There had been an astonishing number of changes to the base since I had last seen it. Large, permanent-looking structures had replaced, for the most part, the frame and thatch that I remembered. It didn't look unlike a large stateside base. The headquarters building looked like something that belonged to SAC headquarters rather than to a wartime command center. Hundreds of vehicles jammed the wide streets, most of which were paved.

The club had changed as well. I remembered a small, open building where you could pick up a hamburger, Vietnamese-style, along with a cold beer for a few piasters. Instead there was a huge air-conditioned structure with several bars, bandstands, and a dress code. Rather than the fly-speckled screened-in porch where you could sit and watch the sun go down and the malaria-bearing mosquitoes arrive, there was plush-chaired, draped-window elegance. We stood in the foyer and wondered if we'd be allowed to enter. Max looked at me curiously and said softly, "Are you sure we're in the same country that you and all those stateside instructors have been talking about?"

Grinning weakly, I said, "Well, things do seem to have changed a little since I was here."

"Hey, I ain't complaining," Max responded. "Maybe this won't be such a bad war after all. Do you think they have any FACs stationed here at Tan Son Nhut? Wonder what you'd have to do to get a job right here?"

"One thing for sure," Larry interjected. "If they do have FACs here, somebody right off the boat ain't going to be one of them, not if I know the Air Force."

"You can bet your bars on that," I said. "Let's see if we can't grab a bite to eat before those commandos from the bar come swarming in here. We'll probably get ranked out of a table if we wait for them to finish their second martini. After we eat we can wander over and see if the medical dispensary is in the same place that I remember. You're about due for your next rabies shot, aren't you?"

"Yeah," Max told Larry. "I think you're starting to foam at the mouth a little bit."

"That's right. It's either that or the meltdown of your brain has finally started and will soon be running out of all your body openings," Joe said.

"Why don't you all blow it out your ass," Larry responded graciously.

A tiny Vietnamese woman directed us to an empty table. She was wearing the traditional *ao dai,* the national dress for all cultured ladies. It had loose, billowy pants covered by a split skirt of silky material that flowed almost to the ground. The blouse was a tight-fitting garment with a choker collar. Most of the women wore high-heeled sandals with it. The naturally graceful tiny females floated about like gaily colored butterflies.

Small luncheon steaks and a can of cold beer did much to wash away the remnants of last night's debauchery. I filled my pipe and enveloped the table in a cumulus of smoke. I had stopped smoking cigarettes a few years before and thought that the pipe made me look scholarly.

"Jesus, Major!" Max said, fanning the air vigorously with his hands. "That goddamned thing ought to be outlawed under the Geneva Convention." I had learned to ignore their childish quips and continued to puff away complacently, admiring the bronzed bodies of the men and some women stretched out around the swimming pool visible through the large window. My experience had been that field troops will do almost anything to stay out of the sun. Here were people actually courting it.

The group began to grow ugly and to actually threaten me with physical violence until I finally promised to put away my briar. I didn't do so before reminding them that only I among them had the vaguest idea about how to reach Bien Hoa, today's ultimate destination. Several of them had already tried and been defeated by the military telephone system. The exchange was almost impossible to use without some knowledge of the routing throughout the country and a willingness to lie about your priority.

We left the club and took a leisurely stroll for the few blocks to the medical dispensary, speculating on how long it would take for Larry's will to be broken by the continued application of needles to his belly. He was not amused. Even less amusing were the occupied body bags being unloaded from ambulances to the rear of the hospital. The bodies were obviously inbound for preparation before being sent back to the States. They would be placed in coffins before they were shipped back. There seemed to be a lot of them.

Considerably sobered, we made our way back to the airport terminal, where we reclaimed our baggage. Carrying our large green canvas parachute bags and trying to look as if we knew exactly what we were doing, we walked back out onto the flight line. There were many different aircraft in various stages of loading or shutting down. I saw a pilot doing a preflight inspection on a Caribou aircraft some distance down the ramp. I left my bags and walked to him, arriving just as he was peering distrustfully into the bowels of the left engine.

"Hi," I said brightly. "Don't suppose you're heading over to Bien Hoa today?"

Glancing at me and then at the others waiting up the ramp, he again leaned his head into the uncowled engine and said, "Yeah, as a matter of fact we are. We'll end up going there twice this afternoon, as well as more than half the damned corps. You guys need a lift?"

"Yeah, we sure do. We're all assigned to the 504th and we got in this morning but nobody showed up to claim us. We'd appreciate a ride over that way, if you've got room."

"Oh, hell yes. We've got room. We're actually picking up most of our cargo over there, then hauling some trash on down to the delta. If you're ready, y'all haul your shit on board, then wait in the shade under the wing. We'll be leaving in about twenty."

"Great, we really do appreciate it. I don't know why no one was here to get us."

"That doesn't surprise me. I think a body could spend his entire tour right here at Tan Son Nhut and never check in anyplace and nobody'd miss him. You could probably take your pay records down to Finance and get paid in a casual status and then when your year was up, you could check in with the Transportation people and get shipment orders home to the base of your choice. I don't know why I never thought of it.'' He seemed genuinely intrigued by the idea.

He walked away to continue the preflight inspection, still muttering possibilities to himself. I waved the group over and we loaded our gear aboard the transport aircraft, then stretched out under the wing of the Caribou. The heat was starting to peak at its normal 100 degree reading and the humidity was very high. Sweat was soaking through our khaki uniforms, which weren't helped any by wallowing in the grit of the concrete ramp. We watched the hustle of the airdrome activity as we waited, following a constant stream of aircraft taking off and landing. There were recce birds; transports of every variety, including a constant stream of civilian airliners; fighters, mostly of the air defense type; navy and air force command and control birds; and more helicopters than any of us would have thought possible. We got a sampling of just about every aircraft in the theater in just those few minutes. The airliners quickly discharged their human cargoes and quickly reloaded with a batch of lucky ones on their way home. The planes stayed on the ground for minimum time, unwilling to risk exposure to rocket attacks.

The Caribou pilot, now joined by his copilot and enlisted loadmasters, came out of a small flight-line building and ambled toward us. He gave us a halfhearted emergency briefing and told us to strap in. Both engines were started before all of us found our seat belts. We taxied immediately, the ramp door partially open for ventilation, for the aircraft had no other ventilation that we could find. There was a lengthy traffic delay, then the ramp door groaned closed and we took the runway to sit for another two minutes before we were cleared for takeoff. With the door closed it was stifling in the cargo bay.

After takeoff we leveled at a low altitude for the short hop to Bien Hoa. I was preening in my newfound prestige for having found transportation to our destination so easily. I was content to let everyone believe that it had all been my doing. No need to let them know that I'd been lucky to find an aircraft going our way on the first try. We just as easily could have remained sitting in the terminal the rest of the day before we found an aircraft to our destination that didn't stop at half the airfields in Vietnam.

After leveling off, the pilot, feeling some compassion for his cargo, again cracked the ramp door, allowing a beautiful draft to cool our wet skin. We were able to get teasing glances of the countryside below through the door and the tiny windows set in the fuselage. We were also able to smell the rising miasma of Vietnam itself—that particular combination of rotting vegetation, wood smoke from a thousand charcoal fires, the human waste on the rice fields, and the rivers with their cargoes of dead vegetation and animal matter that combined to make an aroma readily detectable even at 2,000 feet. The nose soon becomes desensitized to the smell, which, however, is instantly recognizable even years later.

The countryside was dotted with small villages and connecting roads, with the major highway between Saigon and Bien Hoa readily discernible in the flat farmland. The primary forest surrounding the capital city had long since been burned away in charcoal braziers. There was a constant flow of vehicles on the main highway connecting these two principal cities of South Vietnam. It didn't look particularly like a country at war except for the water-filled bomb craters occasionally visible in the rice paddies.

It took only moments of flying before we started our descent into the Bien Hoa airfield traffic pattern. As we taxied toward the in-country terminal, I peered through one of the Caribou's windows at the surrounding flight line. The base was huge compared to what it had been just a couple of years before. There were long rows of revetted fighters, both prop and jet; transport aircraft of every variety; and even an area set aside for OV-10s.

Deplaning allowed us to fully appreciate the late afternoon sun. Once in the terminal, Joe was finally able to make contact on the phone to the 504th. Soon two jeeps arrived to take us to the Transient Officers' Quarters.

"The duty officer said he'd sign us all in," Joe said as we moved in a two-jeep convoy along the crowded streets of the air base. "He told me that they didn't know who was coming anyway. Said they just took anybody who showed up. Funny way to run a war, isn't it?"

The theory held by the Caribou pilot was looking more and more sound. Maybe you really could spend an entire tour over here without ever showing up for duty.

We checked into almost-new, air-conditioned BOQ's, and I headed for the bunk. It occurred to me that, even discounting jet lag, it had been quite awhile since I had had a full night's sleep, what with being in the jungle or in a sleazy bar.

We met with the operations officer the next morning and found that we had yet another school to attend before assignment to our units. They couldn't give us the specific unit assignments, but the decision had already been made to keep me, Larry, and Max somewhere in III Corps. Joe and Willie would be heading north to I Corps. There were no assignments to IV Corps, for there were no OV-10s located down there.

The ops officer, a lieutenant colonel, was a real horse's ass. He acted as if a few months of sitting on his fat bottom at Bien Hoa made him an expert in controlling the aerial war within South Vietnam. Most of the people we met at headquarters had the same superior attitude. During my first tour, all of the headquarters staff had gone out of their way to help those living in the field with the Vietnamese units; most of the staff had served out there themselves. Now, however, everybody seemed to be marking time until they could get out of the country and back to the real world. Jesus, I thought, what can be more real than a shooting war? That "marking time" attitude would sooner or later filter down to the troops, so that before you knew it, getting out of the country would be the sole reason for getting up in the morning. I was determined not to fall into that pit.

The ops officer finished his brief with the usual sermons about avoiding the water, women, drunkenness, and illegal money exchanges. We were to keep our hair cut, mustaches trimmed, uniforms clean, and by God, act like military officers. We left the office to gather our belongings and try to bum a ride to Phan Rang, where our school was located. Max said very solemnly, "That man is truly an inspiration and I *am* going to act like an officer from now on."

"I *am* going to get my hair cut, by God," Joe said reverently.

"I *am* going to do my very best to avoid water," intoned Willie.

"That's not fair," I complained. "You guys have already used up all the good stuff."

"How about this, Maj? You could *not* make a graven image," said Larry.

"Or, how about *fighting* them on the beach, and *never* surrendering," suggested Max. They thought that sounded so nice that they began to end all of their conversations with "We will never surrender!" This finally became a little wearing, so I suggested "Fighting them on the beaches." It had a nice ring to it.

Max tried very hard to be a good officer for the rest of the day, and Joe did his very best to keep his hair cut for the same period. Willie successfully avoided water by drinking beer, and I was fully prepared to fight on any beach that we came across. Larry refused to take a vow, since he couldn't think of one offhand that he wasn't in the mood to break.

The flight to Phan Rang was uneventful except for the turbulence the old C-123 seemed to go out of its way to find. The air base looked like another large stateside base, except for the unusual mix of aircraft, which we had come to expect. Flights of F-100 fighter-bombers were constantly taking off and landing and the usual hordes of helicopters seemed to be everywhere. The base nestled next to the South China Sea, and miles of beautiful beach could be seen on the approach to landing. I would certainly be willing to fight the VC on this beach. To the west, the tall backbone of the Vietnamese cordillera pushed up through the low-lying clouds. I thought the country looked a lot like Hawaii.

On the way to the BOQ we drove past a huge PX and a movie theater showing *Camelot*. The BOQs were individual rooms and, of course, were air-conditioned. The men were starting to look at me strangely. Where were all the hardships and primitive living I had been telling them about for months? So far, every place we'd been had a more-than-adequate supply of good food, cold beer, and refrigerated air.

We relaxed on the beautifully appointed terrace of the O-Club that evening at sundown, sitting in a group with our feet propped against the rail and gazing down at the flight line and the fighters taking off for night strikes. Suddenly, four large explosions erupted, one after the other, in the grassy area adjacent to the runway. Someone shouted "incoming," and almost simultaneously the base siren began to wail. There was a mad rush to the bunkers outside, although Max displayed his well-developed survival instinct by grabbing an armload of beer before he dived in beside the rest of us. We passed our first rocket attack in relative comfort.

The school, "FAC U," according to the sign over the door to the Quonset hut where it was conducted, was tolerable; the procedures taught were at least current and not overtaken by events the way they often were in the States. But, it was still a school with all the characteristic pettiness and boredom. Each student was scheduled for two flights with an instructor, one day and one night, more or less to get current in the aircraft once more and to get some feel for in-country flying. For some reason known only to Seventh Air Force and Saigon, our assignments were also awaiting us at Phan Rang. Within III Corps, Max would be heading to Tay Ninh when we completed our training; Larry would stay with a unit based at Bien Hoa; I would be going to Di An, a stone's throw from Bien Hoa.

Individual instructors were assigned, and by chance mine was a major who had been transferred to the school from Di An, my new home. I questioned him about the base and its area of operations, and it became clear from his response that not a hell of a lot was going on there at the present: Sweeps through the AO had been producing little in the way of NVA or Viet Cong. He reported that about the only contact the brigade had been getting was on far sweeps out into the Indian country of War Zone C and D.

The first day's training mission was a repeat of those at Hurlburt Field—a few aerobatics, an instrument approach, and a few landings. On the night flight, we were expected to follow a tortuous, preplanned navigation course to a destination and then drop one of the flares we carried and find it below us in the shadows.

It was a moonless night, and once we had crossed the perimeter of the base it was so dark that I couldn't even see the ground much less my checkpoints. I went through the motions, however, heading in the general direction I was supposed to go, and flying my legs by time, turning when my expected ETA arrived. As the final second on the last leg ticked by, I announced on the intercom that we were now over the target, the confluence of two largish rivers. The instructor's "Are you sure?" was skeptical and did little to reassure me. Then I figured, what the hell? His eyes weren't any better than mine and he had to be just as lost as I was.

I triggered out the flare and put the aircraft into an easy banking turn around it, waiting for the ground to come into view as it drifted downward. There were two streams joining, looking not unlike those we had briefed.

"Are you sure those are the right streams?" he asked.

"Yup," I answered with all the confidence I could muster. "I've been on the checkpoints all the way, though I did have to compensate for some westerly wind that wasn't briefed correctly." He was silent for a few moments.

"Harrison, you're either the best navigator I've ever seen or the luckiest. You know, I don't think you have the foggiest idea where you are."

"I don't understand, Major," I said. "You mean you weren't following through on your map on the way here? I can probably explain where you went wrong when we get back on the ground. You see, I've always figured that navigation is one of the things that a good pilot understands thoroughly. I mean, there is really entirely too much reliance on electronic hardware these days. We need to get back to basics."

There was another long pause, then: "Jesus Christ, let's go home and get a beer if you can find the way." I could hardly miss it, since the base was visible from halfway to Thailand.

Later as we sat around a large table in the club—students and instructors alike—I modestly sang my own praises to anyone who would listen, comparing my navigating with that of Magellan and Byrd. My instructor looked very sour.

As the evening progressed and the beer continued to flow, Max's instructor became quite philosophical.

"You guys know," he said, "that what we've been doing here tonight was bullshit. We weren't dropping bombs on anybody and we didn't have a troops-in-contact. It was just an exercise to show you how difficult it is to find a real target over here. It seems so simple back in Florida to say that you just have to fly to a certain set of coordinates and drop some bombs on some dinks. But, wait till you've got a really bad one goin' on down there and you're the only FAC around, and some asshole bird colonel is screaming at you to save some poor bunch of grunts getting their asses blown away. And the nineteen-year-old platoon leader doesn't even know where he is, much less the rest of his people. He'll give you a grid that's probably wrong because he doesn't know what else to do and he's getting his butt kicked properly. You're going to put those coordinates on your map and all you're going to see there is green—nothing but heavy tree growth. No landmarks anywhere. And you ain't going to know where to put those bombs. Put just one of them in the wrong place and you can do more damage than a whole NVA regiment. You're going to listen to that kid down there crying to put ordnance within fifty meters of his position because he's being overrun and you look down and there still ain't nothing visible there but triple-canopy forest no matter what's going on underneath it.

"That Green Square is an ass-kicker, I tell you. 'Bout all you can do is put in one bomb and hope for the best . . . that you haven't killed a whole bunch of young American boys. And the responsibility is all yours. The brigade commander sure ain't going to take it, and the fighter pilots don't know dick; all they're trying to do is to hit your smoke. Naw, it's all yours and it'll make an old man out of you before your time. That Green Square is something else, I'll tell you.''

The other instructors nodded sagely. I tried to picture myself in that situation, with a bird colonel yelling in one ear and the pathetic cries for help from troops on the ground, and then not being able to identify the target. It was scary. I tried to correlate it with actions during my previous tour, but then I had been serving in the relatively treeless Mekong Delta, not in primary rain forest. This was going to be a completely new ball game for me and I wasn't sure how I was going to handle it. Considerably sobered by these thoughts, we finally called it a night.

It was with a real regret that we said good-bye to Joe and Willie, who were heading north to I Corps and their new assignments. We'd all become close, particularly with Joe. His Chinese face had appeared so bland and inscrutable until we got to know him; then we found out that he was a small package of mischief. His sense of humor had helped pass many a dull moment during our training.

Max was obviously touched by Joe's departure, for he asked if Joe had considered the reaction of a helicopter rescue crew in the event he went down. ''They'll probably shoot your scrawny ass right off as soon as they get a good look at those slant eyes and gook face.'' Overcome by the sentiment, Joe responded with an erect middle finger. We shook hands and watched as they boarded the aircraft that was to take them north.

In less than an hour our flight arrived to take us back to Bien Hoa, and by noon we were there. The remaining three of us were all assigned to the 19th Tactical Air Support Squadron (TASS), located on the airfield. This would be our parent organization in terms of administrative support. Tactically, TASS had very little to do with any of the assigned FACs. The squadron's area of responsibility covered a considerable distance north and south of Saigon and from the Cambodian border to the South China Sea. In all, it took in about a quarter of the country's land mass. Our operational and tactical control would fall to the army brigade to which we were assigned and to the air force Direct Air Support Center. Larry's unit just happened to have its headquarters on the Bien Hoa airfield and he therefore would be permitted to live in all this splendor.

Max would be going to a hot area, Tay Ninh, located close to the Cambodian border. All I knew about my assignment to Di An was what I had picked up from the instructor at Phan Rang, and he hadn't been all that forthcoming. Di An wasn't very far from Bien Hoa, however.

We met the ops officer in the 19th's orderly room and were told that our assigned units had been notified of our arrival. They were to send aircraft to pick us up, except for Larry, who was only a jeep ride across the base from his new home. He turned and waved as he left. Max was also picked up quickly, for a pilot from Tay Ninh just happened to be coming to Bien Hoa anyway and had been radioed to give him a lift back. Max was ecstatic to see one of his bachelor friends from our training days who had been a couple of classes ahead of us at Hurlburt. Their reunion was enough to make me fear for the Tactical Air Control Party (TACP) at Tay Ninh. As I waited for my ride, I borrowed a roster of all the FACs in III Corps and went through it carefully to see if I knew any of them. Sure enough, I did know several, but they weren't assigned to Di An.

Phil, the pilot from Di An, finally arrived; he was a tall, dark, well-built major who was also the ALO for my brigade and was therefore my boss. The air liaison officer is the chief FAC for the unit and may have up to six other FACs under him. He is also in command of the Tactical Air Control Party and is normally a major at brigade level and a lieutenant colonel at division. The TACP consists of all the assigned air force personnel—pilots, ground crew, and radio operators—and is a semi-independent unit operating at any one of the forward operating locations (FOL). The army unit is responsible for the feeding, housing, and protection of the TACP personnel and aircraft, and the ALO is a member of the brigade or division commander's staff. The system actually works pretty well in spite of the fact that no one is really sure just who controls whom. That's probably the reason that it does work so well.

After introductions, Phil helped me wrestle my gear out to the aircraft. The mountain of equipment that I had been issued had grown considerably since my arrival back in Bien Hoa. I now had a full issue of field gear, including a steel pot and a CAR-15 carbine, web gear and canteens, rucksacks and ponchos, jungle boots and fatigues, a pistol and a knife, a survival vest with radios and a parachute harness, and a flight helmet and gloves. I had finally gotten tired of inventorying the growing pile that the supply sergeant kept pushing at me, and signed his form saying that I had received everything. Half of the crap I knew I'd never be using anyway.

Before I crawled into the aircraft, I carefully checked the .38 Special, loaded it, and slipped the holster and the eleven-inch K-Bar knife onto my web belt. Bristling with knives and guns I figured that I must cut a pretty warriorlike image. In fact, I am the world's poorest pistol shot and would be better off with a club should it come to close combat. Luckily I didn't have to carry a club, because I don't think I could have managed it. I peeked into my survival vest as Phil chatted with one of the crew chiefs, and began to pull out all sorts of interesting items—bullets, fishhooks, flashlights, strobe lights, tracers, whistles, and signaling mirrors. I was like a kid in a toy store. Each pocket had some more good stuff in it. Phil finished his chat and began walking back toward the aircraft, and I hurriedly stuffed everything back into the vest, after making sure that the two survival radios had current batteries. I didn't know if batteries would be available at Di An.

Phil helped me stow all my gear in the rear cargo bay of the Bronco. "Do you want to fly front seat?" he asked.

"Naw, why don't you go ahead. I'd like to look around on the way over there and see what things look like."

"No sweat, I'll give you the dollar tour. We don't have to have this bird back for a couple of hours, so we might as well get started showing you the brigade's AO."

Taking off at Bien Hoa was not that different from doing it at a stateside base. There was a ground controller, tower operators, and, to make things seem even more normal, there were six other aircraft waiting to take the runway before us. Finally cleared to go after a pair of prop-driven A-1s lumbered off carrying huge bomb loads, we taxied onto the long concrete runway and made a rolling takeoff, getting clearance for an immediate turn to the northeast. I noted immediately that Phil was a hell of a pilot. He'd told me that he had more than seven months in-country, so I guess he'd had plenty of chance to practice. Nevertheless, he was smooth as silk, and every motion of the aircraft was as coordinated as if it were being done by the autopilot. He never flew in a straight line but always in a constant, gentle turn in some direction, averaging them out unconsciously to maintain the desired direction. His eyes were always scanning the ground, except for quick glances around the clock to avoid the helicopter traffic, which also seemed to prefer our altitude. Every few minutes he would quickly scan the instrument panel, but immediately his eyes refocused on the ground beneath us.

We were soon out of the more populated area around Bien Hoa, the transition being abrupt from town to countryside. Over the intercom

Phil told me that we were approaching the brigade AO. He passed his map back to me; it had some of the more prominent checkpoints circled in grease pencil. I noticed more grease-pencil scribblings on the edge of his windscreen and asked him why he wrote things there. He chuckled and explained in his slow, gentle drawl, which I later found out was from Alabama.

"Well, we really write on the canopy because it's the handiest thing we've got. Those nice little knee boards the Air Force gives you are fine, except when you need to refer to some number in a hurry and can't find it because it's been written so small to fit on that knee board. This way you scrawl whatever it is you have to remember, like the kinds of ordnance a flight of fighters is carrying, right in front of your eyes in letters as big as you want. Also, you don't have to take your head away from the target to see them. Sometimes, just moving your eyes down into the cockpit is enough to make you lose sight of something in the trees. After a big fight somewhere, I've seen FACs land with their canopy so covered with grease-pencil markings that I don't see how the pilot was able to see."

He began to point out some of the major checkpoints I would be using to rendezvous with the fighters and also to locate myself to the radioman who would plot our position every thirty minutes when on a visual recce flight. About half of the area seemed to have a generous population, while medium-height rain forest covered the remainder. The more densely populated area was mostly covered by paddies, with tree lines separating some of the fields. There were plenty of usable checkpoints throughout the area in addition to a large river running east to west through the approximate center of the AO. The river was obviously at its low stage, for debris from its flood season could be seen as far as 200 meters from the low banks. This area of Southeast Asia would soon see the rains again as the cumulus clouds of the southwest monsoon swept in from the Gulf of Thailand. The late-afternoon battlements of clouds were growing every day and would soon overpower the drier air.

The flight was productive for several reasons. I got to see the area in which I would be flying. More importantly, I had the opportunity to see an experienced pilot fly the area. In addition to his constant turns, he also made frequent changes in his altitude and would often ease in a little rudder and hold it for a while, allowing the aircraft to skid through the air. That, he explained, complicated the tracking problem for a gunner on the ground. Occasionally, he would roll the aircraft inverted and we would head for the ground in a screaming dive, only to immediately climb back to altitude after we had bottomed out.

"Just in case old Charles is watching you from the ground," he explained. "He might think you've seen something and panic and loose off a few rounds. If you see where they came from then you can nail his ass. Just don't do it where any wheels can see you, because we're supposed to stay above 1,500 feet, you know. Generally, that's not a bad idea, 'cause that'll keep you above the effective range of the AK-47, but you have to be damned lucky to see anything from up there. The way I figure it, you do whatever is necessary to get the job done. If that means you have to go down to five feet, then that's where you go. Just don't ever admit it to anybody, including me if I ask you about it. And speaking of wheels, those assholes from the squadron and group like to sneak into the area and do 'spot inspections,' unannounced of course, on what's going on. As if they'd know if someone told them. So, if you see another Bronco flying around the AO or hanging around watching you put in a strike, you can be pretty sure that's who it is, particularly since we're so close to the flagpole. Usually, our radio operators can slip the word to us when one of the colonels decides he wants another mission for an Air Medal and heads into our AO. They usually get the word from the headquarters radiomen. You know those guys stick together like ugly on an ape anyway."

"How about the army big shots?" I asked. "Do you have to worry about them?"

"Shit!" he snorted. "If you listen to them you'll never get above five feet. They don't feel like you're doing your job unless you come back with tree branches hanging on your sponsons. Ignore 'em, politely of course, when they start trying to tell you how to fly, because they're real good at getting their own people killed. And there are plenty of ways to do that over here without inventing any new ones, like listening to some ground-pounding bird colonel telling you all about flying. Just remember, you've already got more flying experience than 95 percent of the army aviators and 100 percent more than that asshole riding in the back of the C and C helicopter. And remember too that a good pilot doesn't suddenly become a bad one just because he's new to this here war. And the reverse as well. Fourteen goddamned years in this war can't make a good pilot out of a bad one, no matter what some of these people think. Some of them seem to think that experience is everything, and I'll admit that it sure does help. But I keep thinking of my roommate back at college. He was probably the most experienced college student I've ever known. I mean he had seven years there and was still a junior—the dumbest son of a bitch I've ever known. If he was over here he'd have been made a general by now, with all his experience. Well, let's head on in. We've got to give the ground crew a chance to refuel this bird before it goes out again.''

The flight was over too soon for me, for I had enjoyed flying with Phil and listening to his running commentaries on the land and the peoples fighting over it. He was one of those rare ones who took his job seriously, but not himself. He had little reverence for rank, and from several of his comments I gathered that he had already been passed over for promotion to lieutenant colonel. That happened to a lot of good people, particularly those who had stayed in the cockpit for most of their careers.

Phil pointed out the sprawling base camp. I was surprised at its size; I had been expecting a tent camp but I saw many permanent buildings and paved roads. I was beginning to wonder if everyone in the war lived in an air-conditioned building. The pierced steel planking runway appeared to be completely adequate in length, although Phil used only a portion as he greased the aircraft onto it. After watching him fly for a couple of hours, I wasn't surprised.

We swung off the runway at the far end and taxied directly into one of the air force revetments. They were built of PSP planks supporting walls of dirt. There were three other revetments, one of which had an OV-10 parked in it. The ground crew quickly had the safing pins placed in the armament. After safing our ejection seats, we crawled out just as a captain pulled up in his jeep. He was wearing a survival vest so I assumed he was taking out one of the aircraft. Phil introduced us.

Jerry was a bit cool and standoffish. Before we had exchanged a dozen sentences he managed to let me know that he had been in-country a considerable amount of time. One of those experience snobs that Phil had been talking about, I thought, but I decided to give him the benefit of the doubt. I was to find later that his coolness was only his manner and had little to do with his real feelings. Before he turned and walked toward his aircraft to begin the preflight inspection, he remarked that we'd probably have a couple of flights together, since he was the instructor pilot for the TACP.

I wandered around introducing myself to the ground crew while Phil and Jerry talked. All of the enlisted men seemed to be as happy as they could be in a place like this. They gave me the impression that they considered Di An to be the Pearl of the Orient when compared to the other brigade base camps at Lai Khe and Dau Tieng. ''Those people get hit nearly every night,'' one of the sergeants said.

We toured the base camp on the way to the hootch; Phil drove the jeep and gave me a rundown of the organizations as we passed them. The major organization was the infantry brigade headquarters to which we were attached, but there were also several batteries of artillery, different army aviation units, a security service detachment, and the odds and sods that make any base function. There was even a civilian construction outfit on the base camp.

The roads that gridded the base were asphalt, and whitewashed rock, so beloved by the army, outlined most of the walkways. There was a large PX and several enlisted clubs. Bunkers and watchtowers manned by guards ringed the perimeter of the base. None of the guards seemed particularly alert, and they chatted with acquaintances who wandered down the road. Except for the guards, no one was in field gear, nor did they carry weapons.

''There's no reason for anybody to be armed around here,'' Phil said disgustedly when I mentioned it to him. ''This base hasn't even taken a mortar round in the last six months. Most of these people could be back at Camp Kilmer for all the danger they're in. Since I've been here this brigade has never had more than one battalion in the field at once and there hasn't been an honest-to-God fight in at least two months. The only kills this brigade gets is by air force air or helicopter gunships, and there aren't many of them. I don't know where the hell Charley went, but if he's around here he's doing a damned good job of hiding. About the only time we'll see any hot stuff is if one of our battalions gets the word to head out into War Zone C or D. There's still plenty of butt-kicking to go around out there. At least you won't be here too long, like me. Maybe you'll get up to one of the other brigades. It's rougher but it makes the time pass faster.''

This was news to me, for I thought I was at my permanent station. I looked at Phil in confusion. Noticing my consternation, he continued: ''Didn't they tell you at Bien Hoa? You're just supposed to be here long enough to get a little experience and until an ALO slot opens up somewhere in III Corps. I've still got too much time to go before they start worrying about replacing me, so you'll go somewhere else for sure. You probably won't be here for more than a month or so before a slot opens up somewhere. This won't be a bad place to break in because most of our AO just isn't that hot. In fact, division is using it to break in new troops. They've got a grunt school here that they all have to attend before they're shipped out to their units. For graduation exercises, some of the more experienced NCOs and officers take them outside the wire for a few nights to let 'em get used to being out in the bush and setting ambushes and all of that kind of grunt shit.''

"How come Charley doesn't kick their asses?" I asked. "Surely he knows they're just green troops that a good VC unit could take apart in about ten minutes."

"I imagine that Mister Charles knows that if he starts running wild in the henhouse, he'll have the entire division of fighting troops hunting his scrawny ass, and the troops ain't all pussycats."

We settled me into the FAC hootch, a screened, open-windowed wooden hut. It wasn't fancy but it was a lot more than I was expecting. Every man had an individual, spacious cubicle with bunk and hot locker, that is, a locker with an electric light burning constantly to prevent the dampness from mildewing your clothing. Most of the flying gear, such as parachute harnesses and survival vests, was stored in a metal Conex on the flight line.

I was introduced to two of the other three pilots whom we found chatting and idly flicking through old magazines in the dayroom at the end of the hootch. Somehow, I wasn't surprised to find the dayroom air-conditioned, with a well-stocked refrigerator humming away in the corner. Phil sent off one of the lieutenants to get me some maps of the area while I unpacked. Later as I copied the pertinent information from his maps to mine, Phil conducted a critique of the day's activities. I was again impressed by his grasp of the situation and by his answers to my questions about the next day's flying. He had scheduled us to fly together on the first sortie of the next day. Included in the mission would be a preplanned fighter strike against some "suspected" NVA bunkers in the northern part of the AO.

"If there's anything there," he said, looking at the map, "it was probably dug by the Viet Minh in 1960 when they were still fighting the French. These target people really piss me off sometimes, but at least it'll give you a chance to get your feet wet directing real fighters rather than other OV-10s, the way we did it back in training."

We discussed the next day's flight over a beer, Phil giving me the benefit of the knowledge he'd picked up in the months of flying in-country.

"The main thing," he said, "is never to get in the habit of clearing a single fighter to release his weapons unless you've got the plane in sight and the run looks right. I've known guys who will clear a flight to release without ever seeing them. I don't know if they're ashamed of the fact that their eyes aren't good enough to pick up the fast movers or what. But, if you get in the habit of cheating that way, I'll guaran-damn-tee you that it'll jump up and bite you right on the ass some day. There was a FAC up in II Corps last month who cleared a flight of F-4s to dump everything right on top of a company of U.S. troops and damned near killed them all. At the investigation it turned out he not only didn't see the fighters on their run-in but he didn't even have the goddamned target in sight. The fighter pukes will bitch if you send 'em through dry, but screw them. They don't know what's going on half the time anyway. Well, enough of this, let's grab some chow.''

As the air liaison officer, Phil was expected to eat at the brigade commander's table every evening, and as a newly assigned officer I was permitted the same privilege for one evening. The colonel's manner was patrician, reeking of the Virginia horse country, and we dined on the regimental silver and china. The wit was electric, as staff officers attempted to establish an intellectual pecking order. It was all quite jolly and a real pain in the ass.

The air was sparkling the next morning as we drove to the flight line. The storm from the previous night—the first one of the rainy season—seemed to have cleared out most of the haze and smoke. We had stopped in the TOC to check on friendly troop locations and for any activity in the brigade AO, but nothing of consequence seemed to be happening. One battalion was sweeping from an intermittently used fire base in the eastern part of the AO. That probably meant there was about one company out walking and the remainder defending the fire base. I was constantly surprised at how few people were actually in the field at one time.

Phil watched me do the preflight inspection without appearing to look. I didn't blame him. I'm the same way when I fly with someone I don't know, although I'm not as subtle about it. He made no pretense over checking the weapons and fuel load; he waited until I was satisfied and then rechecked them right after me. I crawled up the steps and wiggled into the front cockpit, the crew chief right behind me to fasten my parachute harness to the built-in chute in the ejection seat. The start-up went smoothly, with the temperatures coming up just as advertised. After a final check of all the gauges, I gave the signal for the ground crew to remove the safing pins from the rocket pods and machine guns. I counted them as they were held aloft by the crew chief, then held up my own seat safing pin for him to see. We all counted everyone else's pins and decided we were safe to taxi, then called the operator in the abbreviated tower and received his clearance for taxi and takeoff.

The turboprop engines responded quickly as I steadily moved the throttles forward to the stops. We were airborne before half of the PSP runway had gone by. I continued to let the airspeed build until I reached climb speed, then eased the control stick back and let the nose rise gently above the horizon. I blended aileron with rudder pressure to keep the aircraft in a gentle turn, first in one direction, then in the other, duplicating Phil's actions of the previous day. Leveling at 1,500 feet, I switched the UHF radio to our control frequency. The radio operator was located in the army TOC back at Di An and would flight-follow us throughout the entire flight as well as he could.

"Sidewinder Control, this is Sidewinder Two-two. Off Delta Alpha at three-eight. En route to area four. Sidewinder Two-one is in the rear." The radio operator acknowledged. He would be expecting periodic position reports for the remainder of the flight to insure that we were still in the air and not being asked to confess our sins against Uncle Ho by an irate group of citizens from north of the DMZ.

The system of assigning call signs was very simple. All FACs in our division used "Sidewinder." There were three brigades in the division, one through three. Your brigade became the first digit of your call sign. The second digit was anything that was available except the number one, which was always reserved for the ALO. Phil was the ALO for our brigade, which was the second, so his call sign was Sidewinder Two-one. The control room was supposed to be called Sidewinder Two-zero but in fact was universally referred to as Sidewinder Control. Each brigade had their own "Sidewinder Control," but confusion was avoided since they had different operating frequencies.

We were scheduled for a three-hour mission with an air strike planned about halfway into it. Phil directed me to find the target area I had so carefully grease-penciled onto my new map. The maps were covered with plastic, which allowed the marks to be easily removed when they were no longer needed. I mentioned that the maps seemed to show a good representation of the actual land we were flying over.

"Yeah," Phil answered, "it's pretty easy to do that around here. But there are areas in the country where you'd swear that the map and the ground were two different places. Most of it isn't the fault of the cartographers either. It's just that the countryside changes so much, so often, that they can't keep up with it. Take that river down there, for instance. It conforms pretty much to the map, doesn't it?'' I assumed he was asking a rhetorical question and kept my mouth shut.

''One month from now, in the heart of the wet season, that sucker'll be so far out of its banks that you'll be lucky to find one bend you can identify on your map. Then, sometimes they burn down the rain forest or blow it away with Arc Lights, or they plow it up with Rome plows. All you can do is try and do your best. At least everybody is working with the same set of maps. If we're screwed up about a location, then usually everyone else is too.''

Our target was easy to find, having many obvious landmarks from which I could triangulate and find the blob of green below me that should contain the bunkers. Phil advised me to overfly the target only once, lest we give away our intention of blowing it to hell. Having identified the target and marked all the pertinent fighter information onto my windscreen with my faithful grease pencil, I really didn't have anything else to do until the fighters arrived. Some visual recce seemed in order. Under Phil's guidance, we slowly cruised about the area, searching for anything that might indicate enemy activity—movement or evidence of recent movement, fresh tracks along a trail, smoke coming from areas where there should be no smoke, too many farmers toiling in the paddy fields. This was going to be 90 percent of my job for the next year—flying slowly around looking for anything suspicious. They say that after a few months in an area a FAC can tell if there are VC or NVA there by how much laundry the local mama-sans hang out to dry.

I never counted the number of drying black pajamas, but I did learn to look for small, telltale wisps of smoke from early-morning cooking fires and for small vegetable patches where they shouldn't be. The family water buffalo was another good indicator of enemy activity. These animals were much too valuable to be slaughtered in the cross fire of a firefight. At the first hint of trouble the ''water boo'' was taken back to the family hootch, where he could be protected.

The local families almost always knew when something was going down. Even if they were not VC sympathizers, the families' ''bush telegraph'' was effective. The VC and the NVA depended upon the local villagers for food and other supplies. In addition, the VC were most often local people who had families and friends in the villages and on the farms; they didn't want to see them get hurt, so they'd try to warn them if anything was going to happen. No matter whose side they were on, and most of them weren't on either side, the villagers stood to lose. So, they took the sensible precaution of protecting their valuables from both sides.

The thunderstorms that had rolled through the area had cleansed the air of the smoke from the open fires and kilns of the charcoal-makers. Yesterday the huge trees that formed the second and third tier of the rain forest had seemed dusty and dry, particularly when viewed through the smoke-filled air. Today they had taken on new life. Their boughs gleamed with an improbable green and the earth beneath them seemed redder than before. Even the still-sluggish river seemed to have gained a new vitality as it cleaned the flotsam from its banks. The bomb craters pockmarking the countryside were partially filled with water turned a beautiful emerald green from the minerals of the soil. Phil pointed out the muddy footprints now visible in the red mud of the trails wandering in and out of the tree lines. I made a low pass along the main trail where it became visible in a small opening among the trees.

"Those footprints could have been made by woodcutters," he said, "or by old Charley himself. We know the rain ended about three hours ago and the sun's been up for only half an hour, so whoever made them was up awfully early this morning. Mark 'em on your map and we'll let the S-2 shop know about them when we get back. They may have some collateral information that can tell us who's wandering around in these woods. My dollar is on Charles; those woodcutters and farmers are awfully shy about leaving their hootches before daylight, since the Nighthawk helicopters are liable to blow away anything they find wandering around after curfew."

"How could we tell the difference even if we did spot them?" I asked.

"It's almost impossible," Phil said, "unless you see that they're armed or in a sizable group. Believe me, everybody in this country knows that they shouldn't wander around in big groups. Of course, the best way is if they start shooting at you. Most of them have learned not to do that, though, because it generally gets the wrath of God brought down on them real quick. If they keep their cool and stay in small groups of three or four, there really isn't much we can do about it here in this populated area. That's too few people to put in a ground unit to check. Ho Chi Minh himself could probably walk from one side of III Corps to the other in broad daylight without anything being done about it unless he did something dumb.

"If we start seeing too much of this kinda' crap, though, you can bet that our grunts are going to start ambushing the area or putting in LRRP teams to check it out. Fortunately, Charley has a problem using small groups of people, too. It's damned unwieldy to move people around that way, and if they're NVA from north of the DMZ they're probably as lost in these woods as I would be. A good many of them are city boys and they can't put up markers the way they do over in Laos and Cambodia. And if it's a main-force unit, somehow they've got to feed all of them. That's not always easy because the only place they can get food is from the locals, and if they piss off enough people doing that, somebody eventually starts yelling about it. Our biggest identification problem, though, is all those damned kilns down there making charcoal. When they all get cranked up it looks like a bunch of hillbillies in the Smokies making moonshine. There are so many fires it's just impossible to check them all."

It was getting close to our rendezvous time with the fighters, so I turned back toward the RP (rendezvous point). Phil went over the procedures we'd use with them once more. Essentially, it was the same as we had practiced in training, but he said things would be happening much more quickly. Each fighter would have to be cleared in visually on each pass. Their high speeds would make them difficult to see, particularly since the planes were painted subdued colors that blended into the jungle background.

As we approached the rendezvous point, I heard the fighters checking in on our frequency. Our call sign had been prebriefed to them. The flight leader checked in his two wingmen.

"Ford Flight, check in."

"Two."

"Three."

"Sidewinder Two-two, this is Ford Lead. A flight of Fox 100s approaching rendezvous point from the south. Twelve out. Descending through fourteen grand."

"Roger, Ford Lead," I acknowledged. "Sidewinder Two-two is at the RP entering a left orbit. Smoker is going on now." I depressed the toggle switch on the left side panel to generate smoke to aid the fighters in visual identification.

"Go ahead with your lineup, Ford Lead."

"OK, Sidewinder, I've got a visual on you over the rendezvous point in a left turn. We're coming up your nine o'clock about ten out. Lineup follows. We're a flight of three armed with four each of snake-eyes and nape. Each has a full load of twenty mike-mike. We've got beaucoup loiter time. Have you got a visual on us yet?"

"Roger, Ford Lead, I've got you in sight now. I'm turning toward the target at this time. It's about five klicks northeast of here."

I quickly rechecked all the information I would need to pass on to them.

"The target today is a group of suspected enemy bunkers. On an earlier pass over the target I received no ground fire, but you should expect it." Phil had told me to always tell the fighters to expect some opposition whether or not you'd seen any. They tended to get highly annoyed if they were shot at after the FAC had told them to expect a cold target.

"If you're hit," I continued, "the best bailout area looks to be the clearings off to the west. Target elevation is about 150 feet. Let's get as much delay as we can and try to collapse those bunkers. We'll save the nape until after we've seen what we've uncovered with the bombs. I'd like for you to run east to west with a left break off the target. I'll be orbiting directly over the target at 1,500 feet and will clear each pass. If you don't have a positive clearance from me, then go through dry. I'm kinda' new at this so please bear with me. Any questions?"

"Sounds good, Sidewinder. Seems like you're doing fine to me. Let us know when you're ready for us to go to work."

Over the target area once again Phil said, "Just try to forget that I'm back here and work the flight the way you think it ought to be done."

I picked the impact point I wanted for my rocket, then rolled the Bronco almost inverted and let the nose drift down toward the target. Reaching my left hand to the armament panel, I armed one of the four pods of white phosphorous (WP) rockets. I watched the lighted sight in my windscreen come to rest on the target; I neutralized the control forces, then quickly punched the release button on my control stick. I watched the single rocket start toward the target before I put the aircraft into a steep, climbing turn back to 1,500 feet. Looking over my shoulder I saw a ball of dense white smoke begin to rise out of the treetops. It looked as if the smoke were about twenty-five meters too far north of the target. I turned the aircraft sharply to the east, trying to visually pick up the first fighter who had been positioning himself for the run-in as soon as he saw my smoke on the ground.

"Ford Lead is in hot from the east. Where do you want it, Sidewinder?"

My eyes darted frantically around the area to the east where he should be commencing his dive, but I saw nothing. I swiveled my head and checked my heading indicator. Yeah, that was the right direction, but where was he?

"Look at two o'clock going to three," Phil said. "He's just above the horizon."

I saw the sun glint off the canopy of the lead jet fighter just as he rolled out into his dive.

"Hit twenty meters north of my smoke, Lead," I called hurriedly, cursing myself for not giving him enough time to aim properly.

"Rog. Lead has the FAC and the target in sight. Go twenty north on the smoke."

By the time he had finished his transmission he was almost at his release point, but somehow he made a quick correction and the bombs tumbled from his wings, impacting almost exactly where I had planned.

"Lead's off left." "Two's in hot from the east." The calls came almost simultaneously. I had been trying to assess damage done by the lead ship's bombs and as a result had my aircraft pointed the wrong way to see number two's approach. By the time I turned to face him I couldn't identify him in time to give him clearance for release. He went through dry, just as he was supposed to do.

"Three's in from the east. FAC in sight. Where do you want it, Sidewinder?"

"Two's off left."

I finally picked up number three halfway down the run, but it was too late to re-mark for him or to even give him a correction using the lead ship's bomb crater for reference. He went through dry.

"Three's off left, dry."

"Lead's in from the east. FAC in sight." Suddenly, I didn't know where anybody was. The turns the fighters were making were so tight that I had trouble even telling which one was aimed at the target in the unlikely event that I did spot him. Finally I did the only thing I could do in order to bring some sense of order to this shambles.

"Ford Flight, hold high and dry," I said. I could actually hear the grins in the radio transmissions of the fighter pilots. They were enjoying my discomfort too much for my money.

"That's the only thing you've done right in the last fifteen minutes," Phil chuckled over the intercom. "We always let a new guy try it the first time without knowing what the hell he's really doing. It makes him appreciate the job a little more. It also lets the fighter pilots know that without a good FAC, there's not much for them to do over here. I'll take it now and let's see if we can't get this mess straightened out."

I felt like curling into a ball and pulling my flight suit over my head. I was a good pilot, I knew that. There had just been too much to do, too quickly. For one thing, I had been surprised at how fast these experienced fighter pilots could bend their aircraft around in a tight turn and be rolling back into the target in another attack. I wasn't sure that I'd ever be able to pick them up in time to clear them for their runs. How could anyone watch the ground for targets, mark them, and still maintain visual contact on three or four other aircraft? I simply felt overwhelmed.

"All right, Ford Flight," Phil said over the radio. "This is Sidewinder Two-one riding shotgun with Two-two. We've had our fun, but now let's do some bombing. I'm taking control of the strike."

"Roger that, Two-one. Just give us a new mark."

"Sidewinder Two-one is in for the mark."

He rolled the Bronco smoothly to the inverted position and applied enough back pressure on the stick to bring the nose firmly down through the horizon; then he released the pressure and fired the rocket. He had no sight in the rear cockpit, but the rocket went true toward the target. Immediately he pulled the nose above the horizon in a tight climbing turn that almost blacked me out momentarily. Instantly we were back at the proper altitude, facing the inbound fighter head-on as it came barreling down the tube toward the target.

For the next twenty minutes I was treated to an outstanding display of airmanship by the pilot sitting behind me. Somehow, he was able to keep track of all the aircraft as they dove and pulled away from the target, knowing where each of them was in the racetrack pattern. His eyes were usually on the target, smoothly rolling into a dive to re-mark when the white smoke drifted away. Somehow the aircraft was always in the correct position to do the marking or to check the run-in angle of the attackers. He threatened, he cajoled, he chided them until they did exactly what he wanted them to do. He made it sound as if they had committed a mortal sin if their bombs didn't go exactly where he wanted them. They tried to please him the way a child tries to please its parents.

For all the effort, there was nothing worthwhile beneath the trees. The bunkers, now collapsed and plainly visible after we knew what to look for, were probably old and certainly unoccupied.

"Blowing the tops off each of those old bunkers down there probably costs us about fifty grand today," Phil said. "At least no one was shooting at us."

"Do many of the missions have targets like this?" I asked.

"Too damned many," he growled. "A lot of the problem comes from the fact that the pilots have to fly the airplanes if they're going to keep up their proficiency for when we need them. And we never know when we're going to need them. What I don't see is why we can't divert 'em up north where they're needed, but General Westmoreland hasn't asked my opinion on anything yet."

We made one last pass to gather a BDA for the fighters and headed back to Di An with a few detours en route for more VR (visual reconnaissance). I was completely depressed. I had been so confused and lost during the strike that I hadn't known what was going on and wasn't sure that I'd ever have the ability to do it the way Phil had. He tried to lighten my mood before landing.

"Hell, you didn't do that badly for a first flight," he said. "We had one guy who didn't even see the fighters until his third flight. Everybody goes through this. We all come over here knowing that we're pretty damned good pilots and suddenly that's not enough. It seems that everything we learned in training goes right out the window and nothing seems to work. What you've got to remember is that I've been doing this every single day since I got here and so have those fighter jocks. It's that experience factor we talked about.

"But, like I said before, experience alone is not going to make you any good over here unless you were good to start with. The same thing holds true for that grunt walking down there. If he couldn't shoot before, just coming over here ain't going to make him a marksman. And if a guy didn't have guts before he got here, then this sure isn't the place to pick them up. For us, it's mostly a matter of letting your body fly the airplane without any conscious thought. One day you'll be putting in a strike and suddenly realize that you're not giving any thought at all to the flying but that you're using your brain to anticipate what to do next. Hell! Some people say that I haven't had a conscious thought in three months! Just remember, until you think you can handle it, don't let anybody, either the fighters or the troops on the ground, rush you. You're the one who's going to have to bite the bullet if anything goes wrong. And more important than that, it could also hurt some of the folks on the ground real bad if you make too much of a mistake. We all make 'em, of course. Just try to see that they're small ones.'' I thought about this on the way to Di An. The berms of the base came into sight and I descended to enter the traffic pattern at the airstrip. "One more thing," Phil said. "Conserve your rockets. There ain't no law that says you can't bring some of them home. Some guys feel like they've got to clean out all of their tubes on every flight or it's not a successful sortie. But if you get in the habit of using them all up, some day you're going to be stuck with trying to put in three flights of fighters with two willie petes. There's the runway. Let's see you grease this sucker on.''

We stopped at the TOC on the way back to the hootch from the flight line and filled in our after-action reports. Phil discussed the fresh footprints he had seen along the trails and marked them on the S-2's map. The S-2 promised to see if there was anything else to go with it. Phil began updating his maps with all the known friendly locations and suspected enemy activities. I followed suit.

Walking back to the hootch, I asked Phil something that had been bothering me: "What happens if one of our birds goes down and the enemy finds these maps with all of the friendly units marked on them? Wouldn't we compromise their positions?''

He looked at me with some amusement before answering. "Charley knows where everybody's at all the time anyway. He could probably tell you what Westmoreland had for breakfast. In all the time I've been here I've never heard of one instance where we gave him much of a surprise. Oh, we might catch 'em in an ambush or drop some bombs on 'em while they're walking under the trees, but I'm talking big-time surprise. We've got to have too much preparation or too many briefings or some such shit before we do anything. That's the only reason the visual recce that we and the loaches do is so successful. There's nothing planned about it. We fly over and see something and call in the fighters. They don't really have a chance to plan against it. Naw, this is his country and he knows what's going on in it.''

After the noon meal Phil and I waded into the paperwork that seemed to accumulate hourly and from which no military officer can escape. There were effectiveness reports to be written and submitted on every officer and man in the TACP. New and revised regulations arrived at a furious pace; bomb damage assessments had to be forwarded; maintenance and operational reports of every ilk slithered under the door; and inspection reports on morale, haircuts, VD rates, and safety all had to be completed and forwarded to headquarters. In line with this insanity, the Air Force did not provide a single administrative person to the TACPs. At about 1800 Phil announced: "It's getting close to happy hour, and if I have to look at another single piece of paper I'm going to puke."

The other pilots had already gathered in the dayroom and were busily punching holes in cans of beer, then marking their tab on the wall. There was a sign over the bar that read "Duty Pilot" followed by a space. Phil walked over and filled in a name. That pilot would do no drinking that night but would be available should the brigade need a FAC scrambled before the early-morning sortie lifted off at dawn. Jerry told me that the honor of being the duty pilot normally fell on someone who had screwed up somehow in the previous few days. I vowed not to see my name up there.

The talk was the same as that found in any fighter club bar after the day's flying was completed; it was mostly about airplanes and women, usually in that order. Tonight conversation focused on a serious issue: whether the new PX sales clerk's breasts were real or the product of a well-engineered bra and foam rubber. There were a number of liquor bottles on a shelf behind the bar, but I noticed that no one touched them, staying instead with the semicooled cans of beer. In the heat, the thought of scotch almost made me gag, while the beer tasted wonderful, especially when compared to the water.

The pattern of the first flight was followed for the next several days, flying with either Phil or Jerry. We would conduct visual recce, then put in one or more air strikes. I always enjoyed my flights with Phil, for he had a friendly, good-humored way of showing you the best way to do something. Whether you actually chose to use that approach was up to you, for Phil believed in doing things the way they worked best for you. Not always so with Jerry. Although he had logged more than 500 hours flying in-country, he was as rigid in his techniques and training as a fifteen-year SAC aircraft commander. I thought his flying was adequate but uninspired. He had brought little experience with him to Vietnam and had risen to the position of TACP combat instructor pilot due to longevity. Otherwise, he was a pretty nice guy.

Jerry and I were preparing for my night checkout before I was declared ready to fly the FAC missions solo. I was already annoyed, for he seemed to be briefing me as if I were a new cadet getting ready for his first night mission rather than as a senior air force pilot with almost fifteen years of flying in all conditions. I kept my mouth shut as I listened to him explain the dangers of vertigo, just as my first instructor had done years before. I was going to be glad to get him out of my backseat.

We finished the briefing and preflight inspection and strapped in just as the tropical darkness started falling. I was always astounded at how quickly the tropical nights came on. It seemed that dusk had just begun when suddenly full night was upon you. Flyers like this, for it's in the time between daylight and darkness that so many mishaps occur. In the dusk images blend together with shadows and become indistinct. Depth perception is shot to hell; consequently, a landing attempt may be two or three feet too high or too low. Either way is embarrassing.

As we taxied onto the runway, I swung my head back and forth looking for stray aircraft, and noticed the flicker of lightning in the direction of our target area.

"Do you see that crap up toward the northwest?" I asked Jerry. As instructor he was in command of the aircraft even though he was in the back seat. "It looks like a monsoon is about here. I don't care what the weather report says, I think that's a squall line forming out there."

He was silent for a moment while he studied the pattern of the lightning, then answered: "I don't think so. It looks more like several isolated small cells. I don't think we'll have any trouble working around them."

I was not reassured. I might not have his experience conducting fighter strikes, but I knew I had a hell of a lot more weather flying experience than he did. I decided I'd better keep an eye on the storm cells, for experience in the midwestern U.S. had taught me how rapidly a strong storm could build.

Leaving the confines of the base and the town was like flying into an inkwell. Compared to America or Europe, the countryside looked deserted. Occasionally a dim glow pinpointed a village, but there was virtually no traffic on the roads. Miles ahead I could see a bright light in our flight path that I was sure would be our rendezvous point with the fighters; it was a brightly lighted bridge kept that way in hopes that the VC wouldn't be able to blow it. It didn't work, for they blew up spans with depressing regularity. The target was some ten klicks from the bridge and would be difficult to find. A flare ship was assigned to us to help in target identification.

The rendezvous with the fighters and the flare ship went smoothly, and we concluded the prestrike litany. I found the target after the second flare run and marked it well for the fighters. I had worked under flares before, but I had almost forgotten the eerie sensations to the equilibrium produced by diving through the smoke trails of the burning flares into the artificial light flickering on and off as the flares burnt out and were replaced by new ones. At times I felt the flares were hanging sideward or even upside down.

The night air was heavy and moist, so the flare smoke, rather than drifting from the target area, began spreading and finally formed a ceiling through which the flares below glowed dimly as they completed their trip to the ground. Those above the ceiling had their glow reflected back toward us. Each marking pass I made and every bomb run by the fighters had to penetrate the smoke layer, making the pilot transition from light to dark to light once again. My problem was complicated by the fighters who, in accordance with their rules of engagement, turned off their position lights as soon as they started their run-in toward the target, making them virtually impossible for me to pick up. I had to keep my position lights on so that they could see me over the target. Somewhere above all of us, the C-123 flare ship droned away and chucked flares at us. As each fighter pulled off target, he would turn his position lights back on and I would be able to track him around the pattern until he was inbound once again and would turn them off. On several occasions I insisted that the fighters go through dry, since I had been unable to recognize them in time to clear them for bombing. It didn't matter; they still turned off their lights. I hoped they could all see me over the target.

The green tracers began tracking the fighters midway through the strike. There was someone home after all. Why hadn't they fired earlier? Maybe they thought we'd go away or start getting too close to them. Whatever the reason, they had decided to fight back. I watched three trails of the green ground fire try to track the next fighter down the tube before he was off and out of their range. Normally, Charley's tracers were green and the American types were red. This could hardly be taken as a verifiable identity, however, since so much materiel had been captured from the U.S. and its allies. They used ours but we didn't use theirs, so green tracers indicated Charley but red didn't always mean good guys.

I rolled my wing over and shoved the nose down to put in another marking rocket as close to the guns as I could place it. Relaxing all the control pressures, I closed my eyes and punched the firing button on the control stick. Once, back in the States, I had kept my eyes open when firing a rocket at night and had been blinded by the light of the rocket motor. Now, I made sure my eyes were tightly closed until the burning tube was out of range. The marker hit reasonably close to one of the firing guns, which was silenced by the next bomb. One of the other guns continued to bang away at us ineffectually. I decided to ignore him and get on with the job unless his accuracy improved.

"Sidewinder Two-two, this is Spooky Four-three." Our flare ship somewhere overhead was calling. I had forgotten about him.

"I don't know if you guys have noticed while you've been there playing in the weeds, but Spooky is going to have to get his butt out of here pretty quick," he said.

"Spooky, this is Sidewinder Two-two. What's the problem?"

"Well," he said, "if you people will take the time to look back toward Bien Hoa, you'll see what the problem is. We've been watching that weather build and we just can't wait any longer. I don't think we're going to be able to get back now. We hate to spoil the party, but there it is."

I turned toward the southeast. Those "isolated cells" of Jerry's had developed into a full-fledged squall line sweeping toward us and seemingly unbroken in both directions as far as the eye could see. I hadn't noticed the increased lightning because of the glare of the flares and, besides, Jerry should have been watching it. I was furious with him, although I didn't say anything. That wouldn't have helped the situation.

The lances of lightning far above the horizon quickly dispelled any thoughts we might have had of topping the giant cumulonimbus; we had no oxygen aboard and even if we had the service ceiling of our aircraft would be well below the cloud tops. I cleared the fighters for one last pass to clean away their ordnance, then bid them good night and gave them clearance to leave the area. They probably wouldn't have any trouble getting home now that they had depleted their bomb loads, for they would be able to top anything that stood in their way. At worst, they had the airspeed and altitude capability to find an alternate airfield somewhere in the country. Old Spooky, the flare ship, didn't really have any problems either. He had hours of fuel and could fly all the way to Thailand to find a nest for the night. The only people with a real problem was us, since we were down to an hour's fuel before dry tanks. I was almost sure the storms had us cut off from our home base at Di An as well as the Saigon and Bien Hoa areas. There were many small strips scattered around the countryside, but they were, for the most part, unlighted and not suitable for night landings even if we had been able to find them.

I waited for Jerry to say something, but he didn't speak. Twisting around and looking at him over my shoulder, I saw that he was staring at the lightning coming ever closer toward us. Changing the radio frequency, I called our control room back at Di An.

"Sidewinder Control, this is Two-two. How's the weather back there?"

"Sidewinder Two-two, this is Control. It's raining cats and dogs back here. There's a lot of lightning and thunder in all quadrants," he cheerfully responded. "What are your intentions? I don't think you can land here."

"Thanks for letting us know," I said in a flat voice. I ignored his request for information. A large part of our predicament was his fault, since he was supposed to have kept us briefed on the current weather situation. I made a mental promise to take a wide swath of skin off his ass if and when we got back. Neither he nor Jerry, at whom I was equally pissed, seemed to realize the situation we were about to be in. I didn't see how chewing out the radio operator's butt over the air was going to help us at the moment. As for Jerry, it was his responsibility to watch for things like this while the other pilot conducted the strike. That was one reason we almost always flew night strikes with two crew members. More damning was the fact that he was the TACP's instructor pilot and should have enough savvy not to be caught in these situations.

I had passed control of the aircraft to him while I talked to the control room, and now he was orbiting in a racetrack pattern in front of the advancing storm clouds, slowly being pushed farther west and away from safety. I waited a few more moments for him to make some sort of decision, since he was still in command of the aircraft. We continued to orbit, still being forced to the west. I finally thought, enough of this. We could argue the finer points of command after we'd found some place to land.

"Jerry," I said, "in about ten minutes we're going to be over the Cambodian border, and I know there's no place for us to land over there. What do you want to do?"

There was more silence, then: "Maybe we could fly around the end of the storms to the north and maybe Lai Khe is still open."

He's lost it, I thought. Slowly it began to sink in that this was all new to Jerry. He hadn't been in-country long enough to witness a monsoon. Neither had the radio operator. They had no idea of its potential for destruction. I watched as the huge thunderstorms seemed to join together, presenting a unified wall of billowing clouds and lightning that seemed to increase its speed toward us. I estimated that the leading clouds were moving at least forty knots over the ground. It was impossible to try an end run on them.

"We're down to forty-five minutes of fuel," I told Jerry. "By the time we find an open strip and find somebody who can turn on some lights for us, we're either going to be deep inside Cambodia or out of fuel. I don't think we've really got any choice. We're going to have to penetrate the squall line in a direction back toward Di An. Even if we have to eject, we're better off doing it in that direction than out here in Indian country. Besides, we don't really know where we are anymore, do we? There's no way we can get a steer anyplace from out here. We're just going to have to suck it up and do it."

There was no response from the rear cockpit, so I put my hand on the control stick and shook it vigorously, the universal flying signal for "I've got control of the aircraft." I felt a slight vibrating of the stick in response. Turning the aircraft, I flew parallel to the approaching line of storms for a few minutes, studying the pattern of lightning. The closer the clouds got, the more intense they looked. There were no apparent openings, just the bulging cumulus clouds, boiling and rolling, as they neared us.

I cinched my lap belt and shoulder straps as tightly as I could stand them and told Jerry to do the same. He acknowledged quietly, and in the mirror with the lightning providing the illumination, I saw him gathering up the loose items around the cockpit and stowing them. I did the same. I should say something to him to try to salve his injured pride, I thought. To hell with it; I'd worry about that later if we got through this mess. I thought back to my flying experiences: I'd been in only two thunderstorms before this and they were both terrifying. The storms contain every bad thing that can be associated with flying weather: severe turbulence, lightning, hail, unbelievably heavy rain, ice, and maybe lava flow and tidal waves for all I knew. One of the aircraft I had flown into a thunderstorm had never flown again after I got it out. It had hail damage almost three-fourths of an inch deep, and I'd been lucky the canopy hadn't broken. Think cheerful thoughts, I told myself.

Advancing the throttles, I climbed another thousand feet just to give us a little more ground clearance when the turbulence started, then reduced power to the point where the book said the aircraft would have the best chance to avoid breaking into small pieces.

Our aircraft was stressed for eight-plus g's, so I figured we could ride out most turbulence without tearing off the wings. Lightning strikes were fairly common on aircraft penetrating storm areas and as a rule didn't create too much damage. Normally they only left small holes where they struck, though they could easily destroy all of the electrical system. Our biggest problems probably were going to be the rain, which could come down with the force of a waterfall and overwhelm a jet engine, or the turbulence, which could cause me to lose control of the aircraft.

We approached the leading edge of the storm and were dwarfed by its size. I turned the cockpit lights up to full brightness in an attempt to counteract possible momentary blindness caused by a close lightning flash. Another tug on the lap belt and I was as ready as I was going to be. Over the intercom I reminded Jerry to shut his air vents to keep out as much of the water as we could. The airplane was unpressurized and would leak like a sieve anyway. Without the flow of fresh air, the cockpit immediately became oppressively hot and humid. The windscreen fogged over and I turned on the defrost. At the last minute I remembered to turn off the external lights. Should they be on as we entered the turbulence, their reflection off the swirling clouds could easily induce vertigo.

We entered the clouds, and the air was deceptively smooth. I knew that wouldn't last long. The lightning ahead was diffused through the clouds now, and it cast a strange glow over the instrument panel despite the bright cockpit lights. The sharp, well-defined lightning bolts were no longer visible. Instead, an entire cloud would suddenly come alive and glow as the electricity discharged the millions of volts. I began to feel sharp, irregular jolts to the airplane's bottom as we approached the first storm cell. I tried to steer away from the area of heaviest lightning but finally just glued my eyes to my instrument panel.

All hell suddenly broke loose. We were rocked by a swift, violent updraft, then just as quickly slammed down toward the jungle. I attempted to counteract these outside forces with control movements, but the aircraft was outmatched by the fury of the storm. I tried to concentrate on the attitude indicator that would allow me to keep the wings level, I hoped; I ignored the vertical speed indicator, which was alternately showing a maximum-rate climb, then a maximum dive as the fickle storm currents tossed us about. In spite of my attempts to prevent it, one wing suddenly dropped to an almost vertical position. We were slammed into another dizzying ascent with the wing still cocked almost ninety degrees under us; then suddenly it corrected itself as another strong downdraft caught us and sent the other wing plummeting in the other direction. Debris from the floor and from under the ejection seats filled the cabin and water poured in from myriad openings around the cockpit. The lightning was so close that the cockpit was awash in a constant eerie glow, much like the flare lights we had ueen working under earlier.

Glancing at the airspeed indicator, I was momentarily shocked to see that it was no longer operating. The deluge of water had overwhelmed the Pitot tube from which the aircraft instruments drew their information. A sudden gust dropped the left wing past the ninety degree point, and it was easier to complete the roll rather than try to bring the wing back up in the conventional manner. Saint Elmo's fire danced around the windscreen like a scene from a horror movie. It was harmless but did little to help my orientation in a night gone mad. The rain beating against the aircraft sounded as though we were going over a waterfall in a barrel. I was afraid from the noise that the rain had turned to hail but was afraid to look outside the cockpit. Some things you'd just rather not know, especially if there's not a damn thing you can do about it.

A last, huge jolt that actually hurt my tailbone, and the storm cell spat us out of its tempestuous bowels. We were still between cloud layers but in one piece. More lightning flashes directly to our front pointed out that we weren't out of the woods yet. Suddenly, we were back into the clouds for a repeat of the first passage. I found myself talking aloud, negotiating a serious deal with God ("Get me out of this one Lord, and I'll . . ."). I glanced in the mirror at Jerry and all I could see were two huge eyes.

Eventually we did emerge into clearing air, and although flashes in all directions showed the thunderstorms were still about, they now appeared to be isolated cells, easily detoured. The squall line had moved rapidly on through. The automatic direction finder (ADF) worked on a low frequency and would only point toward the storms—an annoying feature. My other navigational instruments were dead, their antennas probably a victim of a lightning strike.

If the fuel gauges were operating and had not frozen in their last position due to the lightning strike, then we were down to about fifteen

minutes' fuel. I calculated that we had been in the storm system for almost twenty minutes, although it had seemed much longer than that.
"Jerry, do you have any idea where we are?" I asked.

Before he could answer, a huge explosion blossomed on the ground about twenty miles in front of us, covering a semicircle of two or three miles. I didn't know what caused it, but it had to mean there were people down there. As we approached the area I was suddenly able to make out the dim outline of a small runway between the showers still drifting about. Closer still, the now-visible dim lights on the ground began to take on a familiar shape—Di An—home!

Dodging the small showers, I struggled to keep the runway in sight. I entered the traffic pattern, still puzzled by the flames surrounding half the base camp. Maybe they're under attack, I thought, but it didn't matter; there wasn't enough fuel to go anywhere else anyway.

Not a great landing but an adequate one. We taxied into the revetment and my lights picked up Phil waiting for us. The ground crew squatted under part of the overhang, trying to keep out of the light rain still falling. As we climbed from the aircraft I became aware of how sore my neck and shoulders were. Probably tension, I thought.

"What are all the fireworks?" I yelled at Phil.

"That was the phu gas going off," he said, laughing. "Seems like a lightning strike hit a barrel of the stuff out on the perimeter and before anyone knew what was happening there was a chain reaction along almost all of the south side. Were you able to see it out very far?"

I caught myself before I said that if it hadn't gone off we'd probably have ejected somewhere over the jungle. I waited for Jerry to speak, but he remained silent. Phil looked from one to the other of us, aware of the tension.

"Yeah," I finally answered. "You could see it a pretty good distance out. What is that stuff, anyway?"

He took another long look at Jerry, then turned to face me.

"They're barrels of some kind of napalm mixture anchored around the perimeter. The top of the barrel faces away from the friendlies and can be detonated with a claymore. It catches the mixture on fire and belches it outward in case of attack. It's got some kind of French name, but I don't know what it is. Sure burns pretty, doesn't it?"

We piled into his jeep and headed to the TOC for debriefing. While I was there I quietly wandered back to our control room to have a few words in private with the duty radio operator. I forcefully explained to him the importance of keeping his pilots informed of all changes, including the weather situation. He became pretty receptive when he saw the expression on my face.

Back at the hootch I opened a beer before hitting the sack. Phil looked at me curiously but didn't pry, although he knew something had happened and, as boss, he had every right to ask. I had decided that I would bring it up only if Jerry did. He didn't, and the situation was soon forgotten.

After two weeks of conducting air strikes alone, I was beginning to feel pretty confident. The FACs normally flew alone unless somebody wanted to take a ride, or unless we were night-flying. Actually, most of us preferred to fly alone rather than have to make corporate decisions. Artillery adjustment was the last item I needed to complete before I became fully qualified. Phil was once more riding in the rear cockpit to complete my training.

There is a time-honored procedure that all forward observers (FO) go through in order to make artillery rounds impact on the desired area. The actions of both the fire direction center at the battery and the FO are as carefully choreographed as a Broadway musical; this makes sense since the battery will be hurling enormous chunks of explosives through the air, often in the proximity of friendly folks. The FO adjusts the azimuth and distance of the impacting rounds to insure proper saturation of the target area. This all seemed simple enough and even logical to me.

I had little difficulty finding the briefed target, a wooded tree line along a streambed. From a trail that crossed the stream, we were to direct the artillery fire 100 meters left and right until it exposed and destroyed the recent bunkers that had been dug beneath the trees. Everything looked good: no friendlies, either military or civilian, within fifteen klicks of the target; the target itself, clear and well-defined; good visibility. I suspected Phil had done as much as he could to arrange an easy first session for me.

There were to be three batteries firing: Lai Khe from the northwest, Phuoc Vinh from the southwest, and Fire Base Betty from the east. Communications established and target and intentions reaffirmed, I ordered Lai Khe to commence the barrage with a willie pete marking round. I planned to feed the other batteries into the fray after I had the first on target.

"Shot. Out," said Lai Khe, indicating a marking round was on the way.

"Roger, shot," I repeated, letting the battery know that I understood a round was in the air on the way to the target and that I was positioned clear of its trajectory. The white phosphorous round impacted just short of the wood line.

"Raise it fifty and work it right and left one hundred meters. Fire for effect." No sweat, this was a cinch. Time to get another battery going.

Phouc Vinh responded immediately and soon I heard "shot" as their marking round was fired toward my wood line. It burst with a cloud of white smoke about seventy-five meters over the target. I felt I needed another marking round before they began firing in earnest. It arrived within thirty meters of the tree line.

"Drop thirty, move it left and right of the target, and fire for effect," I told them.

The battery fire from Lai Khe still looked pretty good; most of it was impacting in the wood line but was straying where the streambed took a severe curve. A small, quick correction seemed to have them back in the ballpark. Now to get Fire Base Betty working.

One willie pete marking round, then another, and Betty was soon happily throwing its projectiles in with the others. Something didn't seem right though. The last correction to Lai Khe had seemed only to make their small error worse. A tiny germ of unease was creeping into my frontal lobe. Let's see now, if I want to move Lai Khe's fire to the south, I would have to give them a correction of right fifty, up twenty. If I wanted to make the same correction for Phouc Vinh, it would be right fifty, down twenty. For Fire Base Betty, it would be left fifty, up twenty.

As I thought about that, I heard, "Lai Khe shot. Out."

"Phouc Vinh, shot. Out."

"Fire Base Betty, shot. Out."

I watched the rounds impact, one cluster behind the other. In a moment of near-panic I realized I had no idea which cluster came from which battery. Lai Khe had called first, but they were the farthest from the target.

"Lai Khe, shot. Out."

"Phouc Vinh, shot. Out."

"Fire Base Betty, shot. Out."

Again the clusters of explosions quickly arrived. Damn! I didn't know artillery could shoot that quickly. The impacts were even farther off target. A correction definitely had to be made now. I tried to adjust Lai Khe's fire, but it turned out to be Fire Base Betty's impacts I had been looking at. Lai Khe continued to churn up the meadow in blissful ignorance. Phouc Vinh's fire now edged toward an area of rice paddies after my last correction, when I had mistaken them for Betty. I quickly called a correction to them but found I was in fact moving Lai Khe in the wrong direction. Within ten minutes I had managed to move all of the batteries' fire away from the target to an area some 200 meters away. Every correction seemed to move them farther. The word "shot" continued to directly assault my nervous system as it seemed to increase in frequency.

Beseechingly, I looked into the rearview mirror, silently asking Phil what I should do. I thought he'd gone mad. He was throwing himself about under the restraining straps of the seat and beating his helmet with his fist. Maybe he'd been hit by ground fire.

"What's wrong? Are you OK?" I asked, the artillery momentarily forgotten. He didn't answer but continued his fit. I glimpsed his face and realized he was almost hysterical with laughter. I'd never seen him act like this. Sulkily, I went back to the artillery adjustment and tried to straighten out the mess I had created before they blew up a small village only 500 meters away—obviously not a safe margin with me directing the fire. The batteries must be wondering what the hell was going on.

Phil was finally calm enough to gasp over the interphone: "You'd better get that stuff shut off before you get it moved all the way to downtown Saigon." He was still wheezing, barely under control. "Call for a check fire. Then we'll start all over again with just one battery at a time, the way I thought we were going to do it."

I gave the cease-fire order and withdrew into a bruised but dignified silence while he explained that we normally worked only one or two batteries at a time, particularly if we were new at the game. His explanation was constantly interrupted by snorts of laughter.

"Whew," he said. "That's the funniest thing I've seen since Uncle Elmer got his pubic hair caught in his zipper at the church social. Look, a guy who's been doing this awhile can handle three batteries at once. We don't do it all that often. And the FOs are sitting in the back of an O-1 or a helicopter and they don't have to worry about flying the damned thing. They can just sit back and keep track of what's going on. An FO on the ground can tell by the noise of the shells coming in which battery has fired them. When we fire arty it's generally an emergency, and the batteries will be glad to work with you any way they can to get the shells on the right target. So, don't try to do more than you can handle. This was pretty funny today, but it wouldn't have been if we'd been blowing American boys outa' their holes. Keep that in mind and let's get back to the batteries before they figure we've crashed.''

It was with a great deal of humility and embarrassment that I called the artillery batteries and told them we'd be taking them one at a time from now on. I heard some good-natured comments in reply, but I think they'd already figured what was going on. After working with them for a while, I realized that it was just like putting in air strikes: Experience was very helpful but common sense was even more so.

It was a bad week. First, Danny, one of the brigade FACs, disappeared. He had checked in with the control room approximately an hour after he became airborne and announced he was over a checkpoint in War Zone C, an old designation from the French days in the country. He hadn't been heard from since. He was on a visual recce mission with no fighters scheduled, and it wasn't unusual for a FAC to miss his check-in time by a few minutes should he get interested in looking at something.

The control room finally initiated a communications check but was unable to raise him. Another FAC working some distance away was diverted to search, but nothing was found of the aircraft, either at any other landing strip or in the jungle of the war zone.

We were a subdued lot that night. I sipped a beer and talked in a low voice to the others. I didn't understand how he could just disappear. His parachute was equipped with an emergency beeper that would have squalled over Guard channel if he had ejected, but nothing had been heard that afternoon. Search planes hadn't discovered any wreckage or even smoke from a crash, and they had been in the area fairly soon after he was missing.

"That's the way FACs usually go," Phil said, staring at the rings that his wet beer can had made on the table. "Usually, when anybody else goes down there's somebody else around to let you know what's happened. They either know that you were shot down or you had engine failure or you ejected or something. But a FAC is usually by himself and it's only luck if somebody sees him in trouble or he gets a chance to call. There's just no way of knowing. Danny might have seen something and made a low pass to check it out and flew into a nest of 12.7s. Or he might have hit a tree on a low pass. He may have been too low to contact the control room and had an engine fire. All you can do is guess. You know, when a fighter squadron loses somebody it's pretty bad, but it's just one guy out of thirty or forty. When we lose one, it's 20 percent of our people.''

Before the week was out, Phil received word from the Red Cross that his wife had been hospitalized in serious condition from an automobile wreck back in Texas. I had just landed from a flight but insisted on taking him to Bien Hoa myself to catch the airliner home. He probably wouldn't be back; he had so much time in-country and, although the prognosis on his wife was still unknown, certainly she would require his presence for an extended period. He discussed the TACP's operation on our short flight, assuming I would be taking his place, since I was the next senior officer. I wanted the job but didn't really know if I had the experience to stand up to the brigade commander and tell him he was wrong, as I had seen Phil do.

I helped him take his baggage to the check-in point after the travel arrangements had been made and he had his boarding pass. We would pack the rest of his belongings and ship them when we found out where he would be going.

"I want you to know," he said, "that I've recommended you to take my place. You don't have too much experience yet, but you know what I think about that. You've got common sense and you don't get unduly excited about things, even if they go wrong. Frankly, it was after you made your mistakes that I decided to recommend you as an air liaison officer. You recover well and that's important over here. Just remember the old cavalry saying: 'First, the horses. Then the men. And only then, the officers.' For us, I guess that'd translate as first looking after your aircraft, because you can't do squat without them. Then, look after the grunts on the ground—they're the reason you're here. Last, take care of the pilots if you have time. Let's face it, we've all been getting flight pay for a long time, and we ought to start earning it whether we're staying in or getting out and going to the airlines as soon as we get home.''

We shook hands, and he turned and started toward the door as his flight was announced. We both knew that he probably would not be back, at least in the near future. Just before he got to the door, he turned and yelled at me: "Just don't shoot any artillery if you can help it!"

I watched the commercial jet take off, feeling as if I had lost a real friend, though I had known Phil for only a few short weeks. But I had to get to the squadron headquarters across the base and find out what was going to happen. Was I really going to get the TACP at Di An? Phil had said only that he had recommended me; that didn't mean the squadron commander was going to go along with it. A telephone call eventually provided an airman with a jeep to give me a ride over to the squadron complex.

It was almost noon, a wait of more than an hour before the CO deigned to acknowledge my presence in his outer orderly room. He was a lanky and sour-looking lieutenant colonel who didn't seem particularly pleased to see me. The rumors had told me to beware of him, that he definitely looked after number one and had sent some good men down to protect himself. It wouldn't be the first time I'd worked for a self-serving officer, I thought, and besides, I shouldn't see that much of him over in Di An.

Standing before his desk, I saluted and he returned it very correctly, not offering to shake hands. I stood at attention while he walked slowly around me. Inspection completed, he sat behind his desk and told me to be at ease, but he still didn't ask me to sit.

"Your flight suit is a mess and you need a haircut," he said by way of greeting. "Your boots are scuffed, and why are you wearing that damned silly baseball cap?"

Actually, I wasn't wearing it but carrying it in my hand, and it was a Dallas Cowboy football cap, not baseball. I didn't expect that he would savor the correction, so I decided not to mention the difference. I also decided to bypass the old "no excuse, sir" crap generally expected from an underling.

"Colonel, I had just gotten in from the first flight when I had to bring the ALO over here for transport back to the States. My uniform is a mess because I've been out in the rain, as well as sweating in it for three hours putting in air strikes. My boots are scuffed as are those of any FAC I know because they get caught under the rudder pedals as I squirm around in the cockpit trying to look over my shoulder while I'm flying. I'm wearing this cap because my air force piss-cutter doesn't keep the rain out of my face. I don't have a haircut because so far I haven't had time to get one, sir."

"You damn people seem to forget you're in the military service once you leave here," he grumped. "Get a haircut before you leave this base."

"Yes sir."

"That's all," he said. I saluted and left the room. Outside, I stopped and sat on one of the empty desks. What happened? He didn't tell me anything except to get a haircut. I was trying to think it through when I noticed a master sergeant grinning at me from another desk across the room.

"Still a little puzzled, Major? Don't worry about it, sir. I've seen strong men weep after waiting all day to see the CO and then finding themselves back out here in about two minutes, not knowing any more than when they went in. Most folks just get in touch with me. I'm the first sergeant, by the way, or the exec when they want to find out what's going on. Like, for example, that you've been made the air liaison officer for the second brigade."

"Is that for real?" I asked my new source of information. "When is it supposed to take effect?"

"Orders are cut right now. They ought to be ready for you by the time you get back from getting your hair cut."

"How did you know about that?"

"Because he tells everybody to get a haircut," he said. "If everybody got one when he told them to, old Choy the barber could retire to the south of France. I would suggest in your case, sir, that you run along and do it. If you don't mind me saying so, you are getting right shaggy around the ears and you might set a bad example for all our young officers and airmen."

Later, with several copies of orders designating me as the ALO for the brigade, I returned to Di An with white scalp showing all the way to the crown of my head. I still wore my Cowboy's football cap, though.

A week after taking over the brigade TACP, I had just completed a preplanned strike into War Zone D, an area that until several months ago had been a hotbed of Viet Cong activity. Although we had discovered and destroyed some old bunkers, there had been no sign of recent activity. I was safing my rockets when the control room called.

"Sidewinder Two-one, this is Sidewinder Control."

"Go ahead Control, this is Two-one," I answered.

"Roger Two-one. There's some ground action just north of Checkpoint Delta if you're interested."

"What do they have going on?" I asked.

"So far as we know now, it looks like one platoon has been hit pretty hard from ambush and is still taking heavy fire. Charley has not withdrawn but is still attempting to close with the platoon. I thought if you were in the vicinity you might want to check it out, although they haven't called for tac air yet."

"OK, good thinking, Control. I'm heading that way now. Pass me the coordinates and call signs. You might also want to check with the DASC and see what they've got scheduled for the rest of the day that we could use if it becomes necessary." The Direct Air Support Center allocated all of our tactical air for the individual units. "It won't hurt to give them a little advance notice even if it turns out to be a false alarm."

I copied the encoded coordinates and frequencies onto my windscreen with a grease pencil, then checked the figures in my Standard Operating Instructions booklet (SOI) for the correct day. I should buy stock in the company that makes grease pencils, I thought, for we used them at a prodigious rate. My heart was starting to beat a little quicker in anticipation, for this was the first real contact in the brigade's AO since my arrival. There had been small ambushes by both sides, of course, which generally lasted only a few minutes before disengagement. There were also the ever-present booby traps to take their toll of the American troops, as well as punji stakes and malaria, but very little actual fighting. The messages competing with one another over the radio frequency indicated that the enemy had not only initiated this ambush but was still sustaining the contact. Very unusual.

I didn't have to use the map to find the scene of action, for the sky was filled with helicopters, mostly slicks carrying brigade and battalion staff. No one had requested USAF support, so I climbed until I felt reasonably confident that I wouldn't be involved in a midair collision. Once there, I pulled the throttles back to conserve fuel, began a lazy orbit, well over everyone, and tried to make sense of the tense messages being flung back and forth. Big Six, the brigade commander, was giving unasked-for advice to the young-sounding platoon leader hidden beneath us in the trees.

"Latigo Six, this is Big Six. How many of your people have been hurt?"

"Big Six, this is Latigo Six." His voice was shaking from fatigue, excitement, or fear—maybe all three. "We've got six KIAs that I know about. We've also got another fourteen or fifteen WIAs that need dusting off real bad. I've lost almost all of my first squad, and second squad has been hit hard. We're taking heavy fire from both flanks and the front. I'm going to try to move my wounded about 500 meters to the rear, where there's an LZ. We're going to need gunships to help us get out. Over."

"Negative, Latigo Six," the colonel replied. "You hold your position. I'm going to have the remainder of your company flank the ambush and we'll have him in a pincer between them and your platoon."

He changed frequencies before the lieutenant could object, and on my other radio I picked him up giving movement instructions to the company commander of the ambushed platoon. My God, I thought, maybe this is what's wrong with the war. We've got a bird colonel trying to play platoon leader. And if he got tired of the role, the air was filled with helicopters carrying assorted military brass willing to take over. They'd all be delighted to give that kid on the ground the benefit of their experience gained at the Battle of the Bulge or on Porkchop Hill in Korea. I was sure they meant well and would have gladly changed places with the platoon leader. But, this was not their war to fight. Denied the combat position on the ground, they chafed at the rank and the middle-aged bodies they had acquired and tried to fight vicariously through that frightened twenty-five-year-old down there beneath the tree canopy. I felt sad for all of them, but especially for the beleaguered company and platoon commanders who were trying to save their people. Before this I had not believed the tales of entire units hiding from command and control helicopters flying in their area.

The drama unfolded over the next hour. Several things became apparent very quickly: The enemy troops were not disengaging but rather closing in in an effort to prevent air or artillery attacks against them. Furthermore, Charley was either feeding more troops into the fight or doing a little flanking of the company himself. The volume of fire from the enemy forces was increasing, which not only prevented the planned American flanking movement but made it impossible to get dust-off helicopters in to pick up the wounded.

By the end of the first hour and a half, the entire company had managed to get itself effectively surrounded. The amount of advice from the circling helicopters had greatly diminished now. There are considerably fewer options when you're surrounded and the people overhead can't locate you beneath the trees.

Resupply was starting to become critical, for the enemy gunners had triangulated fields of fire for their overlocking 12.7s and were now punching holes in those helicopters foolish enough to stay low. If the enemy had been smart, he would have fired only at the resupply ships, for the command and control birds seemed to be valuable allies.

I waylaid one of our FACs who had wandered over to find out what was happening and designated him to stay on station while I went back to Di An for refueling. While I was on the ground I had the armorer fill my empty rocket tubes, and I grabbed a quick sandwich. It already looked to me like it was going to be a very long day.

Back on station I found that two additional companies of U.S. troops had been inserted on one flank and were already getting their butts kicked. Charley either had no place to run or had decided he was through running for a while. Artillery was impacting along a line several klicks to the north of the engagement, not allowing the enemy to withdraw in that direction. Helicopter gunships were making firing passes into the jungle, but they simply didn't carry ordnance large enough to dig out anyone who wanted to stay.

Two smoldering helicopters lay on their sides among the trees, shot down by intense fire from the ground. The courage of the helicopter crews was magnificent, but sometimes that's not enough. As I watched, or rather listened, to the battle taking place beneath me, I felt like a substitute waiting to go into the big game. I knew I'd be called soon, for the helicopters just didn't have the punch to engage the NVA properly. And it was definitely NVA. These boys weren't local rice farmers.

Listening to the confused reports coming over the ground net and to the numerous helicopter pilots' sightings, I tried to place the friendly units as well as I could. I was very conscious that this was my first troops-in-contact (TIC), and I wished for Phil's calm guidance from the rear cockpit.

I called my control room. "Sidewinder Control, this is Sidewinder Two-one. You'd better have them get ready to launch the alert birds. It doesn't look like it's going to be long now."

"Roger, Two-one. This is Control. I've been listening in here in the TOC and I figure the army will be requesting tac air pretty quick. Do you want another FAC standing by?"

I should have thought of that. If I had to leave for any reason or got myself shot down, standard operating procedure says that another FAC should be available. "Yeah, Control. I forgot all about it. Get the next man on the duty roster over to the TOC so he can monitor what's going on and won't have to go into this thing cold, because they're spread out all over the place up here."

Switching back to the ground net, I listened carefully to see if I'd missed anything while talking to the control room. The commander of the platoon that was first ambushed sounded as if he were weeping as he requested the dust-off medevac helicopters to try again for a pickup of his wounded. One dust-off had already been lost and they were understandably reluctant to make another attempt until the LZ was a bit more secure. Right now no one could even stand erect down there, much less expect a chopper to get in.

The helicopter gunships were still madly attacking and continuing to be badly hurt. They'd lost another ship and had two more pull out of the fight—one with extensive battle damage, the other with a dead gunner. Radio discipline on the aviation nets had gone to hell and the ground net continued to be monopolized by the brigade commander and his staff. Excited requests from the ground unit blended with orders, often contradictory, from the airborne staff. Gunship pilots were trying to call out positions from which they were receiving ground fire. An artillery forward observer circled above the battle in his O-1 Birddog trying to get firing coordinates from the troops trapped on the ground. Smoke was starting to obscure the battlefield and a quick glance to the south showed that rain showers and thunderstorms would soon make our day complete. It looked like Dante's version of military hell. Or maybe a sketch by Dali.

"Sidewinder aircraft, this is Big Six." The call I'd been expecting from the CO was coming through.

"Big Six, this is Sidewinder Two-one."

"Roger, Sidewinder Two-one. It looks like we're going to need some tac air to even things up down there. If you've been monitoring, you know that we've now got three companies on the ground, almost line abreast, with their fronts facing north. In the center of the line the forward positions are farther north and there are pockets of people scattered about who don't know where they are. When you get your aircraft here we'll have the forwardmost units pop smoke and let you identify them. We'd like the bombs about one hundred meters north of the main line of resistance. Can you do that?"

"Roger, we ought to get some air here within fifteen minutes and I'll let your people know when to pop smoke. The other thing is that

I'm gonna' need to have this frequency clear of everybody but me and the people on the ground. We're going to be dropping awfully close and I don't want a screwup because somebody overrides his transmission." I had already decided that if they wanted air strikes, I'd have to do it without listening to all the extraneous directions and orders now cluttering the airways. I was too new at this game to try to sort the wheat from the chaff.

Moments of silence followed, perhaps for the first time that day. Big Six was not thrilled to be told that he was not to transmit to his own troops.

"Roger, that," he finally said. "Everyone not involved with the air strike should monitor, repeat monitor, this frequency. Do not transmit unless there is an emergency. Sidewinder, let me know when you're ready for the smoke."

Not too gracious but it would do, I thought. I checked with Sidewinder Control and found that he had requested the launch of the alert birds as soon as he had heard the request from the CO. Bombing within a hundred meters of the troops is tricky. Most of the ground-pounders didn't realize the destructive radius of a 750-pound bomb. Shrapnel and concussion can produce casualties far away from the bomb's actual impact point. I would start them farther out and try to move them closer if the troops needed it.

The fighters were coming out of Bien Hoa, so it would take only a few minutes after takeoff for them to get to the rendezvous point. I turned the aircraft and headed in that direction. I was almost there when I heard the flight leader.

"Devil Flight, check in."

"Two."

"Three."

"Sidewinder, this is Devil Lead. A flight of three approaching the rendezvous point at twelve thou. Negative contact on the FAC."

"Roger, Devil Lead, this is Sidewinder Two-one. Good morning. I'm coming up to the rendezvous point in about one minute. I'll be coming from your eleven o'clock at three thousand. I'll turn my smoke on now for five seconds." I pulled the toggle switch that activated the smoker. "Smoke is on Devil Flight."

"Negative contact . . . no, wait. Lead thinks he has you in sight, but there's so much smoke in the background that it's hard to say for sure. Rock your wings for me. Yeah, Devil Lead has a tallyho on the FAC. Are you ready for our lineup?"

"Rog, Devil Lead, Sidewinder has you in sight now. Go ahead with your lineup."

"OK, Devil Flight is three Fox-One hundreds, each has four snake-eyes and four canisters of nape. Also, a full load of twenty mike-mike all around."

"I copy that, Devil Lead. What we have today is a troops-in-contact situation and they're awfully close to each other. It's important that you adhere closely to the run-in directions. We've got three companies of U.S. friendlies on the ground and an unknown number of dinks. The green-suiters have already lost three choppers and had two others put out of action, so there's lots of ground fire about. The friendlies are fronting north along a more or less east-west line, so we'll be running parallel to them with a north break off target. There are also isolated pockets of friendlies whose location we're not sure about. But, don't worry about them; that's my job. Just drop 'em where I tell you. Target elevation is about 300 feet and the best bailout area will be anywhere to the south of the bombing line. I want you to call rolling in for each pass and off target. Call FAC and target in sight on each run. If you don't get positive clearance for each run, then go through dry. You're going to have to make each run on an east-to-west heading. Sorry 'bout that, but the way the friendlies are stretched out we can't do it any other way without overflying them. Unless you have some questions I'll lead you toward the target and have you hold high and dry until the friendlies can pop some smoke and I'm able to identify it. Then, I'll mark and we can go to work."

"No questions, Sidewinder. Let's get some!"

Devil Lead sounded ready and not particularly daunted by the reports of ground fire. It wasn't worrying me either, but I was very afraid of screwing up and hurting some GI on the ground. I led them back to the target, switching back to the ground radio frequency and telling the colonel to have his men pop smoke canisters. The different colors began to drift up through the trees, diffused but still workable. I identified each color and tried to mark the locations on my map as well as I could for reference after the bomb blasts had blown away the pretty colored smoke.

It was quickly apparent that the troops were nowhere near being in the line the colonel had suggested. Their configuration resembled instead a long "S" with the top toward the west. It was workable, but I remained concerned about those "isolated" pockets of friendly troops invisible somewhere below. The platoon commander was in contact with the survivors of one of the lost squads, but they had no idea of their location in relation to the rest of the platoon. All they knew was that they were pinned down and unable to pull back.

When I thought I pretty well had the main line of friendlies pinpointed, I told the platoon CO that I was going to put in a smoke rocket and that he should check with his lost people to see if they could either hear or see its impact. Still at 3,000 feet, I rolled the aircraft over into a forty-five-degree dive and fired my first rocket well to the north of the forwardmost troop positions.

"Latigo Six, this is Sidewinder. Did any of your people who are pinned down hear that rocket?"

"Stand by," he yelled into the microphone. I could hear the sound of rifle fire crackling in the background when he keyed the radio to transmit.

"Sidewinder, Latigo Six. My people say they heard the rocket impact about a hundred meters north of their position."

"These are the people who aren't sure of their positions, right?" I wanted to make sure that we weren't talking about his forward perimeter people.

"That's affirm, Sidewinder."

"Good enough, Latigo Six. I'm going to put the first bombs in at about that spot. Tell your lost people that when they hear the detonations to start hauling ass back toward your lines, because I'm going to gradually bring it in pretty close. Let me know if they don't get back south of your smoke or they're liable to get a snake-eye dropped on them." I switched back to the fighters, now in a holding pattern above the target area.

"Devil Lead, Sidewinder here. We'll make the first pass where you see my willie pete smoking. There are troops about a hundred meters south of there who'll be hauling back toward the line after your first pass, so I'll have to re-mark for you then. Let's go with the bombs first. I'll want 'em in singles for the first pass, then we'll switch to pairs. If you have me in sight you can start your run-in." Lord, don't let me screw up and kill any of those Americans!

"Devil Lead is in hot from the east, FAC and target in sight."

I flew directly at him until I was assured that his alignment was good and that he wouldn't be able to drop on the friendlies below, then said, "You're cleared, Devil Lead."

The bomb was good, exploding in the middle of the smoke drifting up from my marking rocket. Two trails of green tracers followed the lead ship's break off the target. I quickly changed to the army FM frequency.

"Latigo Six, this is Sidewinder. Are your people heading back now?"

"That's affirm, Sidewinder. All are heading back at this time. Stand by for one and I'll let you know when they're all back."

As I waited for the report, I overflew the target area at 3,000 feet. Then, thinking that I might catch the enemy napping, I did a quick wingover and flung the Bronco at the ground. My tricky maneuver may have fooled them for about three seconds, for that's how long it took for the tracers to begin floating my way. I let the aircraft continue its dive for the trees, leveling off just above the tops, jinking wildly. At such a low altitude I could see only the southern edge of the bomb crater, but the explosion had cleared out enough of the undergrowth to let me peer beneath the tall trees. The enemy was impossible to count in the brief seconds allowed, but there were many of them and they were moving south toward the beleaguered company. Charles was no fool. When the heavy stuff started falling, he knew that the safest place to be was snuggled as close as he could get to the American unit, effectively canceling out the friendly advantage in air and artillery. If we wanted to stop that, we were going to have to do something in a hurry.

"Sidewinder, this is Latigo Six. My people are all back inside the perimeter."

"Understand, Six. Have your northernmost element pop another smoke immediately because we're going to have to bring some stuff in real close to you. The bad guys are moving south in a hurry toward your positions. Your forward elements ought to be seeing them pretty quick. We're going to use the twenty mike-mike cannon to stop the advance. These fast movers are pretty good with them, but pass the word for everybody to get behind something and keep their heads down because we'll be dropping heavy stuff immediately after the gun runs. I'll be monitoring your freq, but don't call unless it's absolutely necessary since we'll be working awfully close to you. Out."

"Devil Lead, this is Sidewinder back with you. Change of plans. We're going to strafe before we do any more bombs. The dinks are trying to close, moving south. We'll try to make them go to ground, then work with the bombs and nape. I'm going to put in a string of three rockets along an east-west line and I want all of you to make gun runs within fifty meters on either side of that line. Any questions?''

"Negative, Sidewinder. Watch your butt, they're shooting pretty good today.''

"OK, Devil Flight, Sidewinder is in for the mark. Hold dry until I can get back into position to clear you. Be careful. We're going to be working very close to the friendlies. If you have to make a mistake, make it to the safe side—north of the line. Remember about the arty going in three klicks north of here and watch out for the helicopters on pull-off; they're all over the place.''

"And let's don't forget about the thunderstorms either,'' Lead answered with a chuckle. I had forgotten about them but could spare only a quick glance. They were still about five kilometers southwest of us but seemed to be tracking truly into the area.

I rolled the Bronco up on one wing, then let the nose slide below the horizon, blending the aileron and rudder forces to align the little aircraft along the firing axis. What a marvelously responsive thing it was, like having a well-trained horse beneath you, responding to your slightest pressure. I held the stick forward to keep the nose down, which was trying to rise with the increasing airspeed. The needle on the airspeed indicator brushed against the red line; I pulled the throttles back slightly, then abruptly shoved the nose down into a sixty-degree dive toward the dark green jungle.

At 1,000 feet I fired the first rocket, then raised the nose a few degrees, waited for a count of three, and fired again. My altimeter showed me to be at 700 feet. I leveled there momentarily, then, shoving the nose down once more and letting the aircraft stabilize in its new attitude, fired once again. Only then did I become conscious of the automatic weapons winking at me from the tree line. Shoving the throttles fully forward once more, I let the aircraft ease down until it felt as if my bottom were dragging through the treetops. I thought I could hear rounds impacting against the fuselage, highly unlikely considering the close-fitting helmet I was wearing.

Out of the area of most intense ground fire, I pulled hard back on the stick, climbing and beginning a turn back toward the run-in line. Smoke from the three rockets was filtering up from the treetops, presenting a passable line for the fighters to follow.

"Sidewinder, this is Devil Lead. We've got your smoke and I'm in from the east with guns, planning a right break off target. FAC's in sight.''

I picked up the glint of his wings as he made his right turn onto base leg toward the target, accelerating in his dive. I waited until he completed his turn and was flying directly at me. I had to be sure that he was correctly aligned. If he were off only a few degrees, his cannon fire would fall into the U.S. positions. He looked good.

"OK, Lead, you're cleared in hot."

I watched the smoke burst from beneath his aircraft. The sun glinted on the brass as it fell away expended, looking like a small rain shower as it tumbled to the ground. I turned the Bronco so I could watch the explosive slugs impacting. They sawed at the trees like an insane woodsman. The fighter pilot was fishtailing his aircraft slightly to increase the swath of fire. There were also the blinking fireflies of the enemy's return fire. It didn't look so bad up here at 1,500 feet.

"Latigo Six, this is Sidewinder," I called to the platoon commander. "How did that look?"

"I think you may be too far north," he responded immediately. "My people report that they have some NVA elements in sight no more than 150 meters to our north front. They say they're not advancing though."

"Rog. I'm going to move it in closer to you. Let me know how it sounds and if I'm getting too close."

Returning quickly to the fighter frequency I told the number two aircraft to move his fire fifty meters farther south. My heart remained in my throat as I moved the attacking aircraft ever closer to the friendly units. It almost stopped beating when, on the last gun pass, the platoon CO began screaming, "Stop them, you're hitting my forward positions!"

The brigade commander was instantly on the radio: "What in hell is going on over there, Sidewinder?"

I was confused and scared. I didn't see how we could possibly be firing into the U.S. positions. I had a good fix on them and had been carefully aligning and following each firing pass by the fighters. Before I could investigate, the lieutenant came back on the radio.

"Disregard that last transmission, Sidewinder. One of the new troops got excited and thought he was being strafed when the brass from the cannon fire began to fall on him. I'm also getting reports that Charley has started moving away from us toward the north."

I breathed a sigh of relief. I explained to the fighters what was happening. They'd heard it before.

"Devil Flight, Charley is moving back toward the north so we'll have a little more room to work, but beware of artillery up that way. I'm going to mark about 150 meters north of the last gun run line.

You'll have to stay on the east-west heading, but let's go to the bombs. I'll want them dropped in pairs and I'll clear you in after the new mark. We're still going to be working close to the friendlies, so be careful.''

I rolled inverted and let the lighted gun sight drift down to the area I'd selected to hit. I had visually marked a large emergent tree with skeletal branches as a reference point for myself. Rain suddenly erased it from sight, along with the ground, and I found myself in the ludicrous position of diving in an inverted aircraft straight for the ground, which was invisible below me and completely enveloped. The thunderstorms had sneaked into the area and caught me completely unaware.

First things first. I brought all of my attention back inside the cockpit and concentrated on my instrument panel. Staring at the attitude horizon indicator, I used it as a reference to level my wings, then began a steady back-pull on the stick. Glancing at the accelerometer I noticed that the needle was nudging past five and was almost at the figure six. Six g's! No wonder I was having trouble focusing on the instrument panel. Releasing a little back pressure on the stick, I felt the blood start to flow to my brain again. As suddenly as I had flown into the squall I popped out into clear air once more in a nearly level flight attitude.

"Sidewinder, you really ought to find a different way to wash your airplane," Devil Lead said. "If you don't get back up here where you belong, you're gonna' have a few too many drain holes in it.''

"Sorry, but I just couldn't pass up the challenge," I said. "I've never been that impressed with the Thunderbirds. Let them try *that* in a cloud! I'm in for the mark for real this time.''

I located my landmark tree once again and did another wingover toward it, this time making sure I was well away from the encroaching storms. I punched the firing button, watched over my shoulder as the rocket impacted, and made a steep, climbing turn back toward a safe altitude. I wondered why there hadn't been as much ground fire that time. I knew we couldn't have hurt the enemy that much with the cannon fire. Maybe they weren't firing as much because they were moving fast to get out of the area. How fast could they move through the jungle? I had no idea. I decided to play the odds that they could move a hell of a lot faster than I thought.

"Devil Flight, put your bombs about 100 meters north of my last smoke. I think they've had time to move beyond my mark.''

It was a guessing game now. Which way were they heading? Between bomb runs I made occasional low passes but was unable to detect any movement, nor was I fired upon. They'd probably broken up into small groups or individuals, making their way back to a predesignated assembly point. At least we had brunted the attack. I could hear the dust-off helicopters beginning their approaches into LZs to pick up the American wounded. The NVA pressure around the beseiged company had disappeared. No one was taking fire. The enemy seemed to have evaporated.

I finally decided, what the hell, and directed the fighters to drop their napalm in a likely-looking area. It was as good as any other place. The army was already taking control of the area once again. Small scout helicopters, covered overhead by Cobra gunships, flitted back and forth over the cratered area like small angry wasps.

"Devil Flight, this is Sidewinder Two-one. I'm going to clear you out of the area now. It looks like the army's taking over again. I'll have to pass along your BDA as soon as I can get it, but I'll give you 100 percent of your ordnance in the target area. It was damned fine bombing and shooting you did, folks, in pretty close quarters. Y'all have a good flight home now."

"Thank you, Sidewinder Two-one. It's been a pleasure working with you, and if you ever get down toward our squadron, look me up and we'll tell each other a few lies. In particular, I want to know how you learned to do aerobatics in a thunderstorm. Adios."

I watched the fighters bank, rejoin, and climb gracefully back to the south. I hung around the area for another few minutes, but it soon became obvious that they had no further need of my services, though no one actually told me to go home. I called Sidewinder Control and gave him my after-action report. We probably wouldn't need additional tac air, but I said they might send the next FAC up this way just to be sure.

I was banking hard to leave the area when I heard a voice transmit on the FM radio: "Sidewinder, this is Latigo Six. Thanks, friend. You saved our asses." The colonel was silent.

Back at the airstrip I surveyed my aircraft, followed by the crew chief. We counted six neat holes in the fuselage just aft of the rear cockpit. Two were from an AK-47. We knew this for sure since one of the slugs was still sticking in the skin of the aircraft, obviously striking at the far end of its range. The others looked like 12.7mm, making clean wounds as they entered but gaping holes as they blew through the other side of the fuselage. Fortunately, except for the control cables, there was little for them to destroy back there. It was the first time I had been hit hard in-country. The crew chief acted more concerned with the state of his aircraft than the fact that I had been in it. However, that's not unusual with crew chiefs anywhere.

For the next several weeks the ground activity continued to pick up throughout the brigade's AO. There was almost daily contact, usually resulting in a small, indecisive fight. The army casualties were caused primarily by booby traps and mines rather than gunfire. One thing concerned me. At the first shot, most of the ground units would call immediately for helicopter or tac air support. I understood their position, and had I been walking with them I probably would have been the first one yelling for help. But I could hardly justify diverting an air strike to fight one sniper. Not that I felt any stronger than anyone else about conserving Uncle Sam's supplies, but I simply felt it was unwise to use up the aircraft when a real emergency might suddenly erupt. I made my views known to the brigade commander and was a bit surprised when he agreed. He, too, felt that this was a silken trap a platoon commander could easily fall into and end up taking more casualties than if they had dealt with it using normal infantry tactics. Since he agreed with me I thought the old boy was smartening up right well!

The rains had fully returned and had turned the jungle into a startling green that almost hurt your eyes. Small streams flowed into the rivers, now swollen and pushing at their banks. Most days would begin with a clear, fresh sky, but by midmorning puffy cumulus clouds would start to pop up, a beautiful contrast to the dark blue background. By noon the clouds would be climbing through ten or twelve thousand feet. The midday heat and humidity made it seem impossible to draw a full breath; it was like living in a sponge. The first rains normally began in early afternoon and continued to grow in scope and intensity throughout the evening hours, often building into vicious squall lines or chains of thunderstorms that raced across the countryside at a frightening pace. In between the storms, which initially cooled things down, brief periods of sunshine turned the country into a sauna. After midnight the storms began to taper off and the skies commenced clearing, so that by dawn the cycle was ready to repeat. Sometimes, as a cyclonic system drifted into the eastern oceans the rains would become constant, pouring down in a torrential waterfall for days at a time, literally putting the country under water.

Afternoon sorties during this period were miserable. The aircraft leaked like sieves and we had to continually wipe the fog off the windscreen so we could see the ground. It was difficult to concentrate on a good ground search because the pilot spent most of his time trying to avoid the monster storm cells that always seemed to be lurking about. Life was even more difficult for the heavily laden U.S. soldiers laboring below. The VC, on the other hand, liked the rainy season. They were more lightly burdened than their American counterparts, and the rain did much to equalize the firepower since it often precluded the use of tactical air. Even the low-flying helicopters sometimes couldn't find a hole to go down through.

I was steadily learning my trade. I knew how many villagers should be in the rice fields surrounding each village. Too many might mean they had visitors. Too few could mean that a VC recruitment campaign was under way, or that trouble was afoot and the villagers had wisely decided to stay home until it was over. New footbridges had to be analyzed to determine what sort of traffic was using them, for the farmers seldom strayed away from their local village. A comparative surveillance of the bridges and trails leading to the villages would almost always show the amount of foot traffic in the area. It was impossible to hide movement in the wet season, since tracks would show in the mud and elephant grass. I was starting to feel like something out of James Fenimore Cooper. I was probably starting to look the role as well after living in these miserable conditions.

Our flight suits and survival vests were constantly wet from the rain and the high humidity. The aircraft had only several ram-air vents for cooling, a serious design flaw for an aircraft built to be flown in Southeast Asia. Neither could we open any windows in flight. It was the same kind of engineering oversight found in a building with hermetically sealed windows and no air-conditioning. The shoulders of our flight suits were rotting through from the moisture and the constant abrasion of the parachute harness. Most of us were growing a fine crop of warts in that area. The inner lining of our helmets had turned green with mildew, and even after a vigorous toweling, moisture would squeeze out and run into our eyes after we put on the helmets. The ground crews worked constantly in an attempt to keep the red mud out of the cockpit, but with little success. They didn't even try to clean the exteriors until the caked mud began to interfere with the aerodynamic efficiency of the aircraft. The roof of the hootches leaked at night, but even so, we all felt lucky to be sleeping under a roof. There were many who weren't.

I landed after an early afternoon flight and found a message waiting for me at our command post. This was not unusual, for we were deluged with messages from squadron headquarters, usually referring to the need to keep up the men's appearance. This, despite the fact that they were always wet and wading in mud up to their cheeks all day. This message was different though. I was to report the next morning to the third brigade of the division at Lai Khe and assume command of the Tactical Air Control Party there. Their ALO had been badly hurt after his aircraft was shot down by NVA gunners. A more junior major would be reporting to Di An to take my place.

I felt a little disoriented, since I was just beginning to feel comfortable with my job and with the AO in which the second brigade worked. The personalities of the pilots were just beginning to emerge and I had a grasp on which ones I could truly depend on. But at least I would be going toward the real war instead of the small-unit actions that were typical of units designated to guard the approaches to Saigon. The brigade at Lai Khe had fought major actions recently, and their base camp itself was the target of frequent attacks.

Back in the hootch I packed my meager belongings into a parachute bag and spent the last evening chatting with the other pilots. There wasn't time for a farewell party, but I was promised one as soon as I could break loose from my new assignment and visit with them. The thunderstorms rumbled through and I went to bed, covered with a soggy poncho liner. During the night Di An was mortared for the first time since my arrival. An omen?

PART 4

Journeyman

I was up early to board the dawn flight which would drop me in Lai Khe. Denny, who would be flying the mission, helped me stow my gear in the cargo bay. There were no strikes scheduled during his mission time, so we passed the time by VR'ing for a couple of hours, then headed to Lai Khe. Ten minutes out he called their control room and told them of my arrival. I looked over the base as Denny made his approach. It was an ugly sprawl of tents and hootches built around an old French villa in the middle of a rubber plantation. The runway had large rubber trees at either end, which necessitated a steep approach. From the air the roads winding in and out of the populated areas looked to be either under water or a quagmire of mud. There were none of the whitewashed rock walkways that were so popular in Di An. Helicopter revetments were scattered haphazardly beside the runway, as if put there by afterthought.

Several gray air force OV-10s squatted behind sandbags at the far end of the runway. A large, muscular redhead directed us to the parking area and already had my baggage out of the cargo bay by the time I had safed my ejection seat and clambered down the steps to the PSP ramp. The rain was starting to fall harder now, but the redhead seemed to be unaware of it. He gave a quick salute and held out a massive paw as he introduced himself as Butch, the line chief and senior NCO at the TACP. Rivers of sweat and rain mingled to form torrents down his broad, naked chest.

Denny cranked the one engine he had shut down to allow me to deplane, then taxied with a wave and a grin for me. Turning to Butch, I said, "Is there anybody around who can run me to the hootch?"

"Yes, sir. One of the Aussies is coming down to get you. He ought to be here pretty quick."

"An Aussie?" I asked. "What the hell are we doing with an Aussie?"

"You've got three of them, Major," he grinned. "Their headquarters is down in Vung Tau but they're assigned here. I think there's a couple more of them over in the first brigade. They're kinda' different but it's good to have them 'cause they can get Aussie beer whenever they get back to Vung Tau. It tastes like real beer, not the horse piss they give us around here. There's your man now.''

"OK, Butch. We'll get together tonight and go over things. Have all your gripes ready. Not that I'll probably do anything about them right away. Try to have all the troops together either then or sometime this afternoon, so I can meet them and have a few words. See you later.''

Shouldering my bag I walked toward the jeep that was slithering into the parking area. The driver was a slender, good-looking man of twenty-five or so. He had the two stripes of a flight lieutenant, if the Royal Australian Air Force (RAAF) was the same as the Royal Air Force (RAF). He was hatless, and his thick brown hair blew back over a wide forehead as he maneuvered the jeep toward me. A large, curve-stemmed pipe was clinched precariously between his teeth. Huge clouds of smoke billowed from it through the open side of the jeep as it skidded to a tight turn in front of me.

"G'dy, Major. Park it in the other seat and we'll have you home in time for lunch. Call me Dougie.'' He extended a hand.

"No, I don't think so," I said, shaking his hand. "I don't think I could possibly call a grown man Dougie. How about Doug?''

"Good enough. What do I call you?''

"How about Major?'' I grinned at him. He grinned back to let me know he wasn't impressed. "Are you a flight lieutenant?''

"Oh, we're all flight leftenants here. All three of us came from the same fighter mob back in Aussie. We don't have any fighters here, so they transitioned us into the Broncos. I think it's worked out better for us anyway. We see a fair bit of action up this way and no one's really sure how to treat us so we get away with bloody murder. Our only real problem is that the bastards won't let us fly within five bloody kilometers of the Cambodian border. Think you can do anything about getting that lot changed?''

"I don't have any idea. Hell, I didn't even know you people were in the division, so I sure didn't know anything about restricting you five klicks from the border. On the other hand, have you considered they may be doing it to keep you from getting lost? I mean, that may put you out of sight of the base camp, and the Australian navigational training might not be up to par. I don't know if I'm strong enough to stand your lot of wild men wandering about the Cambodian countryside, creating diplomatic incident after incident."

He grinned again and disappeared in a great cloud of pipe smoke. I pulled out my briar and joined him. The jeep soon looked as if it were on fire as we skidded along the rutted roadways. He indicated occasional points of local interest but otherwise let me form my own impressions as we drove back through the rain.

It looked like the Vietnam that I had expected. The overall impression was mud and rubber trees. Any air that might have been moved by a breeze was stopped by the long rows of trees, many of which had been cut down so that tents and hootches could be built. The heat was oppressive even with the falling rain. The troops walking on the roadway made no attempt to stay dry, for wearing a poncho would have created a sauna inside it. The men had the look of cattle in a rainstorm—not happy but resigned to their situation. Rain and mud were the natural elements in their life until replaced by the thick red dust of the dry season.

The air force FAC hootch was set back in the rubber trees, a long stone's throw to the brigade headquarters. The enlisted men's hootch was a stone's throw in the other direction. The mud was a thick gumbo in every direction, defying all attempts to keep it from boots or clothing. The rubber thongs worn by the Vietnamese were beginning to make a lot of sense. At least they could take them off and dunk them in the nearest mud puddle before they came indoors, sparing the flooring. In contrast, there was a heavy trail of mud leading through the entrance of our hootch.

The building was the standard army design for Vietnam—one large room on the end that served as space for our headquarters, kitchen, bar, dayroom, reading room, and briefing room. There was no one in it at the moment. Taped to one wall was a large map of the AO. A small desk with two field phones sat against another wall, and a jury-rigged bar made of empty rocket boxes sagged on the opposite side of the room. At the end of the bar another rocket box served as a library shelf for about fifty ragged paperback books. The boards of the walls rose to chest height, where wire screening continued to the bare rafters. Rocket and ammo boxes had been filled with dirt and were stacked atop each other around the hootch, giving it a fortress-like appearance. The rest of the structure provided sleeping space for eight, separated by two metal lockers. At the end of each mosquito-netted bunk was a footlocker.

Outside at the opposite end of the building was a makeshift shower stall semienclosed by more rotting rocket boxes and fed by the drop tank of some aircraft. It was being replenished by a dribbling rubber hose leading from a large olive drab–colored water tank mounted on a trailer. An unenclosed two-hole privy sat in regal isolation marked by a trail through the high grass and weeds. It was a friendly sort of place where you could chat with passersby as you did your morning's business.

"We don't use that at night," said Doug, who had been following me around on my inspection. "There are bloody cobras the size of tree trunks farting about all through those weeds. They generally stay beneath the hootches during the day and come out at night to catch rats. The rats feed off our garbage and the snakes feed off them. I hate both of them."

"Has anyone ever been bitten? Do they ever come into the hootches? The snakes, I mean." I didn't like the sound of this.

"Not since I've been here," Doug answered. "They take rather a lot of getting accustomed to and I haven't been able to manage it yet. I've seen them on the porch several times when I've gone out there at night to take a whiz, but not inside yet. We try to make sure that the screen doors are always closed securely, but there are probably a million bloody ways for them to get in if they wanted to. By the way, did you notice our bunker?"

I hadn't. Behind one of the bunks the flooring had been removed and extensive excavations had been made. The results were an underground room of some six by eight feet in which an electric light had been rigged, backed up by lanterns and battery-powered spotlights for use when the generator was inoperative. In the glow of the small bulb I saw there were cases of C rations as well as weapons and ammunition stacked against the moist walls. It smelled like a tomb.

"Looks like you're ready for an assault," I said.

"It's happened twice since I've been here," Doug answered without a smile. "Once, they got inside the wire and we had a hell of a time getting them out. They ran about, slinging satchel charges in buildings and at helicopters. Badly damaged one of our aircraft, as well. This hole also comes in handy because we generally get rocketed three to four times a week. Sometimes it's only a few rounds, but often they'll spend the whole bloody night at it. Incidentally, there's a brigade SOP that requires a FAC to be launched in the event of attack, no matter what time of day or night it comes. We have to get to the flight line with the ground crew with bloody one-two-two rockets falling about and then take off without bloody runway lights to fart about for an hour or so until Charley gets tired of the game and crawls back into his hole for the rest of the night. Your troops have found that most of the rockets are set off by timers made of the workings of a cheap watch, so even if we were to see one of the rockets launched and could get a strike force together in time, we'd more than likely be bombing a bloody Seiko.''

The rain had stopped for the moment so we trudged toward the brigade mess for lunch. The food was unidentifiable. I made courtesy calls at the staff dining table. The brigade commander was not there; he was out harassing his troops in the field. The S-3 suggested that I attend the staff dinner that evening in one of the old French buildings that served as the staff dining room for the evening meal. There, I supposed, the staff could dine in splendid isolation without inciting their underlings to riot. All staff section leaders were expected to attend, including the ALO.

I rejoined Doug at what looked like the pilots' table, everyone there being an air force or army aviator. The helicopter pilots all looked to be about eighteen years old and were mostly scout pilots flying the light observation helicopter (LOH) called a "Loach." I figured if you were older than eighteen you had more sense than to be flying as a scout. What they had in common with FACs was that both literally "trolled" for enemy ground fire at low level, using themselves as live bait. Many of the scout pilots never finished their year's tour.

I was introduced to the remainder of the FACs, except for one of the Australians who was airborne. I told them to be available after I had the evening meal with the staff and brigade commander. They were in a motley array of uniforms. Some were in army jungle fatigues, others in the standard USAF flight suit, still others in all or parts of camouflage fatigue sets. The Aussies wore their RAAF light green flight suits. Headgear was either army green baseball-style caps or floppy bush hats. While staring at my food, which appeared to be trying to crawl off my tin mess plate, I asked Ed, a young captain, how their last ALO had been shot down.

"No one really knows too much," he said quietly. "He radioed that he was patrolling down the river, then made a broken request for fighters, even if they had to be diverted from another target. He said something about VC in the open trying to cross a river, and that was the last anyone heard from him. The army diverted some gunships, but when they got to his area they didn't see anything or take any ground fire. The major's plane was completely destroyed and he was found unconscious, hanging from his chute on the limb of a big old tree. They damned near killed him just getting him out. They tried to hover over him so they could grab the chute and pull him in, but the Huey's windblast blew the chute loose. He would have fallen about a hundred feet to the ground except the chute snagged again. Finally, the door gunner crawled out on the limb and tied a rope to him. The major is pretty messed up, I hear. The brigade's put in a couple of companies, but all they've found are cold trails. It looks like the VC have split up into smaller units. We'll probably be hearing from them in a few days. The S-2 thinks another NVA unit is moving into the area or through it. Nobody really knows.''

The remainder of the afternoon I spent talking to the enlisted men and listening to their bitches. They had a lot of complaints, mostly about spare-parts availability and things of that sort. Few had requests that would benefit them personally. In theory the TACP at a forward operating location (FOL) was to do minimum aircraft maintenance, sending back to squadron headquarters in Bien Hoa those aircraft needing more sophisticated repair work. In practice, the aircraft couldn't be spared from the flying schedule to shuttle them back and forth to the larger base for repair. Consequently, Butch and his people did everything short of a full engine change. They all—mechanics and radio operators and armorers—grabbed wrenches and attacked the sick Broncos. Their ingenuity was delightful to watch; the results weren't pretty, but the planes held together in flight.

After a cursory inspection of our facilities I spent the remainder of the afternoon in the TOC, familiarizing myself with the brigade's area of operation. I tried to anticipate questions the commander might ask me at dinner that night, but gave it up as a useless exercise and went back to the hootch to unpack. While there, I scribbled a few hurried lines to Mary Ann, letting her know my new address. I still hadn't received any mail from home. I had moved around so much that it still might be weeks before the APO found me. I heard a scurrying in the rafters and looked up to see two huge black rats in trail formation running across a bare brace. A feeling of melancholy enveloped me. No mail, no friends, the new boy on the block, rain and mud, and goddamned rats running around unchallenged over my head. Jesus Christ, this was no way for a man to live.

Lighting my pipe, I walked carefully out through the weeds to our privy, keeping out a wary eye for snakes. None appeared. They were probably high and dry under our hootch, for it had started to rain once more. I lowered my flying suit, sat on the wet wooden plank with the rough hole cut in it, and listened to the rain pounding on the tin roof. At least no one in Vietnam suffered from constipation. I wouldn't have known a solid stool if one had rolled up and introduced himself. I gazed at the graffiti someone had penciled in on one of the beams holding up the tin roof: "If God takes care of fools and drunks, the brigade commander is in for a double dose of divine grace!"

Still smiling, I safely negotiated the path back to the hootch where I heard subdued laughter coming from the dayroom-cum-briefing room. Doug was there with another Aussie I hadn't met. He must have been the one flying during the noon period. His wide grin threatened to shatter his round moon face into fragments. Large freckles covered his face, and tousled, sandy hair hung down over his forehead in an engaging manner. He looked like something created by Norman Rockwell. Unfortunately, the man seemed either to have a speech impediment or be severely retarded, for I couldn't understand a word of the gibberish he was spilling out. I looked to Doug for help in case he became violent and we had to restrain him in the metal Conex outside.

Doug was smiling at him affectionately. "Major, meet Huckleberry," he said. "Pay no mind to his natterings for he grew up in some outlandishly named station in the outback and often even his mates have difficulty understanding what he thinks is speech."

Huckleberry only grinned broader and pumped my hand.

"He's not worth much except for flying," Doug continued, "but that he does very well. However, we do try to keep him hidden away when civilized folk come to call."

"Is Huckleberry your real name?" I asked. He wriggled with joy like a young puppy at being spoken to.

"Neh," I deciphered, "me mates just think I look like 'im in the book. Most folks just call me 'Huck' though."

And well they should, I thought. I had never seen a name and subject match quite so well. He left us for a washup, and I had a few minutes to sit with Doug before I had to leave for dinner.

"How's the AO?" I asked him. "The status board in the TOC indicates there's more activity now than any time in the last three months. How do you see it?"

The smile dropped from his face and he became a different person, this one an all-professional briefing officer.

"There's been a noticeable increase in enemy activity since I arrived here several months ago," he said. "Most of it has been toward the border, where new infiltration routes are constantly being discovered in the thickest part of the bush.

"We've been placing air strikes daily into this area," pointing toward the wall map, "and on every one of them that have been checked by ground units, we've had KBAs [killed by air]. Usually not a lot of them, but you know the NVA and VC aren't so different from the rest of us in that they do try to get their dead and wounded off the battlefield. There's some prevailing bullshit that they remove their dead so that we can't count their casualties, but I fail to understand why people would think they feel differently about their dead than we do. It makes no sense a'tall. One important difference of late is their willingness to take potshots at helicopters and FACs. When I first came here they did their best to avoid us unless they knew they'd been spotted. Now, it seems that if we fly within earshot of them, they begin blasting about.

"We've taken quite a lot of battle damage as of late, not to mention losing the major, and the helicopters have been having an even worse time of it. They've been taking losses by the dozen. There simply aren't enough troops to adequately cover the AO, so they're trying to extend the coverage of the air and artillery to break up any suspected troop concentrations. You can only see so much from the air, however, and we often don't know if our targeting has been successful or not. The special intelligence reports that filter down to us indicate that our thinking is right—that is, there is more infiltration. On the other hand, some members of the staff believe our AO is just a transient area for the NVA moving on farther south."

"What do you think?" I asked.

"Damned if I know!" he said, breaking into a grin once more. "I'm just a lowly flight leftenant and everyone knows you must be at least an air commodore to think like that."

"Thanks for your thoughts, Doug," I said, "and now I have to get to the colonel's dinner. Tell the others I'll be back within an hour or so, hopefully. We'll have a little meeting then."

The staff dinner went about as I had expected. We dined with regimental silver off regimental china after we had our cocktails. The meal was sumptuous, the best I'd had in-country—steak, fresh asparagus, whipped potatoes, delicate carrots, and a green salad with tangy dressing. Dessert was ice cream and strawberries. These guys do OK for their forty-seven-dollar monthly subsistence allowance, I thought.

After the meal, while we had our fresh coffee (not the C-ration variety) and brandy, the commander began asking sharp questions of his staff. His social charm disappeared and his manner became quite abrasive. He briefly outlined the brigade's strategy for the next day. I talked to him about his air requirements, then asked if it would be possible for me to be excused from the evening dining ritual until further notice, pleading the need for time to reorganize and orient myself to the new AO. He appeared relieved not to have to look upon me at meals and suggested I stay in touch with him via the S-3, the operations officer. I think the situation suited both of us, although protocol may have suffered a bit.

All the pilots were gathered in the big room in the hootch when I returned from dinner. Some were drinking warm beers; others had mess cups of C-ration coffee in their hands. I went through all the names again to make sure I had them straight, then reviewed the listing of TACP duties and who was assigned to them. It didn't matter how far forward you were located, the Air Force still wanted all the jobs filled. The operations officer's job was the number-two position in the TACP and would therefore be filled by the next senior officer, in this case Doug. Maintenance was a different story—that could be anyone, and rank had nothing to do with it. Whoever was in the position of maintenance officer would have to work closely with Butch, the senior NCO and line chief. Sometimes this situation could get touchy if the usually older NCO was the type to resent a twenty-year-old second lieutenant getting in his way. Don, a senior captain, now held that position, but he would soon be rotating home. I decided to worry about his replacement later.

Most of the other jobs were make-work positions, except for the awards officer, for decorations were important to all of the men and officers, despite their protestations to the contrary. That position was now held by George the Horrible, but since I hadn't reviewed any of his work I didn't know if I was going to keep him in that position. I had wondered about his name during the earlier introductions but felt it prudent not to delve too deeply at the risk of finding out something I'd just as soon not know. I'd have to check his writing and creativity as soon as possible, for I wanted every man to have some sort of decoration or award before he went home. This usually wasn't a problem with the pilots but could become one with the ground crew.

We went through the problems as the pilots saw them and felt each other out, since I was an enigma to them as well. One thing, you did get to know everyone quickly in combat, the good and the bad things. I had Doug schedule me to ride with the TACP instructor pilot on the early flight the next day and called an end to the meeting.

As I crawled beneath my mosquito net, my head was whirling with things that I needed to accomplish. The rains came immediately, beating on the metal roof with a ferocity that was almost evil. Over the din I could hear the mosquitoes seeking an opening in the net. As my conscious-ness wound down, I heard a large crump down by the flight line. I sat up with a jerk.

"Incoming!" someone down the bay yelled. A stampede swept by me heading in the direction of the bunker. Two more explosions, highly visible through the screen wall of the hootch, made my fight with the mosquito net more frantic. The hateful thing seemed to clutch me tighter the more I scrambled. The brace bar had now pulled free and had cunningly wormed its way under my arm while the net serpentined around my ankle. In a trice I had all but hog-tied myself. This will be a ridiculous position for my body to be found in, I thought sulkily, if one of those rockets blows away this hootch. I slowly began to unwind the net from around my legs, and carefully removed the metal brace that was digging toward my spleen.

Finally freeing myself I charged down the aisle as more explosions edged toward us. Everyone in the bunker seemed to take it as a fact that I should be the last one in. They were hunkered around one of the radios listening to the TOC direct the base defense.

"We'll be getting a call from the TOC in a few minutes telling us to launch a bird," said Doug. "Who's up tonight?"

Huck spouted some sort of outback gibberish that probably translated as "I am." He was lacing his boots and getting into his survival vest when the expected call came through. There had been no explosions for several minutes.

"I counted twenty-two," Ed said. Several of the others nodded affirma-tively.

"Nine rockets and fourteen mortars," George the Horrible said. Everyone nodded. There was silence again for a few moments.

"That makes twenty-three, not twenty-two," said an unseen voice.

"Aw, stick it up your ass," Ed said peevishly. "What difference does it make?"

"I'm sure I counted twenty-two," George the Horrible said. He sounded puzzled, as if someone were pulling a monstrous trick on him and he was determined to get to the bottom of it.

"If you gentlemen don't shut your mouths I'm going to draw my revolver and kill every one of you," Doug announced.

"Huck, hold off on the launch," I said. There was no more incoming fire and I saw no reason to put up an aircraft just for the thrill of getting some night-flying done. The schedule was too tight for that. I could see that we needed a phone to the enlisted hootch to keep them from running to the flight line for no reason.

I grabbed Doug and my CAR-15, and we jumped into the jeep and headed toward the flight line. Trying to drive without lights was too slow so I told Doug to switch them on. There were lights coming from buildings and tents all over the base camp, so I figured our headlights were hardly likely to whip the VC gunners into another frenzy of firing. The rain seemed to be falling almost horizontally, but it stopped as we reached the flight line. Butch and two of his men were crouched in a bunker near the aircraft. As we walked to them the all-clear siren sounded.

Starting tomorrow, I told Butch, I wanted field phones connecting our hootches and in future shellings his men were to stay in their bunker unless one of our officers ordered them to the line. This didn't upset him in the least. The remainder of the night was disturbed only by the thunderstorms roaming the area.

The morning was sparkling clear and the temperature almost pleasant as Ed and I drove toward the flight line. He was driving and I was wrapped in an army poncho trying to escape the mud being flung up by passing trucks. A thought had been gnawing at my mind since breakfast. I thought I remembered from lectures back in training that the TACPs were authorized one jeep per pilot. This was not because USAF believed each FAC should have a personal vehicle, but because each pilot was supposed to have a radio jeep and radio operator ready for use as a mobile ground control in the event that air surveillance was not practical. Supposedly, a FAC would be ready to join his battalion in the field at a moment's notice. It seemed to me, however, that in this TACP every officer and man had his own personal jeep.

"Ed," I asked, "where in hell do all of our people get all these jeeps they're driving? The way I figure, we ought to have a maximum of six assigned to the TACP. I know that I've seen at least twice that many with our people in them. How do we come to have so many and who authorized them anyway?"

He cut his eyes toward me and grinned, then hurriedly looked back toward the road at the six-by truck hurtling toward us, which gave no indication it was going to surrender its position in the middle of the road. At the last possible moment the truck swerved to the right. Ed did the same. A tidal wave of mud splashed against our windscreen. Ed worked the hand wipers a few times in order to completely smear the mud. Satisfied that it was evenly distributed and completely impenetrable, he looked at me again.

"We either reconstitute 'em or we liberate 'em," he said.

"What do you mean 'reconstitute'?" I asked. "I think I understand what the other means."

"Simply that," he said. "The same way they do with the eggs we get. First, you go down to the motor pool and slip whoever's in charge a bottle of something they like. Or we get one of the Aussies to donate one of their hats or an old flying suit or something like that. The grunts like that stuff. Then we get Butch and his merry men to look over the salvaged jeep parts they have laying around down there and select the parts they need, and then about two days later we have a new jeep. You know that Butch and his guys can fix anything and a jeep is a cinch to them. After it's ready you can get gas for it anywhere because nobody pays any attention to the serial numbers stenciled on the jeeps. The army doesn't really care because they've already written the jeep off the books. Butch has a whole Conex filled with spare parts he's scrounged. They don't mind keeping all of them running because we don't say anything about *their* personal jeeps."

"That sounds OK to me," I said. "But, does 'liberating' mean exactly what I think it means?"

" 'Fraid so," he said, as we pulled in by the aircraft revetments. "Sometimes, it's just easier to swipe them from somebody else. For example, if you're clear across the base visiting the helicopter pilots some night and you don't want to walk all the way back, it's easier to cut the chain they use to secure the steering wheel and drive back, courtesy of the helicopter company."

"Why would you have to walk back anyway if everybody in the TACP has a jeep? Besides, doesn't that kinda' hack off your friend, the helicopter pilot? And don't you eventually end up with a whole bunch of stolen jeeps?"

"Well, it doesn't quite work that way," he said as we pulled our gear from the back seat. "You see, the helicopter pilots are pretty good at stealing jeeps, too. There's no way to get them out of the base camp, so it really turns out to be a matter of just swapping them around. There's probably not a single jeep in the entire encampment, including the brigade commander's, that matches up with the registration of the person who originally signed for it."

"I think you're all a bunch of social misfits who have completely perverted the good name of the officers' corps."

"You got it, sir."

Ed and I flew that day to cover the daily truck convoy moving from Lai Khe, up Thunder Road, to An Loc. The road aimed almost straight north through sparsely populated plains and forests, which were scarcely patrolled by the U.S. or South Vietnamese forces. Security for the convoy depended instead upon aerial and artillery support. Normally an air force or army aircraft accompanied the convoy for at least a portion of its trip. The VC, of course, knew the schedule as well as a Connecticut commuter knew the one to the Big Apple. Ambush was always risky, however, and Charley could count on receiving a bloody nose if he tried it too often. About once a week, though, he was unable to withstand the temptation. Often, it was no more than a couple of men with automatic weapons and a command-detonated mine. Other times, for reasons known only to their leaders, who may have relied on phases of the moon or the way bones fell from a shaken container, they would descend upon the trucks in a full-blown assault. Perhaps our intelligence relied on the same methods to decide when and where to do extensive air or arty prep along the road. If Charley was well-mannered enough to be in the location that intelligence had picked, then he would withdraw and no attack was on for the day. If Charley snubbed our intelligence analysts, however, and chose an ambush site not considered by them and thus escaped being blown into oblivion, then he proceeded with his attack.

That day, we flew at 500 feet along either side of the long line of trucks, trying to stay far enough ahead of them to scan the roadside before they passed. Trees and undergrowth had been defoliated as far back as a hundred meters from the road, leaving behind a tangled mess of huge logs and smaller trees. It provided enough cover to hide the entire politburo. Enemy troops would be discovered only if they were so foolish as to shoot at the circling aircraft or move into one of the areas that had been plowed as well as sprayed. No one ever thought Charley was foolish.

Control had informed us that two sets of fighters were being diverted to us because of bad weather in their original target area. Both flights had a full load of cluster bomb units (CBUs) and 20mm cannons. The CBUs were a nasty piece of work consisting of hundreds of small bomblets carried in pods; each bomblet exploded into hundreds of pellets on contact with the ground. One pod could cover an area the size of a football field. Each attacking aircraft carried four pods of the little devils. The CBUs were virtually useless in the heavy foliage of a rain forest, but as antipersonnel weapons for lightly defended troops they were the perfect weapon.

The ambush that day was sprung when the third truck from the leader was blown from the road by an exploding mine. Charley had probably planned on the blown truck effectively blocking the road and stopping the remaining convoy for some easy shooting. Unfortunately for them the exploding truck had either been blown clear of the roadway or had been driven there by an alert driver before overturning. The next truck in line veered around the burning vehicle and, following standard convoy instructions, put his accelerator to the floor and ran out of the killing zone. The remaining trucks followed his lead while the soldiers riding shotgun atop the trucks began unleashing their machine guns in a random pattern, raking the countryside on either side of the road.

The enemy then began a series of very costly mistakes. One of the ambushers began firing at the convoy as it sped by. Those muzzle flashes were picked up by a sharp-eyed gunner who radioed the convoy commander.

"Sidewinder Two-one, this is Mobile Six," the convoy leader called to me.

"Go ahead Mobile Six, this is Sidewinder."

"Roger, we've lost one truck and the rest are didi-ing down the blacktop at maximum speed. We'd like for you to stay with us for a few miles until we're out of the kill zone for sure, and then if you'd like to rain some shit on Charley we think we can tell you where to find him. One of the gunners saw muzzle flashes out about a hundred meters west of the road and opposite the place where the mine went off. As soon as the cleanup truck polices up the survivors from our destroyed truck, you might want to check it out. The gunner said it looked like the gunfire was coming from that area of big dead trees still standing in a clump out to the west.''

"Sounds good, Mobile Six. We'll fly a circle over you wide enough to include the convoy and his hidey-hole and try to keep him from moving out while we act like we don't know where he is. We've got diverted fighters inbound to us anyway and I've been trying to figure out where to put them. Just let me know when you feel like your convoy is OK.''

Ed and I circled slowly, watching the convoy flounder along the muddy road. The last truck and two jeeps with mounted M-60 machine guns stopped at the still-burning truck. The gunners were firing into the area on both sides of the road. We could see two survivors clambering into the back of the truck when, suddenly, one of the jeeps exploded in an orange ball of fire. Charley had decided to take what he could get rather than slide quietly out of the area.

The gunner in the other jeep spun his weapon 180 degrees and recommenced firing, the tracers reaching out to the clump of large dead trees the convoy commander had mentioned as the probable site of the enemy fire. I had been sure there would be no survivors from the flamed jeep, but tracers from a gun in the debris joined the M-60's fire toward the trees.

"I've got them spotted, I think,'' Ed said from the rear cockpit. "Look just to the north of those big bare trees, about thirty meters or so. It looked like tracers coming out of that big tangle where the Rome plows pushed all the trunks together. Look! There it is again.''

"OK, I'm going to try to make them keep their heads down until the fighters get here,'' I said.

Reaching over to the armament panel with my left hand, I armed the four 7.62 machine guns. I wished that we had put explosive rockets on board instead of wall-to-wall willie pete. I rolled the aircraft inverted and pulled the nose well down through the horizon in a forty-five-degree dive. Then I quickly rolled upright while continuing the dive, and nudged the rudders to align the lighted gunsight in the windscreen toward the target. I made myself relax the control pressures to avoid having the bullets skew off to the side. I found I had unconsciously tightened my hand around the control stick handle, so I forced myself to fly with fingertips alone. Squeezing the trigger on the stick grip, I felt the aircraft shudder as the guns fired below and behind me. The tracers flowed toward the ground in what looked like a steady stream. I bumped the rudders slightly to move the gunsight around the area of tangled logs and stumps. The guns were too light to do much damage to a well-dug-in enemy, but I doubted if Charley had made that sort of preparation.

"They're getting after us," Ed said quietly, as if he were asking someone to pass the salt.

I hadn't noticed the ground fire blinking in the tattered landscape below us, concentrating on my own aim instead. Charley's attention had been diverted from the burning vehicles to us. They surely knew that unless we were quickly put out of action, allied artillery and air strikes would soon begin raining down upon them. Their fire concentrated on us as I pulled hard on the aircraft to bring it into position for another firing pass. I glanced quickly toward the road and saw the survivors crawling aboard the truck, which was already slowly moving northward again. Good. I wouldn't have to worry about them. Although I hadn't heard from the convoy commander, it didn't matter anymore. Soon every helicopter and FAC in the area would be homing in on the smoke from the burning trucks; it was unlikely that the enemy would try anything new against the convoy.

I could see the figures on the ground shifting position to gain protection behind the huge logs as I rolled in for the next firing pass. The intensity of the fire was frightening. I momentarily shut my eyes so I wouldn't have to look at it, but they popped back open like a doll's. I stared with horrified fascination as the greenish tracers floated toward me, then veered off sharply.

Just before I pulled the gun trigger, I told Ed, "See if you can mark their positions," more to have something to divert my attention from the ground fire than a real need to know. I could have shot anywhere in the area and been aiming at somebody. My voice sounded shrill to me.

"Right, I'm looking," Ed replied. His voice sounded a little higher as well, but we were both playing the old air force game of "I'm cooler than you, you son of a bitch." We were both actually scared witless.

The strafing run seemed to take forever. Before we pulled out we were close enough to the ground that the automatic weapon fire didn't have the floating look you see when flying higher. This was more like being locked in a small room filled with maniacs firing shotguns. Finally, it was time to pull out. I jerked hard on the stick and got the nose going up almost to the vertical. Thank God we were in a Bronco. An

O-2 would have been dead by now. As the airspeed bled off I let the aircraft roll slowly toward the horizon in low-speed flight. We were flying slowly but we had managed to convert our airspeed into 3,000 feet of altitude to put us above most of the guns.

Ed grunted over the intercom, but I looked at both wings before I responded. I could see two holes in the left wing where some of our fuel tanks were located, although they were supposed to be self-sealing against hits by small-caliber weapons. Nothing seemed to be dribbling out, so I suppose they *were* self-sealing. Inside the cockpit, in the floor beside the control stick, was a hole the size of a pencil; it was about six inches from my booted foot. I looked at the canopy for an exit hole but couldn't find it. The bullet must have spent itself somewhere inside, but all the instruments looked good and the engines were still performing well.

"How does it look back there, Ed?"

"They shot my goddamn heel off!" he said, his voice full of wonder like someone who just witnessed a dog flying or congress voting the military a 10 percent pay raise.

"How bad are you hurt?" I asked. "Can you reach your first-aid pouch?" There was a pouch mounted on each cockpit bulkhead wall, complete even to morphine.

"It didn't touch my foot"—the wonderment still in his voice—"they just shot the goddamn heel right off my boot."

I was spared further discussion about the status of his boots by the arrival of the first fighters.

"Sidewinder, this is Greasy Flight checking in."

"Greasy Flight, this is Sidewinder Two-one. Go ahead with your lineup."

"Rog. Greasy Flight is three F-100s carrying CBUs across the board. We're ten minutes until bingo fuel because we've been diverted from up-country. You got anything for us quick?"

I realized that they didn't know there was a live target, which they would have if our radio operator had been doing his job. He should have been monitoring all of our radio transmissions and letting the fighters know on initial contact that we had a hot target. I made a mental note to check on that when we got back.

"Roger, Greasy Lead, this is Sidewinder. We have a new development. A convoy's been hit along Thunder Road about ten klicks northwest of the rendezvous point. I'm going to stay over the target instead of meeting you at the RP because I think we've got Charley pinned down and I don't want him to slide away. When you get to the RP, just head northeast and you'll see black smoke along the road. We're working just to the west of that smoke. Where the two vehicles are burning are the only possible friendlies in the area; they may be out of there by now, but we won't take a chance until I've got confirmation.''

I suddenly realized that the radio operator wasn't the only one who had dropped the ball. We hadn't reported the burning vehicles to the TOC. I told Ed to call in a sit-rep to the army and to get slicks and gunships en route to the ambush site. I went back to the fighters as he called on the other radio.

"Greasy Flight, this is Sidewinder Two-one. I have you in sight now at four o'clock descending, about five out. I'm putting out smoke now."

"Rog, Sidewinder. We've got you in sight but we're getting skoshi on fuel. We'd like to get to work right away."

"You got it, Hoss. They're hiding in that defoliated mess about 100 meters west of the smoke on the road. Make your runs parallel to the road, either direction, with a west break off target. We'll soon have some helicopters working right over the road. We think Charley is only lightly dug in down there because we can see 'em scamper around. There's a lot of automatic weapon fire all over the place. We've taken several hits ourselves, so watch your ass. Best bailout area is back toward the road. Elevation is about 250 feet. What I'm going to do is put in two markers for each of your runs. I'll want each of you to spread your CBU between those two markers. I want one pass per aircraft, then if you have enough fuel we'll see about strafing. I want each aircraft to call the target and FAC in sight. I'll be orbiting directly over the target at 1,500 feet unless I tell you otherwise. Any questions?''

"Shit hot! Let's get some."

I had mentioned that we had taken hits to emphasize the reality of the ground fire. Many FACs told the fighters to expect fire to cover their own rumps in the event some unexpected VC gunner suddenly opened up on the attackers. Attack pilots had begun to expect the call whether or not ground fire had been observed. Also, some FACs in mild-mannered, well-secured AOs called the possibility of ground fire to spice up their own image as one who always had it hanging out.

"Sidewinder is in for the mark."

I positioned the aircraft on a perpendicular heading to the target so I could make a wingover firing pass, just the way we did it at school. I kept my eyes on the big trees that we were using for a reference point and thrust the stick to the left side of the cockpit, rolling inverted to keep positive g-forces on the aircraft, and trying to ignore the muzzle flashes from the ground. Picking the two points I wanted my rockets to hit, I gently nudged the nose of the aircraft to get them lined up in my sights. Punching the firing button on the stick, I watched one rocket away, then gently raised the sight on my windscreen with a little back pressure on the stick until it was pointing at the new target, then fired again.

At the lower altitude I could easily see the figures running about, then stopping to raise their weapons to fire at me. I didn't know whether or not they had noticed the jets overhead. Probably not or they would have been seeking shelter. There were many more of them than I had expected. I felt the impact of the ground fire as I flew out of the stream of tracers that had found me. I didn't wait to see the second rocket impact, but made a hard pull-up, trying to regain the altitude I'd lost in the dive.

"Greasy Lead, put your CBUs between those two smokes, but watch yourself. I think they've got at least one heavy machine gun down there and we took more hits from it." As I spoke I was busy looking over my aircraft for other battle damage. I twisted in the cockpit and could see Ed doing the same. There were no new holes that I could see, so the slugs must have hit us somewhere in the fuselage, well behind us. They couldn't hurt much back there unless they happened to cut a control cable and I didn't want to think about that. Besides, all the controls felt OK. The odds were that they just punched some holes in the empty cargo bay.

"You're cleared in hot, Lead, if you have the target and the FAC in sight."

"Lead is in hot from the south; FAC and target in sight."

I watched the sleek aircraft make a small correction as the pilot lined it up on the two smoke balls rising from the tangled mass of dead trees below us. As he flew under me I banked the Bronco on its side so I could watch his CBU pods ejecting their lethal bomblets. The small explosions began almost immediately for they didn't have far to fall. They seemed to be in the right area. They were still exploding as I put my aircraft into a shallow dive toward the target. Aiming fifty meters to the west of the smoke I fired two more rockets and cleared the next fighter for his pass. The heavy machine gun on the ground switched from me to the fighter as he began his approach. The AK-47 fire was intense.

I watched the tracers lick at the tail of the second fighter as it pulled off target into a hard climbing turn to re-enter the bombing pattern. He wasn't squealing so I figured he wasn't hurt too badly. That gun had to go, though; he was getting entirely too good.

Rolling inverted, I pulled the aircraft down into a near-vertical dive, squeezing the trigger on my own guns as soon as the sight settled in the target area. With my finger still wrapped around the gun trigger, I hit the rocket-firing button with my thumb and watched two more of them dart toward the ground. They looked as if they'd impact near the gun site, so I began a hard pull on the stick to raise the aircraft's nose. Ed was grunting over the intercom, but because of the g-forces I couldn't make out what he was trying to say. I cut my eyes toward the accelerometer and saw we were pulling more than six g's. Still safe enough but mighty uncomfortable. Through my grayed vision I saw the nose rise above the horizon and let off some of the pressure I'd been holding on the control stick, allowing the blood to begin to flow once more. My vision improved immediately and I looked back over my shoulder at the carnage on the ground. The CBUs and machine-gun fire were taking their toll. Prone bodies lay motionless, no longer interested in the fight.

The last fighter was asking for clearance, but I had been unable to answer because of the g-forces of my pullout. I cleared him in hot and climbed back to my orbit altitude to wait until his attack was over.

"Before you tried to drive my head into my body cavity back there," Ed said over the intercom, "I was trying to tell you to look over your head."

Glancing up I saw a jagged hole the size of a drink coaster directly over my head, next to the fresh air scoop. I hadn't heard the shell hit.

"The shell came up through my side panel," Ed said. "Three inches lower and the damned thing would have taken off my leg at the knee."

"Well, at least then you wouldn't have to worry about your heel," I said.

"A lot of people seem to be taking this damned war too seriously," he grumbled. "It used to be that we could go out and fly our sorties in a refined, gentlemanly sort of way, without everybody and his brother getting mad and starting to shoot and carrying on like a bunch of durned fools. I'm glad I've only got two months to go, unlike some folks, who shall go nameless, who have so long left that they might as well buy a piece of land and start raising crops to sell to the VC."

I grinned at him in the mirror but didn't answer. The other set of fighters was checking in. Diablo Flight was two F-4s also armed with CBUs but no guns. I positioned them for the attack as I cleared Greasy Flight for one strafe run, then cleared them from the area. They were past bingo fuel. It's difficult to judge a pilot's skills when he's using CBU, but I gave them all 100 percent of their ordnance in the target area.

Most of the ground fire seemed to have stopped except for the odd, isolated burst as I flew low over the ravaged area. The rescue helicopters had finished whatever it was they were doing over by the ambushed trucks, and after contacting the convoy commander again, I found that all personnel, both dead and wounded, had been removed from the area. There were no friendlies in the area, so the fighters could attack and pull out in any direction.

"Diablo Lead, there are negative friendlies in the area so I'm going to clear you all for attack anywhere within a box outlined by the four rockets I'm going to put in. You'll be cleared in from any direction, just call FAC and target in sight and direction of attack and break off target. I'm going to perch above the target at 2,000 and stay out of your way. You're both cleared in hot at your discretion. Be advised we have received heavy ground fire, but it's slacked off quite a bit. However, there's still some down there."

"Roger that. Understand we're both cleared hot from any direction. Lead is in hot from the west."

"Just put it anywhere in that square formed by the four smokes," I told him.

Having given them carte blanche, we sat above the target and watched them work. When the fighters were allowed to choose their own axis for attack, they were in relatively little danger from the fire from the ground, for they were in and out before the gunners could react. After the first pass I saw no more ground fire.

"Do you think they got away?" I asked Ed.

"Hard to say. Obviously, we got a bunch of them. Brigade will probably have troops on the ground here within the hour and I suspect they're going to be a bunch of KBAs down there, but I'll also bet that there are a lot we didn't get. I'll bet we hear from the colonel pretty quick because it isn't often that we get the chance to hit back against ambushers along the road. I don't think he's going to let this chance slip by him."

The fighters finished their work and I sent them on their way. Ed had been right about the troops. They were on the ground within half an hour of the last bombing. Before the gunships arrived to start blasting the area in preparation for the assault, we made a final low-level pass over the target. Not many of the prone figures had come to life and slipped away. Short of being in bunkers, there weren't many ways to hide from the bomblets that had been dropped.

At the evening briefing the S-2 reported a body count of more than 150 NVA in the target area, all KBA, and they were still finding them. The brigade commander turned in his chair and looked at me. Removing the cigar from his mouth he said, "Not bad!"

Score one for the Gipper. As I left the briefing room I was thinking that I had been instrumental in bringing death to 150 people. I should have felt sad, but all I felt was pleasure. A conscience is simply too heavy a burden to pack around in combat. Outside, I found somebody had stolen my jeep.

Crazy John was the sanest man I knew. Fairly new to the outfit, having transferred in-country from one of the fighter squadrons when they ran short of FACs, he'd been given a short course in the fine art of forward air controlling and sent to our unit. A tall, blond, good-looking young man, his quiet demeanor and steadiness under fire had already earned him the respect of the other pilots and men. He was often the victim of a ribald joke or horseplay but never the instigator. His drinking was limited to one beer at the end of the day. Taking all of that into consideration, why was he making such preposterous claims?

"Sidewinder Two-five, this is Two-one. Say again your last transmission."

"Roger Two-one, this is Two-five. I've got a convoy of elephants in sight."

"That's what I thought you said," I transmitted. "Just where is this herd of ponderous pachyderms and do you also see clowns and bearded ladies?"

"Negative, no clowns or bearded ladies. I think I do see Nguyen the Human Cannonball, though. At least one of the elephants looks like he's carrying his cannon on his back. They're trying to cross the river about fifteen klicks north of Minh Thanh."

"OK, Two-five, call it in to the TOC and let's find out if we have any friendly elephants working in the AO. I'm about ten klicks west of Minh Thanh and heading your way. I ought to be there in a couple of minutes, so try not to lose sight of them. Hell, it may be the USO about to pay somebody a visit.''

"No problem, Two-one. It looks like it's pretty slow going for them out in the mud flats. So far, I've counted twenty-seven of them, but they're trying to hurry across and some of them look like they're turning back. There's no good cover for quite a distance, though.''

I approached the area, continuing to monitor Crazy John's conversation with the brigade TOC. They assured him there were no friendly elephants in the area and cleared him to fire. As I came to the river I saw we were going to have a problem. The elephants were indeed in the river and they were being hurried along by small people sitting on their necks, just like in the movies. They seemed slow because of their slow-motion steps, but each step covered a large distance. An assessment of their speed quickly told me that, before we could get artillery or air cranked up, these elephants would be history. I had never heard of elephants being used in the war, and I didn't want to make a mistake and wipe out a wandering band of woodcutters or something of that sort. Looking down on them, however, it was apparent that at least one crew-served weapon was indeed being toted by Dumbo. The others carried bales and boxes, and I could see no other people except the handlers topside. The elephants were obviously fleeing the scene, being urged to greater speed by their riders.

Crazy John was circling about 500 feet below me. He waved his hand as I approached to let me know that he had me in sight. I knew we were going to have to shoot those critters down there and I didn't want to. If they had been people, I'd have been on them in a minute, but *elephants,* for God's sake! Who could shoot Dumbo? I could still remember circus parades as a kid with the elephants following one another, holding onto the tail of the one in front. Elephants rank pretty high on the cuteness scale as far as I'm concerned.

"Crazy John," I said over the radio, "you know what we have to do, don't you?"

"I don't want to do it," he said. "You do it."

"We're both going to do it. Let's set up a gunnery pattern; we'll use guns first, then finish with the rockets. Maybe they'll all be dead by then." I sincerely hoped so, for if they were still alive the white-phosphorous marking rockets would burn them horribly. But we had no other weapons to do the job.

Shoving the control stick to the left I rolled into a dive, reaching up with one hand to arm the guns. I wished that we'd had time to call for helicopters because those guys loved to shoot at anything. The large gray bulk closest to the shore filled my sights and I fired a short burst. They were so large it would have been difficult to miss them. Oddly enough, I didn't give the human figures on their back a second thought except to note that they were there. Several of the elephants convulsed, kicking and stirring the water about them. One lifted his trunk and faced toward me, almost defiantly. I killed him for his pains. Looking at the other aircraft I could see that Crazy John wasn't pulling any punches either. More of the gray bulks went down thrashing, then caught in the river current and were pushed gently in to beach on the western bank of the river.

Methodically, we picked the group apart until there were none left on their feet. More than a hundred meters downstream the river's water was stained by their blood. We finished the massacre by firing all of our rockets into the bodies still writhing. As we flew low over the dead bundles, the stench of burning flesh filled the cockpit of the aircraft. Crazy John joined on my wing and I made a waving motion back toward the base camp. He nodded and began his report to the TOC as we flew together. He didn't look or sound any happier than I.

Back in the hootch after debriefing, Crazy John sat on his bunk, staring out through the grenade screen on the wall. He didn't look at me as I walked by, nor did I speak to him. I knew he wished he had never found those elephants, and I think we both felt ashamed.

We never mentioned the incident again, but the elephants had the last laugh. Their huge bodies quickly decayed in the tropical heat, and the miasma that arose from them tainted the air for miles around the scene of the slaughter. Our names were cursed by helicopter crewmen who had to fly through the area at low level, breathing in the fruits of our work.

The AO continued to heat up, with more incidents in all three battalion areas and even a probe of the brigade base camp. The probe was easily beaten back. The FACs were taking ground fire on almost every sortie, with the resulting battle damage stressing our meager mechanical resources to the limit. Butch and his troops worked into the night to get aircraft ready for the next day's flights. But still, any sort of major repair work had to be done at Bien Hoa, some distance to the south. Even on a rush job it meant taking the airplane out of the schedule for a day or so: The squadron had to send up a maintenance inspector to give his blessing before we could ferry the wounded bird for repair work. The Air Force had strict rules about flying damaged aircraft, but it simply wasn't practical to ground an aircraft because of a few bullet holes. Consequently, we patched the holes if they were too bad and left those that didn't interfere with the aircraft's performance. In the event we had a maintenance inspector paying us a visit, all aircraft with battle damage were reported as having taken it the day of his arrival. He knew it was a crock but usually went along with the lie.

Our most serious paperwork problem had to do with the overtime on the pilots and aircraft. Each aircraft was limited to 100 flying hours before undergoing inspection back at the squadron. The pilots were to fly no more than 65 hours per month. We needed to get at least twice that figure from man and machine to meet the scheduled requirements and anything else that popped up. With the increase in enemy activity within the AO, there was often more than one fight going on at a time, requiring the launch of an unscheduled FAC.

Our solution was relatively simple. We stopped reporting flights. This was not as simple as it first appeared. For one thing, the pilots' credit for the award of Air Medal was predicated on the number of combat flying hours they accumulated. In addition, the aircraft would be getting only half of the inspections that the Air Force deemed necessary for safe operation. Tough cheese. A good pilot and mechanic can tell when an aircraft isn't performing well enough to fly—that was the approach we took in lieu of anything sensible coming down to help the situation. A lesser problem was to get the necessary fuel, rockets, and ammo to replenish supplies expended on the bootleg flights. This was easily solved since all of these items were also used by the army and they weren't close with it. We figured to be in good shape unless somebody squealed on us. As Doug told me one day: "You seem to have developed a low animal cunning since your arrival."

He was right, of course. Few military commanders found themselves in the situation of the air liaison officer and his TACP in South Vietnam. Most other units seemed oversupplied, whereas we were cut off almost completely from our logistical base of support. Our aircraft were built for the loving care of an operational maintenance squadron, but they had to make do with the work of a few grimy mechanics and what they carried in their toolboxes. We were using equipment lists designed for the plains of Germany and allocated expendables such as rockets and fuel based on the last month's expenditures. Pilots were expected to comply with requirements and regulations that made sense back in the States but were totally inappropriate for a combat theater. Flying violations were handed out by the squadron CO and the safety officer to FACs flying lower than 1,500 above the ground, despite the fact that neither of them had ever been in a troops-in-contact situation. If a member of the TACP wore out his jungle fatigues, it was easier to trade for an army pair than attempt to get them replaced by the Air Force. Our people were harassed for having their hair or mustaches too long and for wearing ripped or torn clothing and scuffed jungle boots. Consequently, they stayed away from Bien Hoa and Saigon as much as possible and tried to hide when one of the staff visited the fire base.

By and large, most of the pilots and ground crew showed a cheerful acceptance of and a healthy contempt for the mud, rockets, and harassment. Not all of the personnel though. I parked my jeep one night after attending the last briefing of the day, and as I stepped out into the rain I noticed that all the lights were out and none of the pilots were to be seen. I finally made out Doug, pacing back and forth in the darkened dayroom, great billowing clouds of smoke floating over his shoulder from the pipe clenched grimly between his teeth. There was a heavy scowl on his face and I knew there was some kind of trouble. I headed for the door.

"What's going on?" I asked. "You look like you've just heard that Foster's lager is really owned by a pommie."

"Just as bad, I'm afraid. Butch just called to say that Rex is either drunked up or doped up and is on his way here to shoot Ben. He seems to think that Ben's been riding him too hard or some bloody thing and he's decided to take matters into his own hands."

"Where's Ben?" I asked. This didn't sound good at all. "Has anyone notified the MPs yet?" Rex was a three striper, not noted for his industry, and one I had marked early to get rid of. He had served a previous enlistment in the navy and had been a competent enough mechanic with Butch staying on his case constantly. Ben, I knew, had been riding him, trying to light a fire. Hell, I'd done it myself a few times, trying to get him to straighten out.

"Ben's barricaded himself in the bunker with his M-16 and his flak jacket," Doug said. "I told everyone else to go to their bunks until we had this thing sorted out. I also told Butch and his people to keep away from Rex and not to attempt to stop him."

"Good thinking. How long ago did he leave their hootch?"

"Long enough to be over here by now if he hasn't passed out somewhere. How do you want to handle it, Major?"

"Get on the line to the military police and tell them not to come in here with their lights flashing and sirens blaring. Let's try to keep this thing as low key as possible and try to keep anyone from getting hurt. You meet the MPs and I'll walk on down the road and try to meet Rex. You keep everyone inside and I'll try to talk some sense into him. If I can't, it might not be a bad idea for you to have a weapon. Here, take mine. I don't want to have it on me when I meet him anyway. It might seem too hostile."

Doug took the CAR-15 I handed him and chambered a round, then walked over and pulled the string hanging from the one low-burning bulb dangling from the ceiling. He unfolded the stock and thrust the muzzle through the RPG (rocket propelled grenade) screen that made up the walls of the hootch, settling his haunches down below the level of the sandbags. He should have a good view of the path.

I took a deep breath and walked from the hootch toward the dark rubber trees. I heard Rex before I could pick up his shadow against the dark background of the trees. He wasn't trying to keep hidden, but then he wasn't lurching about like a drunk either.

"Rex," I called. "It's Major Harrison. What's going on?" Oh, great, I thought to myself with a grimace, you're a wonderful shrink—why not just come right out and ask him why he's going to shoot Ben. He pulled up abruptly in front of me, weaving just the slightest bit. I tried to keep my eye on the M-16 he was carrying like a squirrel hunter, cuddled in one arm with the other hand on the handle. It was too dark to tell if his finger was on the trigger. He raised the muzzle a bit but didn't point it at me.

"Where's that goddamn Ben?" he shouted. "That sumbitch has been riding me hard ever since I got here and it's going to stop right now. You just tell 'im to get his sorry ass out here right now and we'll settle this like men, or I'll come in and get him."

"Now, Rex," I said, making little patting motions in the air with my hands. "We've already told the captain to leave the hootch, so he's not even here. Why don't you just put down that rifle and let's talk this over before someone gets hurt. Neither one of us wants that, now do we?"

He looked at me as if I were insane. Didn't I understand what he'd just said? Of course he wanted someone to get hurt. He wanted to kill Ben. He wasn't buying this at all. He tightened his grip on the rifle and his tone of voice became harder.

"Get him out here right now. I've had all the shit I'm going to put up with from anybody, and him and me are going to settle it right now. We'll just see if we've both got the same color blood. Now, you just get out of my way, Major, 'cause I've got no argument with you unless you decide to screw around with this. Get away from me, right now!''

My mind seems to have a habit of trying to avoid unpleasantness by taking off on flights of fancy. In this instance it was mentally circling all the "right nows" of his little speech with a blue pencil like Mrs. Stewart used to do on all my English themes. She would have said: "You've made your point, don't belabor it.'' I was starting to feel giddy and more than a little frightened. I was suddenly up against the situation every officer dreads. You tell someone to do something and he refuses. There aren't that many options open to you. Obviously the threat of a court-martial was useless in this situation, since it hadn't already stopped him from making threats to kill a senior officer. I guess I could challenge him to a duel, but he had a weapon and I didn't. Perhaps I could offer to arm wrestle him, or threaten to take away his Captain Midnight secret decoder ring and make him go to bed without his C-ration supper. Instead, I kicked him in the knee.

I had been walking slowly toward him as we talked, having no real plan in mind, until I was within reach of him. My mind was whirling but I couldn't seem to come up with any solution to the problem I had in front of me. My size twelve jungle boot thought for me and lashed out at him. I quickly grabbed the muzzle of the M-16 and pulled it toward the ground with both hands. Rex was putting up only a feeble resistance, being more interested in hopping around on one leg and holding his injured knee, effectively surrendering the rifle to me. The screen door of the hootch banged and Doug charged out holding my carbine like a cricket bat and looking at Rex as if he were going to use his head to score. He released one of his hands from the weapon and grabbed a large handful of Rex's hair. The MPs must have been lurking close by, for now they made their appearance and rushed into the fray. Soon, Rex was manacled, buckled, and generally trussed up like a hog. I asked them to keep him in the stockade until I could get some air force cops up to take him back to the squadron.

We walked back into the dayroom and popped open beers without a word. Cautious faces began to appear in the doorway and finally the birthday boy himself walked warily into the room, still stylishly clad in his steel pot, flak jacket, and M-16. Ben peered into the darkness as the MP jeep bounced out of sight.

"Call Butch," I said to Ben, "and let him know that everything is all right. Have them all write out statements immediately about what happened, putting in as much detail as possible. I want all of you," indicating the pilots gathered in the room, "to do the same. Before you write everything down, Ben, I want you to call the squadron duty officer, on the radio if you can't get through by land line, and tell him exactly what's going on and that I want transportation up here first thing in the morning to get Rex out of here. We'll be down later to file the charges. Go!"

Ben put down his weapon and began the ordeal of trying to get an open telephone to Bien Hoa. My hands were shaking as I raised the beer can. Moments later, Ben was talking to someone in the squadron. He must have gotten lucky. Turning from the phone he said to me, "They want to know if we can fly Rex down there tomorrow?"

"Do you want him to ride in your rear cockpit?" I asked. His face turned pale at the thought. "Well, I don't either." I grabbed the phone from his hands and found that the squadron adjutant was on the other end.

"Major, the only way we're taking that man in one of my airplanes is if we tie him up and throw him in the cargo hold, and I doubt the inspector general would care too much for that. If somebody down there wants him in their backseat after he threatened to kill an officer, then let them fly on up here and get him. I'd suggest an alternate means of transportation."

The squadron adjutant thought on this for a few moments, then allowed that he would dispatch a pair of air policemen on the early morning courier flight to remove Rex from Lai Khe.

Another bad week. Both Bob and Chris had been shot down within hours of each other, and though neither was seriously injured, Bob was sporting a huge swath of tape covering his broken nose. He used his story to cadge drinks from all who would listen.

Bob had been directing an air strike against a bunker complex and things seemed to be pretty straightforward. The absence of ground fire and movement in the complex lulled both him and the fighters into believing they had a cold target. As he rolled inverted to make another marking pass, a heavy gun, probably a .57mm, opened up from below—figuring most likely that they weren't getting anywhere by being silent since the running dogs were already bombing their complex. Bob hurriedly completed his "split-S" maneuver and leveled off just above the treetops, one of the best places to hide from a heavy gun according to the conventional FAC wisdom. Not so wise in this instance, for he flew into an interlocking pattern of 14.5 and 12.7 guns that knocked out one engine and severed most of his control cables. The resulting yaw from the loss of the cables made the aircraft virtually uncontrollable, particularly on one engine. He wobbled it around until he was pointing away from the target area, feeling that those on the ground might be understandably pissed at him should he fall into their hands; then he punched out.

The fighter lead put out the Mayday call, then set up a protective CAP over him, waiting for somebody to respond. They had enough ordnance and fuel to discourage Charley from taking the initiative in the rescue. The response to a call for help in South Vietnam was overwhelming; normally within minutes there was more traffic over a downed airman than could be accommodated. They tended to get in each other's way until someone took control, often a FAC. Pilots would listen to the FAC simply because they were accustomed to listening to him and having him direct traffic. It was much like the response to a cop on a beat. That sort of authority comes with practice.

An army helicopter gun team arrived at the scene within minutes and were ready to help in Bob's defense, along with the fighters who were still on station. Unfortunately, the biggest threat to his life wasn't from the enemy, but from his own aircraft. The damned thing refused to die gracefully, acting instead as if it were putting on a low-level aerobatic performance for the enjoyment of the spectators—in this case, Bob and members of the 307th NVA Regiment. The helicopters had to do some fancy footwork to avoid the erratic maneuvers of the pilotless Bronco as it pulled into a series of chandelles and lazy-eights over the battlefield. After one spectacular pull-up it finally rolled inverted into the trees, missing Bob by about fifty meters.

The helicopters completed the rescue, a replacement FAC arrived, and the fighters went back to bombing the bunker complex—the war continued with scarcely a break.

Back in our care after his nose and other contusions had been dressed,

Bob was displaying the classic survivor behavior. There was wild exhilaration and the inability to sit quietly; he would plant himself and open a beer, then pop up and pace around the hootch, then back into the chair for a few squirming moments. His eyes were bright as a puppy's and the words tumbled from his mouth often without meaning or context. We let him babble and after two more beers he virtually collapsed. We helped him to his bunk and stripped off his clothing. He slept for almost twelve hours.

Chris's shoot-down had far more serious ramifications. Not that he was hurt, for he didn't receive a scratch. He decided to get shot down in Cambodia, though. The Australian Rules of Engagement prohibited their pilots from flying within five kilometers of either the Laotian or Cambodian borders, and their command was serious about it. They wanted no international incidents with a supposedly-neutral country; this situation was one of the more paradoxical things in the war, since we knew with certainty that the North Vietnamese had completely taken over the border area to a depth of at least twenty kilometers. We would see their trucks or troops blatantly marching southward, as effectively removed from our attacks as if they were moving through Picadilly Circus. It was difficult to stop the hot-blooded young pilots from taking an occasional crack at them if they became too brazen. Hell, I'd shot a rocket or two across the border myself when the roads became too crowded with NVA vehicles. It was difficult to feel repentant when the countryside across the border was often covered with B-52 bomb craters. It was obvious that our government wasn't against all attacks over there, just ours.

Chris was a superb pilot but, like many of the Aussies, his blood easily reached the boiling point. He had spent the best part of a three-hour flight doing a visual recce, with no results. He told me that he had carefully watched his map to avoid the five-mile buffer between our AO and the Cambodian border.

Made careless by their apparent sanctuary, an NVA antiaircraft gun crew made the mistake of taking a few potshots at Chris as he flew past, minding his own business. It was a senseless sort of firing, for he was well out of the range of the gun and had made no apparent attempt to take it on. Chris was infuriated when he saw the puffs of flak exploding and he was fortunate enough to see the small flashes of the gun muzzle as the rounds left it.

Chris immediately turned his aircraft and attacked the gun and its crew with his own weapons. He got the gun, but another one, more canny than the first, that had remained silent during the shootout, ambushed him as he pulled out of the attack, right over its position. With a wing gone, and with it any hopes of returning to friendlier climes, Chris ejected. His beeper was immediately picked up by another FAC as well as several other radio stations in the area who passed the approximate location on to our FAC as being the closest to the action.

The FAC who was given the responsibility of coordinating the rescue was, in fact, Chris's relief. As he arrived at the scene he faced an immediate dilemma, for the beeper returns clearly indicated that Chris was well over the border, and the smoke from his recent attack against the gun site was visible in the wrong place. The smoke from the burning aircraft confirmed what the FAC already knew.

Chris suddenly came up on the survival radio, transmitting on Guard frequency, and the Abbott and Costello routine began.

"Well," he said, "here I am alive on the ground and a good five kilometers inside South Vietnam. Does the Bronco orbiting have me in sight?"

"Yeah, Chris," the FAC said, taking his cue from the man on the ground. "This is Sidewinder Two-eight. I've got you in sight, at least five klicks inside Vietnam. Are you OK?"

"Roger, I'm fine, Two-eight. Just get me out of here as quickly as you possibly can. You do understand, I hope, the urgency of the situation."

"Yes, I think I know what you're talking about," said the FAC. "I've got rescue choppers inbound to get you there, well inside Vietnam." It sounded as if they were trying to prepare a defense for a court-martial.

The FAC directed the choppers in the area "well inside Vietnam" and pointed out the downed pilot to them. They could read a map as well as the FAC, but they played along with the game without even knowing the reason for it, even going so far as to inquire of the FAC the correct set of coordinates of the rescue for their report. A set of fighters had been dispatched to fly cover for the FAC who was down close to the border but "well inside Vietnam." Random offers of help came from other aircraft drawn to the scene of the rescue like moths to a flame, offers to help out the Aussie who was down "well inside Vietnam." In a short time the entire affair had become an airborne joke.

Unfortunately, these jokes and offers to help were also monitored by the DASC radios in Saigon, and they in turn passed the news to the Australian Forces. They were not amused but didn't really know what was going on, only that a number of pilots were making buffoons of themselves, not unusual in itself, and that an Australian happened to be involved.

The rescue went without a hitch and Chris was soon on his way back to us. I was called to the control room to take a message that a representative of the Australian Forces and one from Seventh Air Force would soon be arriving, and that my and Chris's presence would be required.

I found Chris on the back porch of the hootch, buck naked, washing himself down.

"Are you OK?" I asked him.

"Well," he said, as he continued scrubbing, "to tell you the truth, Major, when I realized where I was going to land, I shit meself. All I could think was that I'd never get back into fighters after this bloody balls-up. I'll probably spend the rest of me bloody life in a bloody C-130."

"Well, there is that possibility after pulling such a head-up-your-ass stunt like that." I was getting the red-ass myself after I saw that he was uninjured. "But cheer up! They may only court-martial you, and me as well, and we can spend the rest of our lives telling everyone about your across-the-border adventure, while we're serving our time in the stockade."

He looked very forlorn. I smiled and clapped him on his shoulder: "Keep smiling, maybe miracles will happen. Remember Dunkirk!"

Doug and I sat in our little air force command post, brooding at the wall map of our area of operations. The radio operator turned and removed his headset and told us that the brass was due to arrive in twenty minutes. The three of us looked at each other, then went back to our brooding. Suddenly, Doug sat erect, then sprang to his feet with a broad grin on his face.

"I've got it! By God, I think I've got it!" he exclaimed.

"Got what, you silly bastard?" I asked.

"Just you try to stay away from them as much as you can," he said. "Be sure to put me in charge of taking them around and interviewing Chris and all that sort of thing. That shouldn't be too much of a problem since I'm the senior Australian here. If you can keep that Yank bloke out of my hair, I might just have a solution for all of this. Just don't get too involved, Major, and don't ask too many questions. There are times one is better off not having direct knowledge. I'm only asking you to trust me.''

His innocent blue eyes stared at me with the intensity of the sinless. Sometimes, I thought, you just have to trust in whatever the fates have in store. I nodded and walked from the command post and unlocked my jeep. Absentmindedly, I noted that someone had been trying to cut the heavy chain I used to lock the steering wheel to the post.

The C-123 was right on ETA and I watched an RAAF squadron leader and a USAF lieutenant colonel deplane. Both looked uncomfortable in their new jungle fatigues. Revolvers sagged around their waists, making them both look ludicrous. It was interesting to note that a particular uniform for a particular job simply looks right on the person doing that job and wrong on someone trying to imitate him. Grunts looked natural and even cocky in their mud-splattered jungle fatigues. FACs looked right in flight suits or cammo fatigues. The two staff men now wading toward me would have looked correct in the khaki working uniform they wore in their offices in Saigon. They looked wrong here and they knew it.

"Good morning, gentlemen," I said and saluted. "Welcome to Lai Khe. Let's drive back to the hootch and maybe we can rustle up some coffee. Did you have a good flight?"

"Quite nice, thank you," murmured the squadron leader. Thinking of Doug's request, I kept the conversation away from the incident they were here to investigate as we drove back toward the hootch. It wasn't that difficult, for they appeared fascinated by the ordinary workings of the base camp. Then the rain started again, which dampened us and further conversation. I watched them big-eye the country and knew that neither had been far from the flagpole. That may or may not work to our advantage, I thought, for a shrewd man can tell when he's being conned. I began to sweat when I thought of the things Doug could be trying to pull. Suddenly, I wanted to blurt out everything I knew about what had happened, for that's what I had been trained to do. I kept silent.

"Mai, you number ten, lazy girl! You bring coffee now. Chop! Chop!" I yelled as we walked into the hootch. Mai was assigned to clean our hootch and wash our clothes. She lived in a village outside the wire with her parents and may have been anywhere from sixteen to forty years old. Our eyes were level only when I was sitting and she was standing. She'd only worked for the Americans a few months and, like most Vietnamese women, she was soon running our hootch like it was her own. She was cute as a kitten, with a devilish sense of humor, and we would have cut the heart out of anyone who tried to make a move on her. We made a point of picking her up and depositing her at the gate each day.

"Majah, you make noise like hurt water boo," she said. She was not impressed by our yelling and bluster. "You sit nice now and I make you nice cup number one coffee." She had picked up English very quickly. We settled in the dayroom and the officers looked at me expectantly. I waited until Mai served us each a cup of C-ration coffee.

"I suppose you want to know about the crash as soon as you can. Just let me call my senior Australian FAC and we'll let you get right to it. Unfortunately, I have a meeting with the brigade commander, but I'm sure Doug will be able to help you out." As if on cue, Doug's jeep pulled in front of the hootch.

We finished our coffee while Doug filled them in on the details of the flight. There weren't very many and those he did give out were vague and general in nature. When asked about the location of the crash, he brushed aside the question and said he would show them straightaway since he'd just lined up a helicopter for that purpose. In a panic I watched him hand each of them a map and ask if they were ready for the flight. My God! I thought. Surely he can't be planning on flying them into Cambodia to view the wreckage. I was afraid things were getting out of hand and had about decided to step in and square things away, letting the chips fall where they may. At that point Doug gave me a cheerful grin and a hidden wink and began hustling them from the hootch into his jeep. I remained behind, moodily drinking coffee through the rainy afternoon. Mai, ever sensitive to my moods, slipped quietly from the hootch, leaving me alone.

A little after 1700 Doug pulled up alone in his jeep and came whistling into the room. I watched as he popped the top off one of the Foster lagers the Aussies were so fond of. I couldn't stand it.

"What in the hell happened?" I asked.

"Oh, I took them to see the crash site," he said casually.

"Doug, please don't tell me you took those men into Cambodia or I'll kill you with my bare hands. I'll have you tied between two jeeps and torn apart and personally shove your mutilated body into the shit barrel and set it afire. I will have . . ." He held up both hands to interrupt my tirade.

"They said they wanted to see the crash site but they never actually specified which one, you know. We've actually two of them. So, I took them to see the one I thought they wanted. You know, the one by the river.''

The one by the river, I thought? But, that's not where Chris was hit. That's where Bob crashed.

"But, you gave them a map of the area," I stuttered. "Couldn't they see they were in the wrong place?"

"Neh," he said, complacently filling the bowl of his pipe. "It was obvious they'd never been to the field and you know what that country's like out there. Even we have trouble map reading at times. And besides, they saw a Bronco, still smoldering, and they were reasonably sure it was in Vietnam so they were satisfied. They just never got the coordinates of Chris's wreck hooked up to the place on the map. They seemed happy enough when I dropped them off at the strip to catch the courier bird back to Saigon. I don't think they really wanted to stay out here any longer anyway.''

We looked at each other in silence for a few moments, then he said it for both of us: "The bloody Green Square strikes again!"

I raised my coffee cup to him in salute. "Thanks mate.''

I knew that I was going to have to get rid of George, but unfortunately I couldn't think of a way to do it without ruining his air force career. One of the other FACs had suggested quietly that I might want to fly in George's rear cockpit on the next troops-in-contact. He was reluctant to say more, even when I reminded him that we were not the Boy Scouts of America and that the ground troops were laying their lives on the line every time we brought in an aerial bombardment close to their positions. They trusted us not to kill them and I felt that they deserved the best we could give them.

I had flown with George, as I had with every pilot in the TACP, and thought he was neither the best nor the worst. His control of the aircraft was far from perfect, but all in all he seemed an average pilot. On the day I had ridden with him he put in two strikes against an old bunker complex that turned out to be unoccupied and seemed to handle the fighters pretty well. Of course, we hadn't received any ground fire and there were no friendly troops in close proximity.

Another opportunity to fly with him came a few days later when a six-man LRRP team was compromised and running for their lives. The FAC overhead was trying to orchestrate the gunships and the rescue helicopters, and all were receiving heavy fire from well-entrenched enemy positions. The FAC had reached bingo fuel and was running out of rockets as well.

I grabbed George and we made our best time for the flight line. That wasn't too fast, for the mud on the roads almost covered the wheels of the jeep. Motioning him toward the front cockpit, I clambered into the rear, the crew chief helping both of us to quickly buckle into the ejection seats and parachutes. We had the turboprop engines spooling up even before we got to the end of the runway. Alerting the controller that we were on a hot scramble, we hit the runway running as other aircraft and helicopters were directed out of our flight path.

"Do you want to handle the radios or fly?" George asked.

"Why don't you do it all," I suggested. "I'm just along for the ride, so forget I'm even back here." Normally, I would have been delighted to handle the radios or whatever might be needed to make things run smoother. God knows, it was easy enough for one man to get overloaded in a hurry in a TIC. This time, however, I needed to know if George was up to the task we all normally had to handle alone.

His flight path took us unerringly toward the last reported position of the team. Certainly no problem in his navigation. We monitored the continuing fight as we neared the target area, checking in with the station FAC who was preparing to leave the area with near fuel exhaustion. He said that we'd probably be needing tac air, but he hadn't called for any since he didn't know if he'd be able to stay on station until it arrived. George rogered the information but made no effort to alert the control room that we might need help very shortly. This was SOP at the first sign of trouble. If you couldn't use the fighters, you could always hand them off to someone else or put them in against one of the preplanned targets we all carried in our hip pocket for such situations. It might be wasteful, but so then were 50 percent of the targets we struck.

George looked up the team's frequency for the day in his SOI and called, "Pattycake, this is Sidewinder Two-seven. What's your position and situation?"

"Sidewinder, this is Pattycake," a gasping voice answered. It sounded as if he were running hard. "We're moving sierra-echo from the november bend in the blue line, about fifty meters whiskey of it. They're right behind us and gaining. We're going to have to laager up as soon as we can find a good place."

"OK, Pattycake. Understand you're going to hole up. Can you pop a smoke for me?"

Pop a smoke? Was he crazy? A team was running for its life with the little people so close behind them that they were going to have to form a final defensive circle and hope for the best. And he wanted them to pop a smoke for identification? He was nuts!

Pattycake obviously thought so as well. His answer came back quickly: "Negative, no smoke! We'll put out panels around our position when we can get to an LZ."

The team members all carried varied-hued panels to be used for identification from the air, but they were often very difficult to see. Visibility depended on the viewing angle and the amount of foliage in the way. Often, from the ground, the grunts felt that they were in a position to be observed, whereas from the air it would be impossible to make out the small panels. This could lead to critical comments being thrown back and forth. Smoke grenades were a much more positive ID, but you couldn't always choose your situation. Like now.

George still hadn't called for the alert fighters and I reminded him of it, breaking my pledge to keep quiet in the back seat. We screwed around for another few minutes getting this call in, wasting time that could have been better used trying to locate the team. We flew over their approximate position, quartering the area as George made repeated requests for them to key their mike button so we could home in on them, using their radio signal for a guide. They made no response. Finally, I could stay quiet no longer.

"George," I said, "there's probably a pretty good reason for them not answering. They might have little people walking all over them, so let's don't compromise them any more than we have to by circling directly over their position. Maybe if we moved on downstream a hundred meters or so, old Charley just might think they're down that way. Even if you did see their markers now, they'd be too close to the Vietnamese for us to engage them. Why don't you call off those two choppers and tell them what we're going to try? It looked obvious to me that none of us are going to be able to help the team till they've got a little breathing room, and if they are discovered we'll be right here to do whatever we can for them."

George was silent but turned us down river, away from the team. We continued to monitor the team's radio frequency. It was all we could do. I was confident that they were laying low, for if they'd been discovered we'd have heard about it on the radio.

The fighters arrived on station and were parked in a holding orbit south of the target area, far enough away not to make anyone nervous but close enough to attack within moments. So far I hadn't been overly impressed with George. His judgment looked shaky and that was why we had FACs after all, to make the judgment calls, otherwise the fighters could simply bomb a set of coordinates. Yet, he hadn't really done anything to disqualify him for the job.

A whispered voice came over the radio: "Sidewinder, we heard them go by us down the river and since then we've heard no movement. We're going to put out the panels now. What's the plan?"

"I need to get a fix on you. Key your mike for thirty seconds," George transmitted.

"Negative!" I cut in on the radio. Jesus! Didn't it occur to him that the NVA just might have a homer as well? We knew that they listened to all of our radio transmissions unless we were using secure voice. "Just put your panels out and we'll widen our orbit to include your location. We ought to be able to pick them up without any keying of the damned mike."

"Sounds good," Pattycake replied. "Who's running the show? You or Sidewinder Two-seven?"

"Sidewinder Two-seven. Out!" I replied grumpily, and sat back in my ejection seat, promising myself that I wouldn't say another word for the remainder of the flight.

On the second orbit around their area I picked up the panels through the treetops but didn't say anything to George. The next time around I pointed them out to him, deciding it was silly to jeopardize lives just to make an evaluation of a pilot's visual acuity. I listened as he passed the target information to the waiting attack aircraft and helicopters.

The attack and subsequent pickup of the team qualified as a near-disaster from my perspective. George did everything wrong, from having the fighters attack in the wrong direction to selecting bombs instead of guns for the close work. His efforts to coordinate the pickup by the helicopters while still adjusting the fighters' attacks were a joke. Where was the pilot, I wondered, with whom I had flown before and who seemed so confident and relaxed while handling an air strike against the bunker complex. Was he nervous because I was observing from the rear cockpit? If so, tough shit. If he let something that trivial screw up his judgment and perspective, he was in the wrong job. Things could and probably would get a lot worse than this before his tour was up. I was seeing what the other FAC had hinted at—a perfectly adequate pilot who under normal circumstances accomplished his job, but did not function well under pressure. What if there had been several companies of friendlies strung out in every direction, rather than a small group of six? It was conceivable that he could have ended up bombing his own troops, or even worse, putting the bombs where they were useless in their defense. Either way, some people could have been needlessly killed.

All of us make mistakes learning our trade, and as long as we can play through them, little harm is done. George had been at it too long to be making mistakes of this magnitude. With the new guys, you watched like a hawk to make sure they weren't put in a position beyond their capabilities, but you couldn't supervise them for their entire tour. No, George had to go. I would have respected him more if he had requested to be relieved from this assignment.

On the ground once again we headed for debriefing, and afterward I asked him to walk back to the hootch with me. On the way we wandered down toward the concertina wire that surrounded the base camp and we sat atop a crumbling, sandbagged bunker. All the foliage outside the wire had been cut back to a depth of some hundred meters or so. Beyond that the primary rain forest formed a dark backdrop.

"You know you made several bad calls today, don't you?" I began. "A couple of them could have gotten someone hurt real badly. We were lucky to get out of it without doing that. How do you like this job, anyway?"

He stared into the dark forest for a few long moments before answering. "The truth of the matter is that I like the idea of the job better than the job itself. I guess I like the FAC image and I've been willing to put up with the inconveniences to keep it. But, do I really like the job? No, I don't suppose I do. You know, Major, I've always scored high in everything I've tried to do since I left the Academy. Even there, I was in the top 20 percent of my class. I started on the football team and was an honors student my last two years. I ranked number five in my class at pilot training, and even in gunnery school with guys of your age and experience I finished pretty high up. But, this job is something else. I'm so afraid I'll make a mistake that I choke up and do stupid things that I normally would never dream of doing. The harder I try, the worse I actually seem to do. The problem is that if I do something wrong here, I'm going to end up hurting somebody else. If it were just me it'd be OK, but everything we do here seems to affect somebody else. And it seems like the entire world is watching you do it. Every goof is right out there to be seen by either the brigade commander, or the helicopters, or the fighters, or most important, the people on the ground.''

He watched me as if fascinated by the way I filled my pipe and lit it. I remained quiet, content to hear his thinking.

"Anyway," he continued, "it seems like we ought to sell tickets every time we take off. I spend more time looking around to see who's watching me than I do handling my job. No, I don't think I like this job very much, but I do like the Air Force and have always planned on making it a career. I'm also smart enough to know that if I request a transfer I'll be refused because we're always short of FACs, and if I tell them the truth I'll never get another flying assignment. And damn it! I do like to fly. I just don't like the kind of flying that we do here.''

I drummed my fingers on the rotten sandbags as I thought. He was partially right, of course. Most of our mistakes were hung out like dirty linen for all the neighbors to see. But, he was getting credit for the great work done by other forward air controllers and damned if I would let him continue to receive that credit while we hid his problems by giving him the easy, pressureless targets. Too bad that he liked to fly and considered himself a great pilot and a good officer. We weren't here to fly for the fun of it. We were here to put in air strikes, and if he couldn't do that properly he was of no use to us.

"Pack your gear," I told him. "Tomorrow I'm flying you to Bien Hoa. I'll talk to the squadron commander about the situation, but I make no promises. I'll do what I can to let you come out of this clean, but I can't and won't keep you here any longer. I think you realize that.''

He nodded slowly, keeping his eyes on my face. Jesus, I thought, I'm not handing the guy a white feather; I'm not even saying that he's not a good pilot. All I'm saying is that he's not right for this job, and the Air Force will probably kick him out.

That was not to be, though. Standing in front of the squadron commander the next day and braced at attention, I found myself being reamed not only for trying to destroy a young officer's career but for attempting to further deplete an already lean group of FACs. Consequently, George was transferred to the Direct Air Support Center in Saigon, where he would sleep in air-conditioned quarters, eat steak every night, see USO shows, and be as safe as if he were stateside. When his DEROS was up he would go home wearing his medals and campaign ribbons and with a full fund of war stories about the time he spent as a forward air controller. I guess I showed him.

They were suckers; they never learned.

"OK, Sidewinder," I heard the helicopter gunship pilot tell Doug over the radio, "let me make sure I've got the bet right. We're talking about that bomb crater with the blue-green water in it as the target, right?"

"That's the one, mate," Doug answered. "We each get three rockets and the one rocket that is nearest the crater wins two cases of beer. We'll alternate shots and you may even go first," he said graciously.

Flying several thousand feet over them as I returned from patrol, I watched them as they circled over a well-defoliated area. The teenaged gunship pilots were the answer to a thirsty FAC's dreams. Their large macho egos were incapable of turning down a challenge to their shooting prowess even though they must have figured out by now that the deck was stacked against them. An obvious shortcoming in the army aviation training program.

The Cobra began his first run at the bomb crater target; meanwhile, Doug was straining for all the altitude he could muster, well outside the scan of the helicopter pilot. The chopper shot and quickly a small explosion bloomed into view, perhaps twenty meters long on the target. Doug immediately rolled his aircraft into a vertical dive from about 4,000 feet. The rocket streaked away from the belly of his plane and disappeared into the crater. A direct hit.

The helicopter pilot was silent as he commenced his second run, and again a good shot, but still over by ten meters or so. Doug had zoomed back to altitude and was already into his second vertical dive. This time his rocket impacted on the lip of the crater.

"I got a bit careless on that one," Doug said casually over the radio. "I do hope none of the other FACs saw it, for it would be frightfully embarrassing." Nothing like rubbing their noses in it.

Doug's accuracy must have rattled the helicopter pilot, for his last rocket was off by a good twenty-five meters even though he was almost on top of the target before he fired. Doug put his last shot right into the crater again.

"That's the damnedest shooting I've ever seen!" the chopper pilot said. "I'll bring your beer over tonight and I'll also help you drink it, you Australian bastard."

"We'd be pleased to entertain you," Doug replied with the grace of a lord.

We rode to the hootch together after landing, laughing over suckering the army again. In fact, Doug was a very good rocket shot, but he could scarcely have missed the crater when firing from a vertical dive. From that attitude, the sight picture could easily be off a few degrees without it affecting the impact of the rocket by more than a few feet. The helicopters always shot from a low angle, and if they were off that same few degrees it produced an error of many meters. They would indeed have to make a perfect shot to equal even a fair shot by a fixed-wing aircraft firing from the vertical. And the helicopters didn't have that dive capability. It kept us in beer.

I'd been daydreaming about my R and R for weeks, thinking of meeting Mary Ann in Hawaii, the location chosen by nearly all the married men. The single troops preferred the fleshpots of Bangkok, Penang, Taipei, and Sydney. However, most of the commercial airlines had special rates for dependents meeting their spouses in Hawaii.

Everyone was in their best khaki, not always neatly pressed, but looking as presentable as we could be made to look. Money was exchanged and those with illegal-length mustaches were not allowed to process for the flight until the mustaches were trimmed to regulation size. An army captain was close to tears when told that his gigantic handlebar mustache would have to go before he was allowed on the aircraft. Most of the men, though, were in excellent spirits as they boarded the flight to Oahu.

The flight over the Pacific was long but the anticipation of seeing loved ones again made it palatable. The stewardesses looked wonderful, but large, after months of seeing only tiny Vietnamese women. The airline food that I had once despised now tasted like nectar. We ran their tiny galley out of fresh milk by the time we were two hours out of Saigon. Card games sprang up to help pass the hours.

As we taxied in after landing at the civilian airport in Honolulu, I looked through the window at the American females lined up outside the gate waiting for their uniformed men. They looked odd, and after a few moments of reflection I realized that it was because they were all so pale. It was, after all, midwinter in the States. I glanced down at my own arms hanging from the short-sleeved uniform shirt and realized for the first time that I undoubtedly had the finest tan I'd ever had in my life, at least on the face and upper torso. Almost everyone on the aircraft was the same. At Lai Khe most of us went shirtless when we weren't flying, not to soak up the sun but to try to stay a bit cooler in the high temperatures and humidity. I seldom purposely went into the sun, being blond and fair and having a tendency to burn to a crisp. I now looked like a beachboy with hair bleached almost white by the sun.

Any inhibitions that anyone may have built up due to the long separations vanished as soon as we deplaned. There was a mad stampede as husbands and wives charged at each other across the tarmac. Mary Ann looked wonderful—pale, but slimmer than I remembered. Or had I imagined her as more voluptuous after the months of separation? It didn't matter, she was perfect. As we checked into our expensive hotel, I thought of the old joke making the rounds in Vietnam: "What's the *second* thing you plan to do in Hawaii?" The answers varied but were some form of "Put down my bags!"

Much later, as we were lying in bed and still marveling at being with each other again, Mary Ann ran her hand over my chest, admiring my new surfer look. I did look rather dashing, I thought, with my near-white hair and golden tan. Almost like Troy Donahue.

Taking my glass of wine, I headed for the bathroom and the first hot shower I'd had in some months. Turning the water up as hot as I could stand it, I edged gradually under the cascading shower until my body acclimated to the temperature and I was able to totally immerse myself. It was bliss to stand there, my head covered with clean-smelling shampoo and my body covered with a rich lather of soap.

Mary Ann's shriek almost made me slip from the tub. Clutching the shower curtain to keep from·falling, I stared at her as she stood there wrapped in a towel, staring at the bottom of the tub.

"Are you all right?" she asked, her eyes wide.

"Sure," I stammered, "what's wrong?"

Mutely, she pointed to the bottom of the tub. Looking down I saw that the water had turned into a rusty-red viscous liquid resembling hydraulic fluid. At first glance it appeared to be a bloody froth swirling in the bottom of the tub. Glancing down at my body, half expecting to see an open wound, I discovered instead that my golden tan was disappearing forever into the sewers of Waikiki. Washed clean of the red dirt that had become embedded in my pores, my magnificent surfer's body became instead the pale, freckled, odd-looking assortment of bones and sinew that it had always been. Even more disgusting, now with the pale skin as a backdrop, was the unattractive row of seed warts festooning my shoulders like tiny white raisins, nurtured by the constant dampness and irritation of my parachute harness. What tan I had stopped abruptly at my collarbone and at the juncture of my elbows where I kept my sleeves rolled. All in all, a sorry-looking sight.

The week of freedom sped by far too rapidly. We ate good food, saw the other islands, and touched each other constantly as if to make sure the other was really there. We speculated on our next duty station—where it would be, what sort of job it would be, how expensive the housing would be. For the time being it didn't really matter, for though neither of us spoke of it, primarily I wanted to be alive at the end of my tour to be able to go to a new station. Back in Vietnam things had been bad for the previous month or so. We had all been taking hits, and everyone feared that sooner or later the big one would take him. I couldn't mention that to her though. I could hardly stand to think about it myself.

Too soon, the time was up and we were standing on the ramp watching Pan American disgorge yet another horde of GIs to take our places on the sands of Waikiki. Humanely brief, the out-processing took only moments and very quickly we were westbound once more to the war.

Most of the people on the civilian airliner taking us back to Vietnam didn't even bother to look as we started our descent into Saigon's Tan Son Nhut airport. They'd seen enough of it before. Pilots always look out though. They are physiologically programmed to look outside the aircraft if they have the chance.

The view hadn't changed much since I'd been gone. Somehow the troops seemed able to carry on the war without me. Even at thirty-odd thousand feet I could see thin wisps of smoke drifting up from an air or artillery strike down in the Mekong Delta. Before we entered a cloud layer I fancied I could see all the way south to the Cau Mau peninsula. More likely, it was one of the many bays or deltas that delineate the coastline.

I asked my seatmate, an army major, if he thought that was indeed the tip of the country we were seeing.

"Who gives a shit?" he replied—an indication of the caliber of our conversation for the past few hours. He was right, though. Who, indeed, did give a shit? I stared at the unfamiliar toes of my low-quartered shoes. I had managed to get most of the mildew off of them before my trip to Hawaii. They still looked as if they'd been polished with a Snickers bar. I stared at my morose seatmate.

"I don't give a shit either," I said. He stared at me as if I were crazy. You just can't please some people.

Our in-processing at Tan Son Nhut airport took only a few minutes, the military being remarkably more able at getting you into something than out of it. After changing my American greenbacks for MPC—the military pay certificates used in-country—I escaped the clutter to wander toward the transient aircraft parking area. I was sure that someone from the TACP would be there to pick me up. Not that they were especially anxious to have me back, but it gave the pilot a little slack time in Saigon, away from the base camp.

Immediately, I spotted one of our Broncos parked among the rows of sleek jets, looking like a poor orphan. I looked at it with new eyes after having been reabsorbed into civilization, albeit for only a week. It sat there like a wounded animal, various hues of leaking internal fluids staining its body like blood. These stains contrasted colorfully with its coating of mud, covering it as high up as the vertical stabilizers, obscuring even part of the canopy. Black powder burns covered the sponsons protruding from its belly, where the four machine guns were housed. Irregularly shaped patches covered battle damage, the repair of which had never seen a sheet-metal shop. Some of the rockets were missing from the pods slung beneath the belly of the aircraft, indicating that the pilot had put in an air strike on the way. Our Bronco looked like a tramp trying to crash a society garden party. It looked almost as bad as its pilot, who was now approaching from the transient building.

"Hi, Major," Ed said with a grin. "How were things in paradise?"

"Hi, Ed," I responded. "I couldn't wait to get back. You know how quickly you can get tired of all that crap. Good food, good drink, clean sheets, a beautiful woman. Naw, that stuff's not for a real fighting man like me." We shook hands. "By the way, you look terrible. Have you always looked that bad or did you just dress up for my benefit?"

His grin broadened. "Oh, how fast they forget. I know what you mean though. When Rocky picked me up from my Sydney R and R, I thought he'd made up to play a part or something. I could smell his flying suit before I ever saw him. Don't worry about it though, your nose will soon surrender. Let's get your stuff and get out of here before they start charging us a tie-down fee."

He threw my bag into the cargo bay while I strapped my parachute harness over my rumpled khakis. The transient line crew had us started and on our way in minimum time, glad I think to get the tattered ruffian off their pristine flight line. The amount of traffic using the Saigon airport was staggering. We joined the queue awaiting takeoff clearance and Ed passed the time by getting me up to date on what had happened in our AO during the past week.

There were strong indications, according to Ed's report, that the NVA was moving into the AO in strength. During my absence there had been a limited ground attack against our base camp, which destroyed several helicopters and damaged others. One of the NVA rockets had virtually destroyed an old French building used by the brigade, which was located a few meters from our hootch. None of our people or aircraft had been hurt.

Saving the worst until last, he told me that one of our friends, an army warrant officer who flew the fixed-wing Birddog, was to be court-martialed. He had been trying to get from one small strip back to Lai Khe when he was caught in a severe thunderstorm, with only a small piece of the squall line barring his path to a safe return to base. Rather than returning to the original takeoff point, he had attempted to go beneath the storm, navigating by the road that connected the two bases. In his attempt to keep the road in sight, he had to go so low that his prop decapitated a Vietnamese civilian riding a bike.

An incident like that would have merited a strong ass-chewing by his commander and an admonishment not to do it again, perhaps even some type of low-grade punishment for violating safe flying regulations. Our friend, though, made the mistake of not reporting the incident. A Vietnamese soldier in a fortified position along the road happened to be staring in the right direction when the aircraft swooped by, knocking the bike rider almost into his lap. He reported the incident to Lai Khe by radio. When found, the young warrant officer was attempting to clean the remaining evidence from his aircraft. We never heard what happened to him after he was transferred to headquarters for his trial.

Within a day it was as if I had never been away—the heat, bugs, humidity, and mud felt normal again. Doug, nearing the end of his tour, was leaving a little early to finish up his year with a month or so at Australian Forces headquarters in Vung Tau. Chris would be going with him and Huck had already departed for his new assignment in

Australia. Huck had been a real source of pleasure for all of us, and I had even reached the point that I could make out enough of his speech to dispense with the translator. We floated him on his way with a veritable tide of Foster's lager. There were rumors that the Aussies would not be replaced in our brigade but only where the AO didn't abut Cambodia or Laos, probably the legacy of Chris's bailout location.

I would miss Doug terribly. He had been a good right hand, and his unfailing good humor and intelligence had done a great deal to keep our little band reasonably happy despite some trying times. In addition, he had the greatest command of profanity it had ever been my privilege to witness. He could even make Butch, our senior NCO, stand in awe when he unleashed his scabrous tongue. I suspected that the men would often screw something up just to hear Doug blast into another bravura performance. When he commenced, no one was left unoffended, rank went unnoticed, and vegetation wilted in the immediate area. Only his aura of supreme self-confidence kept him from real trouble with the senior officers. When not blaspheming, he was the most charming person I'd ever known. The Aussies were all good people and we hated to see them go.

I had turned over the AO to the replacement FAC and was killing time on my way back to the base when I received word from the control room that the base was under rocket attack. They needed to know if I had enough fuel to put in fighters against the suspected sites. I agreed and pushed the throttles forward to get into position. By the time I had the base camp in sight the attack was over, however, so I passed off the fighters to the other FAC and landed.

No more than thirteen or fourteen rockets had impacted, but even one of the large 122mm Russian-made rockets could do a great deal of damage. There was no damage near the flight line, so they must have been aiming at the other side of the camp—they were normally very accurate. Two of the new pilots were standing in front of the hootch as I drove up. They had worried looks on their faces. I glanced around quickly but could see no new rocket damage, so it had to be something else.

"You'd better come around back and see this, Major," one of them said. "The hootch girl got hit this morning and she won't let anybody look at it."

I ran through the hootch, slamming open the back screen door. Mai was there, squatting in the Vietnamese fashion, scrubbing at a wet flight suit with one hand. Her left hand clutched at her left side where blood dribbled to puddle on the floor beneath her. She turned her head toward me, eyes large and frightened. Tears rolled down her high-boned cheeks, which were normally dimpled with fun and mischief. She continued to scrub futilely with the one hand as I walked slowly toward her.

"Are you badly hurt?" I asked as I knelt beside her. "Let me see how bad it is, Mai." The shock of the wound seemed to have driven her newly won English from her. She continued to stare at me with unblinking, tear-filled eyes, the pain making her mute. Gently forcing her back on her bottom, I carefully peeled the shredded cloth from her side. Some of the blood had clotted, forcing me to jerk the cloth harder than I wished, but she made no complaint. Through the jagged six-inch wound I could see the white end of a broken rib. I tried to take off her blouse, but she suddenly came to life and clutched it to her very modest bosom. For the first time she moved her eyes from me to the other two pilots kneeling beside me.

"Make go away!" she cried, waving her good arm at them.

"Go get a couple of blankets," I told them. "Let me look her over and then we'll see if we can get her to the doc's or if we need to send for a meat wagon. How in hell did this happen, anyway?"

"Well," one of them said, "it was my turn to pick her up at the gate this morning, and just as I got there one of those goddamned rockets landed right in the middle of the crowd of Vietnamese waiting to come onto the base. I found her and was able to get her into the jeep and was trying to take her to the hospital, but she began raising so much hell about seeing you that I decided to try to find you before I did anything else. I was afraid she was going to jump out or something. Then, when we got here she hobbled around back and said she was going to wait for you. Every time one of us tried to check her out, she'd scream like crazy."

"OK, let me see what I can do."

After they left to get the blankets, Mai docilely allowed me to cut the remnants of her blouse from her body. I gingerly probed the bloody mess of her side. She didn't flinch or change expressions. Wrapping her in the GI blankets that the other pilots had brought, I picked her up as gently as I could and walked to the jeep, telling them to drive us to the hospital. She couldn't have weighed more than eighty pounds.

Holding her hand, I sat with her as the doctor cut and sewed her bedraggled side. Her eyes remained fastened on mine or the doctor's until he had finished. He gave me three bottles of pills for infection and pain.

"You'd better ration these out to her yourself," he said, "or have one of your people do it. If she's allowed to take them home with her, her family will more than likely sell them on the black market or give them to the VC. That's what normally happens."

"How am I supposed to do that?" I asked. "We could pass them out to her during the day if she were able to come on base and work, but shouldn't she stay in bed? You know that she can't work until that wound heals, and she can't stay on base overnight."

"Beats me," he said cheerfully. "Take it up with Westmoreland. He's the one that makes policy. I don't have a solution for anything except gunshot wounds."

Well, shit, I thought as I carried her back to the jeep. She was almost unconscious from the shock and the pain pills.

"Where to?" Ron asked as I slid into the seat beside him, still cradling Mai like a baby.

"Back to the hootch," I said.

Most of the other pilots had gathered by the time we arrived. They were truly fond of her, I knew.

"Who's the junior man?" I asked. Ted admitted that he was. He was one of the newer replacements. "OK, she takes your bunk until she's well enough to go home. You can bunk down in the dayroom. Ed, go next door and tell their hootch girl that Mai's going to be OK and will be staying here for a few days. Tell her to let Mai's family know what's happened and that we'll take good care of her. I know this is against the rules, but we all know she isn't carrying anything to blow up the base so let's just keep it to ourselves. Don't even tell the enlisted men, because if the word does get out there's no reason for them to be involved. We'll take turns getting food for her, and let's drape some blankets around her bunk so she can have a little privacy."

Mai healed rapidly and was ready to go home at night after only a week of bed rest and medication. In the meantime, the pilots spoiled her relentlessly. Caches of goodies that had been hidden away from the greedy hands of the rest of us began appearing as if by magic on her bunk. We even tolerated the Vietnamese music she loved so much, which to us sounded like monkeys being castrated. She grew sleek and sassy as a kitten and, true to her sex, she was soon trying to boss around everyone except me. The Vietnamese had great respect for age!

It was Ted's turn to clean up after our evening meal. This was a simple enough chore—he scraped the C-ration cans into an empty carton and dumped them in a mortar hole outside the backdoor. We could have eaten in the brigade mess hootch, but we would have had about the same food. The trip didn't seem worth the effort, unless we heard a rumor that something special might be cooked. We had made the trip over in a gaggle yesterday, since it had been Thanksgiving and the U.S. military practically guarantees that everyone gets a hot turkey dinner.

The night before Thanksgiving had been active and dreary. A heavy fog had developed in the early evening and hung on through the remainder of the night. Just before midnight the NVA had unleashed the first rocket of a continuous all-night attack. They timed the rockets so that the medics and others who had to expose themselves were usually caught in the open. After the initial salvo, the gunners would wait ten to fifteen seconds, long enough for rescuers to get there, then fire another quick salvo at the same target.

The dreary dawn brought an uneasy peace to the base camp. The cooks, who had been up all night trying to prepare the Thanksgiving dinner, were frantic. Their processing of the frozen turkeys had been continually interrupted and now they found themselves with no way to bake the large, twenty-five-pound birds before the traditional noon meal. The mess sergeant's plea for a postponement fell on deaf ears. He was told frostily by the brigade commander that his troops *always* had their turkey dinners and that a few rockets from Charley, or an incompetent mess sergeant, were not going to break that tradition. In addition, if a certain mess sergeant couldn't find a way to feed a drumstick to every man jack on the Lai Khe base camp by 1300, then aforementioned sergeant would find himself humping the boonies as a rifleman until the day of his retirement, or death. And it didn't much matter which came first. Newly inspired, the mess sergeant returned to his field kitchen.

By noon a long line of men snaked through the rubber trees to the mess hall door. Our group had arrived early to establish a good position in the line, since most of us were scheduled to fly an afternoon sortie. Doug, our Australian, was visiting us for the day from Vung Tau and his staff job. He looked at me with some skepticism as I extolled the virtues of the American Pilgrim fathers and described how such a holiday came about. He decided that the Pilgrim fathers were a bunch of twits but was willing to go along with the story if it would get him a decent meal.

As we approached the serving table, a rancid smell assaulted my nostrils. Doug looked into the serving trays with shocked interest. Strange lumps lay in pools of grease. The normally boisterous troops became silent as they stared at them. The lumps seemed to stare back, grease bubbling around them.

"I can't believe it," the young trooper in front of me whispered in disbelief. "They fried the goddamned turkey. Who ever heard of fried turkey?"

The mess sergeant stood with folded arms behind the serving table. He glared at the trooper. "The goddamned colonel said we were going to have this goddamned turkey today, one way or another. Well, we didn't have time to bake it. Hell! We didn't even have time for some of it to thaw out. Frying was the only way to get it even part-way cooked by dinnertime, so quit your bitching. If you don't want it, don't eat it."

Most of us chose not to eat it, for the temperature was well over a hundred degrees inside the mess hall and the smell of the frying birds made many of the soldiers actively ill. Doug showed the same enthusiasm for the partially cooked bird as he did for any new project, attacking it with gusto. As we walked back toward our hootch his only comment was, "Interesting concept."

The last flight of the day had landed, and no mortar or rocket sites had been located. The brigade commander was about to bust a gut in frustration. I knew the feeling, for we'd devoted three sorties to the job ourselves. The old man was pissed; I was pissed; the pilots were pissed. The day had been a total loss, and now with the darkness it appeared that the fog was settling in, almost a guarantee that we would be hit again tonight. We sat around a rickety, old wooden table and groused at the world, squinting at one another in the dim glow of one dangling light bulb.

There was a moment of silence as everyone cocked their head, listening to the new discordant sound. "Incoming!" someone yelled and we hit the floor, stacked like cordwood on one another. Charley was back in business and early too.

"Everybody to the bunker!" I yelled when there was a lull in the explosions, reaching up to pull the string on the light to plunge the hootch into total darkness. I crouched at the head of the homemade stairs leading into our subterranean bastion, trying to keep the silhouette of my body below the sandbags. I counted the bodies as the pilots jogged past me into the darkness below, only one flashlight to guide them. I had begun counting bodies when, during an earlier attack, one of our new men had stayed above ground trying to record the battle with his camera. A piece of shrapnel had cut through the RPG screen covering the upper portion of the hootch and had almost taken off his head. Many commanders from the field had told me that they had men killed or wounded while attempting to photograph artillery or air strikes. One company CO lost a man who had tried to take Charley's picture during a ground attack. He had been shot in the head for his effort.

Our bunker was the best in the base camp. We had bribed a bulldozer operator to scoop out a room-sized excavation, then move the hootch over it so we could enter it without leaving the building. We constructed three Z-shaped air vents for ventilation; theoretically the abrupt turns made it very difficult to hurl a grenade into the bunker, yet still provided adequate air. There were also firing ports in three directions, which could be sealed off from inside the bunker. The walls seeped groundwater, but we had placed wooden pallets on the floor to keep us out of the pools of water. We had stocked the place with weapons, food, ammo, and a radio. If necessary, we could exist for quite a long time down there.

Out loud, I counted the six hunched forms as they stumbled by me in the dark, then I swung in behind the last man to join the parade. Suddenly, I was thrust violently aside as first one man, then an entire stream of people, erupted from the tunneled stairway. They were yelling and crawling over one another trying to be the first person out of the bunker. My God! I thought. The sappers have managed to get inside the bunker. But, other than an occasional exploding rocket, I heard no other gunfire.

"Did you see the size of that son of a bitch?" someone said, after everybody had returned to the floor of the hootch, sprawling beneath the layer of sandbags.

"For God's sake," I yelled, "what's going on?" I had followed the stampede back up the stairs, confirming my belief in mob psychology. There was silence, and my temper was starting to stretch beyond the point of reason. I was taking a great lungful of air to bellow at someone when Ted spoke: "That is the biggest snake I've ever seen in my entire life!"

The story was finally sorted out. Each man had switched on his flashlight in the bunker when he was well below the sight of any observer outside. The third man down had seen the snake and immediately had given the alarm. Unfortunately, the descending herd behind him had prevented him from ascending the steps until they had acquired enough beef to first stem, then reverse, the tide.

The snake, which had appeared to be a rather largish cobra, had been aroused by the lights and motion in his adopted lair, and was ready to aggressively defend its domain. It pulled its upper body erect and flared its hood as the disturbance increased. This sight was more than enough to scatter my stalwart warriors, who decided in a flash that they preferred rocket and mortar fire to a confrontation with the angered snake.

We formed a loose square around the bunker entrance with all lights focused on the hole, disregarding any Viet Cong observer.

"I don't think he can come up the stairs," I said. "Do you think he can?" I asked the hunched figures around me. "Maybe we'd better try to get the entrance covered though, just in case I'm wrong."

We slithered around the floor, dragging footlockers and anything else we could find that was rigid enough to cover the hole. Outside, a cascade of rockets illuminated the flight line with their exploding warheads. I could hear transmissions from the radio seeping through the hastily erected barricade, the voices too muted to determine the message content. I sent one of the pilots to listen to the other radio across the room.

Eventually, the rockets ceased and the all-clear sounded. We turned on our light, looking sheepishly at one another. Ed heated a pot of water, and we settled down with our C-rat coffee to do some heavy thinking. No one wanted to sack out until we had a solution to the problem below us. We had sealed the entrance, but we knew that there were many crevices through which our fanged friend could infiltrate the hootch. We knew that snakes rarely attacked without provocation, and we were not particularly frightened of them outside since they normally had plenty of time to get out of our way. If, though, we surprised this one while he was catching some z's behind a footlocker, his inclination may be to strike first and then fade away.

"Well, obviously we've got to get rid of him," I said. "Otherwise, we might as well move out ourselves. Does anyone have any ideas?"

"I wonder if we could CS him?" Crazy John asked. CS, a virulent tear-gas agent that came in canisters the same size as smoke grenades, was as common in Vietnam as popcorn on the floor of the Bijou theater in Omaha. It came in handy for the troops in the field when they had to flush out a tunnel. It was a slow night when someone didn't roll a can of CS into someone's hootch. It would, of course, empty a hootch of humans, but would it work on the fanged avenger?

"It's worth a try, I guess. Does anybody have any?"

"I can get some from the chopper pilots across the road," Crazy John said.

He scurried away to find the gas while the attack party made ready for the assault. Led by the senior captain, they put on flak vests and armed themselves according to their personal view of the warrior's code. Their leader had an M-16, complete with bayonet, his flashlight flaring from his flak jacket so as to leave both hands free. Others had service revolvers and machetes. We gently disarmed one of the volunteers who, in the spirit of aggressiveness, had clutched two frag grenades in his hands. No doubt they would take care of the snake, along with anyone else who ventured down the stairs. Besides, the bunker was packed with various types of ammo and explosives. He was devolunteered from the raiding party on the grounds of mental instability.

Crazy John arrived with the CS and was pressed into service to fill out the ranks. Donning gas masks, they formed a single file before the entrance and nodded that they were ready. The rest of us withdrew the barriers and leaped back, not only to get out of their way but with a genuine fear of the snake.

Flashlights on, they descended slowly into the dark bunker, beams of light flashing crazily on the walls as they moved them about, trying to thwart an ambush. Their muffled voices filtered up to us. I heard the hiss as the CS canisters were popped and then muffled shouts and curses. The group crawled all over each other attempting to get quickly back up the stairs in a repeat of the earlier parody.

The barricade was hastily reassembled and the rest of us put on our masks as the fumes began seeping up from below. I motioned everyone outside, where we sank in a ragged circle in the fog. By now, our activities had drawn spectators from the neighboring hootches. They were, of course, filled with advice and laughter.

"I don't believe it!" Ed said after he quit coughing. "There are two of the bastards down there."

"Yeah, and one of them has got to be at least twelve feet long," Crazy John added. I believed him, for he was the most stable of any of the group and least likely to fall prey to his imagination. "They must have come in through the air vents," he continued.

"That must mean the screens are down," Ed said.

"We'll give it about five minutes and then take a check," I said.

The attack party felt they had proven their manhood sufficiently for the evening and respectfully declined to have another go at it. I chose one of the new FACs, and we girded our loins, assembling again in front of the hatch to the bunker. I had an old rusty machete in one hand and my flashlight in the other. My partner carried his M-16.

The men slowly removed the blockade and we hunkered by the entrance while the CS cleared. There would be enough residual gas to force us to wear our masks below. I cautiously put one foot on the stairway, then paused to listen for any snake movements in the darkness below. All I could hear was my own breath in the mask and my heart pounding. I crept down the stairs, playing my beam of light into every darkened cranny. As it fell across a stacked case of ration boxes in the near corner, I heard a gasp behind me and a clawlike hand clutched my shoulder, almost driving me into cardiac arrest. I had seen it too, though.

The snake's head was raised a good yard off the ground and the magnificent hood flared like an airfoil. My partner, quick to guard his leader, immediately bolted upstairs, leaving me with only my flashlight for illumination. I knew there were two snakes down here, but I was afraid to move my light from the one glaring at me from the corner. Suddenly, my peripheral vision detected movement only a few feet away in the gloom. That was enough. My nerve broke and I whirled and scampered back up the stairs. The pilots quickly covered the hole once more.

Again, we sat glumly in our muddy circle outside the hootch. We had switched to hot beer by this time and the crowd had grown to something the size of a rock concert. We decided it was going to have to be an all-out frontal assault or nothing. Rounding up a few army volunteers to bolster our shrinking strike force, we made our plans. We would station one man outside by each air vent in case Snake and Friend should try to escape the way they came in. Then, two men armed with automatic weapons would make the assault. The decision was made to limit it to two men because of the narrow stairway. At a given signal, a large searchlight, borrowed from the Nighthawk helicopter crew, would be turned on and the pair of men would attack. I cleared away everyone not needed in the plan in case there was errant gunfire.

Crazy John and the army volunteer took their positions near the entrance, their faces as determined as if they were going up against the 307th NVA Regiment. I leaned over as far as I could to watch their descending forms and snapped on the large light. The largest snake was on the stairs below but had been hidden by the shadows of the steps. Caught in the light, it drew itself into loose coils and lifted its flared head. The coils were so long that they spilled off the stairway and looped onto the bunker floor. Both men began firing wildly, their rounds impacting all over the bunker. Only the dirt floor and walls kept them from being killed by the ricochets. When their clips were empty, they both fled up the stairs. We covered the opening and gaped at each other.

"Do you think you got them?" I asked.

They looked at each other and slowly shook their heads. We trudged outside to the crowd that was re-forming after the gunfight. As we sank to the mud again, a jeep pulled up, driven by a young Special Forces captain. At his query we explained the circus that was growing larger by the moment. With the aplomb of someone bred to an elite unit, he waved everyone aside.

"I'll take care of it for you," he told me.

"We'd all be most appreciative if you would," I answered. "But there are two of them down there and one is really a big bastard."

He breezily dismissed that and started into the hootch. I followed him until he waved me back with a casual movement of his hand. He strode confidently to the entrance of the bunker and began moving the covering away. Jesus, I thought, maybe these guys *can* handle anything, just the way they claim. He dragged the last footlocker from the entrance and reached for his web gear. I realized what he was about to do just as he rolled one grenade, then another, into the hole.

The muffled explosions came in seconds followed by a tremendous eruption as the boxes of grenades and ammo we had stored there exploded in sympathetic detonation. The floor beneath his feet bulged upward, then collapsed upon itself, taking floor, several bunks, and assorted detritus to the lower level. When the pieces stopped falling we ran inside. Looking into the gaping hole, we saw the captain who lay groaning on the shattered planks of what had been our floor. He was cut and bruised but had little serious damage. He was also very vocal in his opinions of dumb-assed air force pilots who didn't know enough to warn a body about stored ammo.

There was a sudden stirring in the rubble of the corner and the sleek head of our adversary poked up through the flotsam. He had survived. This time, however, he didn't extend his hood or even pay a great deal of attention to us. If a snake could shrug, he did. He inspected his surroundings and, as if finding them wanting, gracefully serpentined out through one of the new holes, showing no apparent injuries.

We bunked down in the chopper pilots' hootch that night and began putting things back together the next morning. We never found the other snake.

The AO was hot and some of the older aircraft were starting to show the wear and tear of continual service. There were homemade patches all over the wings and fuselages. Things often got hectic, but I realized that I and the rest of the pilots were flying and conducting operations like real professionals. The airplane now felt like an extension of my body and I never had to give a thought to its operation. It simply seemed to respond to my wishes. For all its ugliness, I had developed a deep affection for the little aircraft.

All things considered, I was fairly content with my lot. I wasn't unhappy with the job I had, and the grunts seemed to appreciate it as well. While I wasn't living elegantly, I at least had a reasonably dry place to sleep. I should have known that my situation was going to change.

The group commander called our control room to inform me that he would be on the ground within fifteen minutes. It went without saying that I should make myself available to meet him if I was on the ground. I was. I sat in my jeep and watched him flying the rectangular pattern required at our airstrip. Something had to be in the wind; this was his first visit to Lai Khe since my appointment as ALO, and he normally preferred staying pretty close to the flagpole.

I watched the colonel bank his Bronco into precise turns around the pattern, squaring off the corners nicely. One of our FACs would have been on the ground in half the time it took him, but the colonel didn't fly that much anymore. He made a decent touchdown and taxied toward our revetments. His square jaw protruded from his helmet and swung back and forth as he watched his wingtip clearance. He still looked like the old fighter pilot he had once been. He returned my salute with a lazy wave of his hand as the crew chief helped unbuckle him from the aircraft. We shook hands and crawled into my jeep.

"Let's just sit and talk awhile," he said. That didn't sound good. He obviously didn't want any witnesses. In the military service, if a senior officer wants to talk to you in private it usually means you're in for an ass-chewing, praise, or a really shitty job. My mind raced frantically over my misdeeds of the past few weeks. There were so many of them that I couldn't settle on any one to begin building a defense.

"Harrison," he began, "we've got a little problem up north of here. I don't know if you knew but the air liaison officer of one of the cav's brigades was killed a few days ago." The cavalry's AO abutted ours to the north.

"He was killed but that's not the real problem. Hell, we're always losing people, and we can usually replace them fairly quickly, although it is harder when it's the ALO. The problem comes in because that particular ALO was flying for the brigade simply as cover for his real job. He and two of the FACs up there are really assigned to duty with the MACSOG outfit, the Military Assistance Command, Studies and Observation Group. They support their covert border-crossing teams as well as doing most of the BDA for those Arc Lights that don't exist in either Cambodia or Laos. This is not the kind of thing where I'd send anybody but a volunteer because whoever goes is going to be catching it from both sides, theirs and ours. I'm not going to tell you any more about it unless you accept the job, and I need to know that before I leave here today. I've got a young captain and a lieutenant up there trying to hold things together, but between them they don't have the kind of experience that's needed. Besides, I'm afraid those assholes at SOG will eat them alive and get both of them killed within a week. So, what do you think?"

I filled and lit my pipe to give myself time to think. I didn't really want to go. If anyone in the Air Force lived worse than we did, it was the FACs assigned to the cav, and I knew that their third brigade was based at Quan Loi, close to the border. Consequently they were all the more susceptible to ground and rocket attacks. Most importantly, I would be operating in either Cambodia or Laos. It was hardly a secret that we had agency and Special Forces people roaming around the hills of Laos. Cambodia was a different story, however. As far as I knew we were not at war with them, although the NVA used their countryside as a sanctuary and roadway into South Vietnam. Neither the American people nor the average military man in South Vietnam knew that we had covert operations going on there. I had suspected it but had not known for sure myself, and I flew by the border every day. That brought another point to mind. What happened if one of our people went down over there. Who was going to try to get them out? Somehow, I couldn't see MACV rushing in U.S. troops to pull a downed pilot out of a neutral country. Maybe MACSOG would do it. They had a pretty scurvy reputation, but most outfits like that looked after their own.

I peered at the colonel through the billowing clouds of my pipe. He was polite enough not to overtly gag on the smoke enveloping his face.

"Just how badly do you need me up there, Colonel? And does it have to be me? Why not someone else? I'd hate to give up the good unit that I know I've got here."

"That's one of the reasons I'd like to have you go up," he said, staring at a helicopter coming in to land. "You have built a good unit here. Good enough, in fact, to put you out of a job. I think we could move a relatively inexperienced man up here to replace you, and the combat effectiveness of the unit wouldn't suffer. I need a real experienced ball-breaker up there, and with this damned one-year tour we're stuck with, it's hard to find a man of the right rank who does have the experience. Besides, I was particularly impressed with the way you folks handled that Aussie who was shot down, where was it, just inside Vietnam and not Cambodia?"

Ahh, did I hear the opening line of a blackmail campaign rearing its ugly head?

"Listen," he continued. "Everybody and his brother knew that crazy damned Australian was shot down over the border. It just suited our purposes to let your band of hooligans get away with hiding it. We weren't any more anxious for the entire goddamned world to find out about it than you were. Just don't think that everybody bought that damned cock-and-bull story you people put out. Incidentally, the innocu-ous-looking air force lieutenant colonel that you had the other nutty Aussie squire around probably knows more about the countryside than your entire pack of pilots. He told me he could hardly keep from laughing out loud when he was shown the *other* wrecked OV-10."

"I'm sure that I don't know what you're talking about, Colonel, but if it would help you out any, I'd be glad to go up to Quan Loi for a while." The old bastard had me and he knew it.

He smiled, a little grimly, I thought. "Good! I'm going to want you up there tomorrow, so you can get your gear together right now and fly back to Bien Hoa with me this afternoon. Spend the night down there and we'll talk. Who do you want to relieve you here until we can get a new ALO in place?''

"Uh, Ed, I guess. He could handle it permanently, but I'm afraid the army brass would try to push him around, since he's only a captain.''

"I agree. Tell him he's got command and get your crap together and get it aboard my plane. I'll go on over to the command post and let everybody concerned know what's going on. Don't be too long. I've got a lot of things going on this afternoon.''

After dropping him off at the brigade TOC, I drove back to the hootch to gather my belongings, my mind churning with things I needed to tell Ed before he took over. Naw, to hell with it. Ed knew the general requirements of the job and what needed to be done. No need saddling him with advice that may or may not work for him. He was going to have to learn the same way everyone else did, by doing it.

My belongings fit easily into a parachute kit bag. Not much for a thirty-two-year-old man to call his own. I sat on my bunk and watched Mai, who had been helping me get things organized. I reached out and took both of her small hands. She hung back like a reluctant child, eyes brimming with tears. I could feel my own begin to moisten. She kept her left arm tucked in a little, protecting the still-healing wound. I reached into my wallet, pulled out a handful of MPC and Vietnamese piasters, and handed them to her without counting them. She pushed them away and turned her head, now crying openly.

"Take it, Mai," I said. "Keep it for yourself and don't give it to papa-san. Maybe some day you'll need it for yourself, so hide it away and don't let anybody know you have it. I have to go now.''

I wrapped my arms around her and hugged her as if she were one of my own children. She clutched at me fiercely, never uttering a sound. Shouldering my bag, I picked up my rifle and started for the door. I looked back at her as I stepped outside; she hadn't moved. My God, I thought, what will happen to her if the Americans ever do leave?

PART 5

Over the Fence

They found me a bunk for the night in the squadron quarters in Bien Hoa. The air-conditioning and tile floors felt as if I were on another planet. The CO allowed me time for a lengthy hot shower before his jeep driver tracked me down and ferried me to his office. The CO returned my salute and introduced me to an army lieutenant colonel sitting in one of the wing chairs before the glossy desk. The commander saw me eyeing the expanse of glistening wood after we had been invited to sit.

"I'll be damned if I apologize for this," he said. "I've had two wars before this one—that in itself ought to allow me to sit this one out in as much comfort as I can find."

"No argument there, sir," I replied. "I just wish I had one like it."

"Like hell, you do! You'd squawk like a goddamned wounded buzzard if I tried to pull you in out of the mud." He turned to the army lieutenant colonel and continued. "I'm going to let the colonel fill you in on what's happening in Quan Loi. I'm just here to make sure that they don't overwhelm you with that SOG bullshit." He waved his hand vaguely at the army type, who took his cue and strode purposefully toward the large wall map. It showed most of the Vietnamese-Cambodian border all the way to the tri-border where Laos joined the two countries.

"Major, your new assignment is going to be with MACSOG, the Military Assistance Command, Studies and Observation Group. If that sounds more like some kind of an entertainment group than anything else, good; that's exactly what we hoped. Originally, SOG were the initials for Special Operations Group, but that seemed to attract a little too much attention. Our group is responsible for a good part of the covert activity in and out of the country. We'll limit this brief to that part in which you'll play an active role. Specifically, I'm talking about this area here." He moved his briefing stick from a point south of the Parrot's Beak, an enclave jutting from Cambodia into South Vietnam, to a point just south of the tri-border area.

"We're funded and targeted by a nameless agency in Washington that's known by its initials most of the time. I'd like to emphasize at this point that all our missions have the approval of the very highest authority. It can't get any higher. And I mean every target."

"Just who is this 'highest authority'?" I was already getting pissed and I hadn't listened to this man for more than two minutes.

He looked annoyed. He probably didn't like me either. "I'm not at liberty to say his name. Take my word for it, he really is the highest authority you can need."

"I didn't know that God was directing SOG now," I said, facetiously. "I guess that's who you're talking about though. Unless you're nonreligious, of course. Then, it could be any number of people or things, like gold to the gnomes of Zurich or polar bears to the Eskimos. For a marine it might be Chesty Puller, or . . ."

"Cut out the crap, Major. You've made your point," said my CO.

"Colonel," I said, turning toward him from the wall map, "I just want to make sure that I've got everything clear, because it sounds to me like this bunch of spooks are planning on dropping me in the shit somewhere we're not even supposed to be. I'm already wondering just who's going to be there to help pull me out. Is it this mystical higher authority the Colonel keeps referring to? If the spooks want to play games, that's fine, but I just don't want to be left at the mercy of some fat-ass at that initialed agency back in Washington who made his rep in World War Two parachuting into France and saving Madame de Gaulle's chamber pot. Neither one of us is just off the boat, Colonel. We both know how these guys play the game over here, and frankly most of us had just as soon not be associated with it. I'll do my bit for God and Country but I'm just a simple pilot who needs to know exactly who I'm working for."

"It's not too late to back out, you know," the army officer said with a sour look on his face. "With that attitude I'm not sure we can use you."

The group commander was on him like ugly on an ape. "I think I'm quite capable of deciding who'll fill that slot, Colonel! Should you feel it necessary to make further attempts at deciding my personnel policy, we'll call Seventh Air Force headquarters right now. Perhaps the general there can persuade your group commander that you're overstepping your brief." He turned to glare at me as the army officer's face went into the West Point, no-expression mode. "Harrison, if it will make you happier, then, for the record, I know who this 'highest authority' is and it satisfies me. Therefore, it *will* satisfy you. But, let's get one thing straight from the outset. You'll be involved in some things that you might find strange and sometimes even a little bizarre. I know I volunteered you, but if you don't think you can do it without getting up everyone's nose all the time, then I'd like to hear about it right now before we get into it any deeper.''

"Of course I'll do it, Colonel," I said with a breezy wave of my hand. "It's just that I don't like name-droppers. But, if it's good enough for you then it's certainly good enough for me."

He looked as if he wanted to strangle me. The army officer's facade had cracked and he was looking alternately disgusted and bewildered. Maybe he was afraid that if he mentioned CIA I'd swoon away with an attack of the vapors. It was common knowledge that they were running the out-country war in Laos, and I wouldn't have been surprised to find their fine hand behind covert activity in Cambodia, utilizing the army's Special Forces for most of the dirty work. I didn't know enough about that activity to come to any rational decision on its effectiveness. My objection to the agency was more personal. They seemed to take an inordinate amount of space in Saigon and other metropolitan areas. When they ventured into the countryside they cleverly camouflaged themselves by driving blue jeeps and carrying Swedish-K submachine guns. This insured that they would stand out from the zillion other men around them dressed in jungle fatigues and carrying M-16s. I mean, where's the glory of being a spook if people can't tell that you're one? Most of the ones I had contact with were a royal pain in the ass.

"Do you think we could possibly continue this now?" the army lieutenant colonel said. "I would like to finish it before my DEROS."

"Of course, sir," I said graciously. My boss continued to glare at me.

"Thank you," he said. "Major, you'll be in charge of the air force support for our cross-border teams operating in the AO shown on this map. These operations are controlled by an organization known as CCS, Command and Control South. There is an army Special Forces major in command of the Mobile Launch Site (MLS) of CCS at Quan Loi who will issue pertinent orders for your aircraft to carry out. He also has operational control over the teams sent there from Pleiku or Ban Me Thuot. In conjunction with the army fixed-wing and helicopter assets in place at Quan Loi and assigned to CCS, you will be responsible for providing air support during insertion or extraction of the recon teams, as well as acting as their radio relay while they're on the ground. The OV-10 was chosen for this mission because of its endurance, armament, and other unique features. You will also be expected to provide bomb damage assessments of the B-52 Arc Light strikes across the border. Question?''

"No, a statement," said my group commander. "I want you people to understand that Major Harrison has full discretion as to whether or not to launch his aircraft. I think he probably knows more about weather and flying than everybody up there combined, so I don't want some half-assed leg telling him he's *got* to fly if, in his judgment, it's not a good idea. If he or his people abort a flight, I can assure you it won't be for a frivolous reason."

"Understood, sir," said the army lieutenant colonel, who then turned back to me. "On paper, your job is going to be the ALO for the air cavalry brigade stationed there. You'll probably find that you're too busy to do much work with them. We've already been in touch with the brigade commander there and explained the situation to him. He's aware of the real reason that the Air Force has assigned additional men and aircraft there. I'd like to stress, however, that he and the two pilots assigned to the mission are the only people up there who have knowledge of the cross-border operations, except for the SOG people in the Special Forces compound, of course. For that matter, except for the colonel here, no one in your chain of command is briefed on these operations. It's a very closely held item. We realize that can make for some awkward situations, but it's best for all concerned that we keep a lid firmly on it. This has the approval of the commander, Seventh Air Force. Your biggest problem is probably going to be trying to keep the other pilots in the dark about it, since your group will be blended right into the brigade structure."

If I knew my pilots, I thought, every FAC at Quan Loi already had a pretty good idea about what was going on. It wasn't the kind of thing you could keep quiet, no matter what headquarters thought.

Noting my skeptical look, the group commander interrupted: "I know what you're thinking—that the entire thing is already compromised, and it may well be. As I see it, though, the thing to do is to neither confirm it nor deny it. Just don't allow anyone to speculate aloud on it. There's no way you're going to keep the other people from knowing what's going on if they see one of their friends driving a plane straight across the border into Cambodia. Just try to keep it in as low a profile as you can."

That made sense, I guess. If it was indeed necessary to keep the operation secret—and I was far from convinced that it was—then brush off the talk rather than denying it and looking like a fool. If you told the troops that it was something they couldn't talk about, they'd respect that, for they'd been in situations like that during most of their military careers.

"You should be aware," the army officer continued, "the area in which you will be operating is well defended and we are not authorized to ask for friendly air or artillery support from South Vietnam. We can use only our organic aircraft and personnel—that is, any support the teams may need can be provided only by the army Charley-model gunships and your Broncos. The helicopter crews are on lengthy temporary duty from Long Binh; all of them are good, experienced volunteers. The ground recon missions are scheduled for ten days unless it's a special situation such as a prisoner snatch. In that case they normally try to get in and out in minimum time for obvious reasons. The primary mission, though, is recon—trail-watching, planting listening devices, that sort of thing."

"Do they usually stay in for the full ten days?" I asked.

"Negative." He looked glum. "In fact, it's rare that we have one that stays more than a couple of days. The compromise rate has been running very high."

"What's been the problem?"

"Primarily, getting them in. Almost every possible helicopter LZ has an NVA 'watcher' who fires off a few rounds if a landing attempt is made on his turf. This alerts the base camps, which immediately send out many patrols in that direction. Consequently, even if we do get the teams in, they find they're being pursued from the outset. But we're working on a few things that should help, and they'll fill you in at Quan Loi if they think you have a need to know."

"Which touches on a rather important point to me and I'm sure to the other pilots as well. Supposing someone goes down over there. How do we go about getting them out?"

"Like I said before, it all has to be done with organic resources. We're not authorized to call for help from friendly units across the border. That might be construed as invasion of a neutral country. Only COMUSMACV or his deputy can authorize anyone to cross over on a rescue mission, and they've done so on only a very few occasions. But it's not as bleak as it may appear. We do have a Mike-Force reaction team of some thirty or forty people we can scrape together from the mobile launch site at Quan Loi, permanently assigned there, who have quite a bit of experience with that sort of thing. We can usually get them airborne within half an hour if we have to."

"Sounds to me as if they may have too much experience," I said. "Do you lose a lot of people up there?"

He ignored my question and continued his briefing. "We normally have only one team at a time on the ground, but in exceptional circumstances there have been as many as three. In that instance, resources are stretched pretty thin. We just have to do the best we can with what we've got."

I noticed he kept saying "we," but I doubted seriously if he went across himself.

"If you have specific questions," he finished, "I suggest you hold them until tomorrow when you get to Quan Loi. We've notified the officer in charge of CCS that you'll be arriving. And I think the colonel has notified your new Tactical Air Control Party."

I stared at the map for a few more moments. There were a lot of things I wanted to ask, but I decided to wait until I could get it from the horse's mouth. My commander nodded to the army officer and rose from his chair to shake his hand. I did the same, and he turned on his heel and immediately left the room. The colonel sat and stared at me in silence.

"I get the feeling that you're not too crazy about this new job," he said. "I wouldn't have asked you to do it if I didn't think you could."

"Oh, I think I can do it all right," I said. "It's just that I think we may be hiding these operations from the wrong people. Like the American public. Hell, sir. The North Vietnamese know we're in there, so it can hardly be a secret to them. We're hiding something from our own people, and I don't know how crazy I am about that."

"Well, if it's any consolation, the people who insist on keeping it a secret are about as high up in our government as it's possible to get. The monkey's squarely on their shoulders if it breaks into the open."

"With all respect, Colonel, we've both been around too long to believe that's how the system works. If one of my people gets himself dinged over there and some hotshot correspondent finds out about it, the pilot will be lucky to get away with a general court-martial for overflying a neutral country without permission. Somehow, I just can't see the President or the Secretary of Defense rising to take the blame for it. Hell, it's not that I think we ought to stay out of Cambodia or Laos. Everybody knows that the NVA have made them into their own private reservations without consulting the leaders of either country. It just seems that we're making a mistake in trying to do this like spooks rather than military men. If our government doesn't think we should put in the military, then fine, we'll just take our lumps like we always have. If we have to do it like thieves in the night to hide it from our own people or world opinion, then we both know it isn't right."

"You may be right," he said. "I confess that I've had my doubts about the whole thing, but that's the way our superiors, whom we've sworn to obey, want it done, so by God, that's the way we're going to do it."

"Sir, then I guess that's the way we'll, by God, do it," I echoed.

That evening at the O-Club I met Jake, one of the air force CCS pilots, down to exchange an aircraft. I would be flying to Quan Loi with him in the morning. There were too many people around to talk about the work, so we held our conversation to the general conditions at the base camp. Jake impressed me. Almost at the end of his year's tour, he had spent his first six months in-country as a fighter-bomber pilot before transferring to the OV-10. He had a slight frame, and the year of heat seemed to have burned off any spare flesh he once might have carried. He was wearing sweat-encrusted camouflage fatigues. They were issued to all FACs but few of us wore them, preferring our familiar light-green flight suits. We refrained from wearing the jungle fatigues, plain green or camouflage, because of our fear of fire in the cockpit. The two-piece fatigue uniform could leave an opening around the middle for flames to lick at. Fear of fire has an almost mystic quality to a fighter pilot, for fire leaves him with only two choices, eject or die. There's really nothing else he can do. With an engine failure or battle damage, the pilot normally has time to steer his aircraft toward friendly troops or at least away from the people he's been dumping bombs on. Those few seconds just may get him to a safe area. Fire allows no such luxuries.

"Jake," I told him, "I think you're the first pilot I've seen wearing that charming outfit outside of somebody dressing up to have his picture taken. Or trying to impress some visitor from the rear."

His teeth flashed in the darkness of the club, his sun-browned face indistinguishable from the dark wooden paneling to his rear.

"Steve and I both wear them. He's the other CCS pilot. He was shot down about three months ago, and though he was only on the ground for less than an hour, he was running the whole time. When they lifted him out, the only thing he still had on was his jungle boots, one sleeve of his air force flight suit, and his jockey shorts. Oh yeah, he still had on his survival vest and his pistol belt. The bushes and bamboo ripped everything else off him as he was scampering through the boonies. When we got him back, we had a long talk about it. We decided the smartest thing you can do if you have to step out of the airplane over there," he winked to let me know he was talking about across the border, "is to act like a tree. Over here there's a good chance you might run into some friendly unit. There aren't any that way. I heard in the squadron today that we're all supposed to be getting some kind of new Nomex, flame-resistant flight suit, but the only people I saw wearing them were the staff pukes."

"Yeah, I heard that too. Maybe I'd better get a couple of extra sets of cammies before we leave. What time are you planning on getting us out of here?"

"I figure about 1000 ought to do it," he glanced around, then continued. "We're going to have to relieve Steve up in the AO before we can go into Quan Loi." He lowered his voice to a whisper. "We're covering the team all morning and the army Birddogs will take over after we leave. I was over them this afternoon before I recovered here and they were running then, so they might have to bring 'em out before we get on station. There's really not any way of knowing until we get up there. Meanwhile, lemme get us a couple more beers. Take my advice, Major, and enjoy this while you can. Your new home is going to be real different."

The next morning I sat in the rear cockpit, the compleat passenger. I enjoyed watching Jake writhe the plane through the air, never on the same heading or altitude for more than a few moments. I could tell it was instinctive now, honed by a year of flying over hostile areas. He probably wasn't even aware he was doing it. With all the twisting and turning, the small black ball stayed dead center in its race, showing coordinated flight. His head was always pressed against one side of the canopy or the other as he watched the ground flow beneath us. This wasn't his territory but he automatically cataloged everything he saw.

Lai Khe, my home until yesterday, drifted by beneath the left wing.

I thought of the people I knew and cared for down there and already it seemed like history. Little Mai pushed her way into my thoughts, but I pushed her back. It was her country and she was going to have to come to terms with it.

Twenty minutes later we watched Quan Loi float beneath us as we continued our flight northward toward the border. I barely glanced down at it, my thoughts focused on the unbroken jungle that stretched before us into Cambodia. I felt Jake pushing the throttles forward and lowering the nose into a shallow dive. The airspeed was building up quickly as we descended from our safe and much cooler 4,000 feet.

"We'll cross just north of Bu Dop," Jake said over the intercom. "We try to go over at treetop level to reduce the tracking time of any gunner. They know we usually cross about there, so sometimes they just wait for us and shoot at the noise overhead. I know it doesn't seem to make a lot of sense to always cross at the same point, but we figure that it lessens the chances of us compromising the team's position." The aircraft was shuddering now as the needle on the airspeed indicator caressed the red line.

"There's a crossroads we usually aim for about twenty klicks on the other side," he continued. "When we get there we can start a wide orbit around the team, trying to stay at least ten klicks away from them after we've made contact. Actually, Charley usually has a pretty good idea where they are anyway. We haven't had a team stay more than a few days in a long time. The extractions can get real hairy, and they're almost always hot. You may want to change it, but the way we've been working is that we don't do any shooting until the gunships are through and the air commander requests it. The ground situation is generally so fluid, what with the team and the NVA running around in every direction, that it's really hard to tell if you've got the right target. We do most of our shooting before the guns get here, just trying to keep them off the team's back until the choppers arrive. But, that's why they love to have the Bronco covering them rather than the army O-1s."

I looked over my shoulder and watched the huge tree limbs sway with the air currents of our passing. Jake had a deft touch on the stick.

"The choppers," he went on, "generally stay on ground alert in a little burned-out Special Forces camp at Bu Dop during the daylight hours while the team's on the ground. They go back to Quan Loi at night after the team has called in to one of the radio relay aircraft, either us or the army, that they're OK and settled in for the night. Thank God we've never had to try to pull them out at night. It's bad enough during the day. Anyway, after the choppers go on home for the day we either VR the area if we've got the fuel or go on home ourselves.''

''What sort of armament do you usually carry?''

''Well, we don't have a big need for smoke rockets, so we generally put only one pod of them on board and use the other three pods for high-explosive rockets. That gives us twenty-one HEs, which isn't bad because we use those with the larger warhead. Then, we've got the four guns, although the 7.62 round sometimes has a little trouble penetrating the trees. I'd better get set up on the team's frequency now.'' A not-so-subtle hint to stop pestering him with questions so that he could get on with his work.

Jake kicked the rudder sharply to crab away from one of the tall emergents poking up through the green canopy just below the belly of the aircraft. This time the black ball skewed to one side of the instrument, showing a flat, uncoordinated turn. A proper turn would have put our wing into the treetops.

The radio began to crackle with the slightly stilted, controlled voices that pilots tend to use in combat. Jake was listening intently, trying to make sense of the various conversations. It was all gibberish to me. He glanced in the mirror at me, waved a hand at our one o'clock position, and said, ''Bu Dop.''

At first I had trouble picking it out but then saw the raw red earth scars through the trees. I could see the destroyed Special Forces camp and a few crumbling hootches. There was a short overgrown runway next to the old campsite that obviously hadn't been used for a time except for helicopter laagers. The village had never been large, and since it had been overrun all the people had been located elsewhere. Maybe the VC slept in it at night. Who could say.

Jake barely glanced at Bu Dop, his attention focused on the radio activity.

''The choppers are gone, so they must be trying to pull the team,'' he said. ''That's why all the radio chatter. We're just about over the border now so we'll head for the crossroads and then on to the team's position. We ought to be able to see that gaggle of choppers up there, but if we can't find them I'll give Steve a call on our discrete UHF frequency. He's our other pilot who should be flying cover for them now.''

I had no idea what was going on but we were *low!* No more than ten feet above the trees. Jake was following their undulating, uneven tops with stick movements so small as to be unnoticeable. He had to be flying a heading, for there was no way he could have been picking up landmarks at our altitude.

Over the radio, voices began to call reports to one another about taking ground fire and hits. Terse calls between ships told of spotted enemy positions and directions for the supporting fire of the gunships. One authoritative voice could be distinguished, directing the slicks and the gunships. I would have thought it was a FAC except the vibrating transmission identified its source as a helicopter. It must have been the army air commander.

"They've already got the team and they're coming out," Jake said. "I'll let them clear the area and then give Steve a call and find out what's going on. We'll be there in a couple of minutes because we're coming up on the crossroads."

Peering over his shoulder I saw the two bisecting dirt roads ahead of us. We flashed over them quickly, and Jake pulled the stick back sharply, sending us into a near-vertical climb. At 4,000 feet, he gently allowed the nose to roll inverted toward the nearest horizon, then drift slowly down through it where he smoothly rolled the aircraft upright with gentle aileron pressure.

"There they come," he said, pointing low to the northeast. I quickly picked up their whirling rotors against the green background of the tree canopy. There were two slicks, or troop carriers, escorted by three of the old Charley-model gunships. About a thousand feet above and slightly aft of the helicopter formation was another slick. That must have been the one directing traffic. A thousand feet or so above the entire gaggle was an OV-10, circling easily so as not to overrun them.

Jake talked to the radio. "Two-two, this is Two-three. I'm at your one o'clock, level. Let's go Secure Voice."

Bronco radios were equipped with a scrambling device to prevent anyone from intercepting readable radio transmissions unless they had a similar device, as well as the proper day's code.

"Pretzel Two-three, this is Pretzel Two-two, up Secure."

The voice was slow and measured. Arkansas, maybe. Jake joined onto his left wing as we continued a slow circle around the helicopters heading directly toward the border.

"Got you loud and clear, Steve," Jake said. "I've got the new Pretzel Two-one on board. What happened back there?"

"Same old stuff. They stepped in a pile of dog shit and couldn't get away. They thought they'd lost Charley last night, but then they almost got themselves ambushed when they tried to move out this morning. One of the team seen 'em just in time and they tried to didi out the back door. They've been haulin' ass ever since. They finally got to a little opening and called for a pickup, but of course ole' Luke the Gook had an LZ watcher. Things got pretty sticky for the pickup chopper for a few minutes until they could get the fire suppressed. They pulled the team out on strings and I don't think any of them got hurt very bad. We all emptied our tubes after they left and are now running home with our tails between our legs."

"Sounds like a normal mission. Are you heading back?"

"Yeah, I might as well. I'm about outa' beebees and getting a little skoshi on fuel. I'll see you all back at the hootch."

"Rog," Jake answered. "Tell the guys to clear out some space and put up another bunk for the new ALO. See you."

Jake put the plane into a hard, smooth turn to the north. "We might as well show you some of your new AO. Here, you can use my maps. I've circled that crossroads we came over to help you get oriented."

He passed the maps back over his shoulder. I noticed immediately that he had put no markings on them except for the grease-pencil circle around the crossroads. They wouldn't give away a team's position even if they did fall into the wrong hands.

"The green beanies don't usually go much farther into the interior than that river about twenty klicks from the crossroads. They'll use about any opening they can find in the jungle for an LZ except the roads—they know the roads are watched. Unfortunately, old Charles knows about all the openings too and he watches them. Hell, we've tried to call in B-52 strikes just to create more LZs. While we're in the area we're always on the lookout for new ones. Then, before the team's inserted, the air commander overflies the general area and selects several LZs for possible use." We had descended to about 1,500 feet now. Jake was peering intently at the foliage, first over one shoulder, then the other.

"Whoops!" he exclaimed. "Somebody's not happy that we're flying over him. We've got ground fire coming from about three o'clock, out about half a klick."

Several small, dirty gray clouds of flak appeared off the right wing. Jake continued to fly straight ahead and soon the ground fire was well to our rear.

"You might want to mark that location on the map," he said. "It probably won't be there tomorrow, but that was either a .57 or a .37 and he'd rip a new asshole for the choppers if they came this way. Actually, the heavier guns usually don't do that much damage here in the rain forest because they're so restricted in traversing against a target. Our biggest headache is the 12.7s and the 14.5s. If you happen to fly into one of their interlocking fields of fire, they'll put your lights out in a minute. They've knocked down 90 percent of the helicopters we've lost. That doesn't look bad down there." He pointed to a small indentation in the trees. In South Vietnam a helicopter would never attempt to make a landing in such an area.

"Actually," Jake continued, "if we can get in a team without anyone seeing them, then they've generally got it made. They're skillful enough not to be found if no one's hunting them. There are usually six on a team, three Americans and three SCU, Special Commando Unit. They're normally indigenous to the part of the country they're working. Like here, they'd be Khmers. On up-country they use a lot of the hill tribesmen. Some of the guys also take at least one of the Nung Chinese mercenaries. That's not unusual 'cause the Chinese have always been all over Southeast Asia.

"They go in with sterile uniforms and gear, ready to stay for about ten days, but generally around here no one gets to stay that long. One of the Americans always wears the radio headset that looks like a stethoscope with a boom mike to keep his hands free. You sometimes have to listen hard to what they're saying because they never speak above a whisper unless they have to. The SCU usually don't speak much English, so you'll almost always be talking to one of the Americans unless things have really gone to hell. Look over there at about four o'clock and you'll see another one of our jobs. We do the BDA for the B-52 Arc Light strikes, which, incidentally, are not supposed to be taking place over here."

I looked at the long lines of bomb craters that had been dug by the bombers flying from Guam or Thailand. It seemed obvious to me that they were directed against military targets. Why all the secrecy? Charley sure as hell knew they were falling on him. Why keep it from the American public? I really didn't understand and still had a bad feeling about it.

Jake pointed out prominent landmarks as we cruised over the area. He identified the mountains and ridges that contained known antiaircraft defenses. Today, they remained silent. He said, "You really have to watch yourself when you're working in this mountain and hill area. They have interlocking fields of fire on damned near every inch of real estate around here. You'll find yourself taking fire from above sometimes. The first time it happened to me I thought I had fighters attacking me! Another thing you'll notice over here is that when the teams call for suppressive fire, they want it *close!* Much closer than any troops back across the border call for it. I once had a team in trouble call for fire within thirty meters and 360 degrees of their position. My God! Thirty meters. That's enough to make you get down real low before you squeeze the trigger or punch the button. Before I got here I figured I was giving real close air support if I fired within a hundred meters of the friendlies. If these guys have a hundred meters they don't even bother asking for fire support. They figure they can either outrun or evade whoever's after them!''

We cruised for another half hour until I was reasonably confident that I could find my way about. It was to be my first and last dual flight into the area, since we didn't have the manpower available to squander in that fashion. It would be strictly on-the-job training from now on.

The Quan Loi airstrip appeared as a red scar on one of the old rubber plantations. Jake greased the airplane onto the pitted strip and immediately pulled the turboprops into full reverse as soon as the gear was on the ground. I soon saw why. Halfway down the runway there were several deep holes and ruts where the thin layer of asphalt had worn through to expose the bare red earth. There were refilled mortar holes that had sunken again with the rains, leaving a circular rim of ten to twelve inches to negotiate on landing. Semiliquid mud from a recent rain created several speed bumps across the strip.

Jake steered the aircraft from one side to the other, trying to miss the larger puddles and holes. Mud had been flung up by the reversing props and now nearly covered the windscreen. He taxied us into a small revetment only a few meters from the strip. Several muddy wraiths appeared from behind a sandbagged wall and one of them directed us to a stop. They were all shirtless and covered with a layer of red mud, ranging from the thickness of butter on toast to about an inch. The only relatively clear spots were their faces, which they had wiped with the muddy GI towels they wore around their necks.

"You ought to see it here in the main part of the wet season," Jake said as he shut down the engines. "The dry season is almost ready to start up."

I opened my canopy and almost recoiled from the supersaturated air as it hit my lungs. My God, I thought it was hot at Lai Khe! This was almost unbearable. I could feel sweat gushing from every pore. A grimy face grinned at me from the ground below the cockpit. I handed him my map case, inserted my safing pins into the ejection seat, then clambered down. My boots sank six inches into the red muck.

Jake introduced the ground crew. They stood in an awkward circle around me, grinning like schoolboys. One even dug the toe of his boot into the mud and squirmed it around, digging a small hole. Are these the people, I wondered, that the squadron commander expects to be in pressed uniforms and freshly shaven? How could anybody tell under that mud? I wondered if the CO ever came up this way.

"Are you black?" I asked one of them. He had so much mud on him it was difficult to tell.

"We're all red up here, Major," he giggled. The others thought he was Bill Cosby. They repeated it to one another a few times. It seemed to get funnier with the retelling. We chatted and joshed for a few more minutes until Jake came up with the jeep and they helped me pitch my gear aboard. We drove toward the hootch, trying to beat another thunderstorm that didn't know the rainy season was supposed to be over. I could imagine what the place would look like after a couple of months of dry weather. Dustbowlville.

The base camp was a miserable place, with sagging tents and rain-rotted hootches randomly thrown back under the rubber trees. Bunkers collapsed of their own weight as the rain soaked in. A strong miasma of burning feces, held close to the ground by the heavy air, assaulted the nose. But it was not strong enough to drive back the hordes of mosquitoes that attacked in a shimmering wave from their breeding places outside the wire. Shell holes dotted the base camp like pimples on a teenager. Above all, though, was the mud. It was everywhere and in everything. It got on you and in you. There was no way to get away from it. Take a step and it was sucking at your boots. Reach for something and it would be covered with mud. Swallow something and it would be in your mouth. I thought with longing of the clean, dry club at Bien Hoa with the air-conditioned motel-like rooms. Di An had been good. Lai Khe had been tolerable. Quan Loi was like something out of a Conrad novel. I half expected Kurtz to come scowling out of the trees.

Yet, everyone I had met and seen thus far seemed cocky and full of vinegar. There was a certain strut to the young air cavalry troops we met along the muddy road, a sauciness that I hadn't seen before. They whipped up sharp salutes as if they were doing it because it was their idea, not because they had to. They looked good. I commented on this to Jake.

"Yeah, they *are* good. They're aggressive, and you won't find any of that crap about faking patrols and stuff like that, the way you do in some of the other units. I FACed for them for a couple of months before I came on board with the spooks, and I don't think there's a better bunch of soldiers in this army. Well, here's home!"

It was difficult to distinguish the hootch from its surroundings. Rotten sandbags and rocket boxes filled with soil almost completely covered the sides of the tin-roofed structure. A huge aircraft drop tank stood on a rickety frame behind the building, probably constituting the water supply. More crumbling sandbags and boxes covered an underground bunker outside the front entrance. A well-worn trail leading to it from the hootch attested to its use. Supply pallets were placed by the parking area to keep the vehicle drivers and passengers from disappearing into the churned mud as they dehorsed.

Stepping out onto one of the wooden pallets, I felt it settle further into the mud as I gazed around my new home. It looked as if nature were trying to reclaim it and hide the man-made ugliness, for small bushes and grasses fought to keep their heads above the red muck. Incongruously, a beautiful red flame tree bloomed gloriously behind the hootch. Helicopter web seats sat forlornly under the tree's meager branches. Some sort of metal apparatus, which looked as if it had started life as part of the springs in a jeep seat, formed a homemade grill standing on legs constructed of C-ration cans. A lidless porcelain commode stood in splendid isolation atop a small man-made hill, with only a thatched roof to keep out the elements. Farther back toward the perimeter wire was a standard GI outhouse, leaning outward as if it were trying to escape. A nearby hole most likely created by a mortar round provided a handy trash receptacle. A sullen Vietnamese woman scrubbed lackadaisically at a mud-encrusted set of fatigue pants, hardly bothering to give us a glance.

Inside, the normally open-bayed concept in GI living had been modified into an arrangement of single rooms, divided by sandbags and more filled boxes stacked to create many smaller bunkers within the building. The heat inside was almost unbearable. Unchanged from the standard model hootch was the one large dayroom at the end of the building—

except the walls of sandbags made it dark and gloomy. The walls, where visible, were tastefully done in a collage of nude women torn from magazines, most of whom showed some damage from shell fragments, thrown knives, and in one case what appeared to be teeth marks. Several cases of beer were stacked in one corner, and schedule boards for aircraft, men, and maintenance leaned against the sandbagged walls. The planks of the floor were wet, indicating that the Vietnamese woman had made some effort to remove the mud. She hadn't been very successful.

"Charming," I told Jake.

He grinned. "I thought you'd like it. Especially after we spruced it up for you."

"Just what was it you did to spruce it up? I'd hate to miss that."

"You mean you didn't notice the fresh fronds over the crapper? Baby Henry will be hurt."

"Well, let's just let it be our little secret then. I'd hate to get off on the wrong foot with someone named Baby Henry."

I retired to my minifortress to unpack, which consisted of putting the pictures of Mary Ann and the kids on top of the tiny field desk, a luxury that was mine by right of command. Everyone else had to make his own. I hung my gear and spare clothes from several nails and spikes that had been driven into the wooden beams and sandbags. I walked outside, past Jake who was on the field phone trying to get everyone together, to the spot opposite my cubicle. I began tossing the sandbags and boxes aside until the outside air could once again flow into my sleeping area. The enemy may kill me, but damned if I was going to live like a complete mole.

By the time I had everything to my satisfaction, most of the TACP had turned up and were busy trying to make enough coffee to go around. I rejoined them in the dayroom. Some were in flight suits, others in camouflage fatigues. Most had on flop hats and there was an abundant supply of knives and revolvers in view. I already had heard that on this base camp everyone was required to be armed at all times. The officers were young for the most part and very muddy. Mustaches, thick and thin, sprouted under their noses like caterpillars trying to get out of the rain. It looked like a clan meeting between the Kallikaks and the Jukes.

Introducing myself, I gave the usual "I'm so happy to be here in Quan Loi . . ." speech. They didn't believe it any more than I did. We discussed how things would run with Jack, the next senior man, continuing to act as the brigade ALO as he had been doing since the loss of their commander. I assured them that as the senior officer I retained all rights and responsibilities that went with the position and that they would have my support in operational and administrative matters. But I would be flying with the Pretzel group, and its operation would take up most of my time. They didn't bat an eye. They knew to a man exactly what was going on, just as I had suspected.

"Look," I said. "I came up here to run the Pretzel program. You all may know or think you know what it's all about. That's fine. Just don't discuss it among yourselves or with anyone else. The mission is highly classified, and American lives could be put into jeopardy if the wrong people get wind of it. Those of us flying the mission will try to be as discreet as we can, but obviously we don't have a secure briefing room and storage area for our maps. Just try to keep your eyes and ears away from us when it's obvious we have something to discuss. From time to time we may have to take replacement aircraft away from you, but that'll be done only in emergencies. Any operational policy questions you have, take 'em to Jack. For all practical purposes he's your ALO and the one you have to please. I'll still make those decisions that affect the entire group of us. It's unorthodox, but that's the way it's going to have to work. Any questions?"

We talked a few things through, and I spent the rest of the day getting the feel of the place. A courtesy call to the brigade went smoothly. The commander had spent a previous tour with SOG and obviously wanted the teams to secure as much information as possible about those enemy units facing his across the border. We discussed the command setup, and I was relieved to find that he had no objections to our arrangements.

My final stop of the evening was the 1900 briefing at the Mobile Launch Site (MLS) of Command and Control South, accompanied by Steve and Jake. It was actually a compound within a compound. The Special Forces had staffed it with hired Nung Chinese mercenaries.

As I walked down into their bunkered command post, ducking into the low-roofed room, I immediately felt the sweet coolness of two large air-conditioners squeezing the water from the air. Confident, fit-looking Americans, most wearing their green berets, bustled around the maps on the wall. Their jungle fatigues were crisp and clean and their boots were shined. They were about my age, in their early thirties, and their sleeves were covered with chevrons of rank. You could almost smell the excess testosterone they generated.

The commander of the permanent American cadre at Quan Loi, Burl, was a short, stocky man with a well-developed sense of humor. I was to find in the months to come that he was perhaps the hardest man I'd ever known. He was assisted by another officer, his XO, and several sergeants to run the different sections. They were all veterans of the cross-border operation. The teams were only at CCS in a temporary status for the preparation, the mission, and its debriefing. They were then returned to their parent headquarters, Command and Control South, up-country.

Helicopter support was provided by one of the army aviation groups at Long Binh, the crew members permanently stationed at CCS, as was the air force OV-10 faction. The Broncos had only been in use in this sector for a short time. The army also provided two O-1 Birddog aircraft and pilots for radio relay.

We sat through the briefing, and it became obvious that this was a skilled and competent group. The NCO briefers were tough, cocky men, each very sure of himself. Burl kept things moving with an occasional caustic remark delivered in a slow speech hinting of the deep south. Two new teams were in camp preparing for the next insertion; only the American members of the team were attending the briefing.

A critique of the day's hot extraction began the briefing, with the team leader, a master sergeant, starting off. I was surprised to see that a member of his team was a first lieutenant. I was to find that this was not unusual. The sergeant was blunt in his criticism and praise. Each team member in turn described his view of the operation. The helicopter air commander took the small stage after the team had aired their views and was equally candid about everything he had observed. Steve, as the air force FAC overhead, followed him, although he had little to add since he was involved only to a minor degree in the day's festivities.

At that point Burl took over and recapped the mission—its good and bad points and lessons learned. Then he began the brief for the next day's operations. Following the other pilots' lead, I too began to make note of places, times, and altitudes. I checked them against my maps without actually copying anything onto them. Everyone seemed terribly casual about the whole thing, including the team members who joined a poker game after the brief was over.

Burl took me by the arm and steered me toward the new hootch he'd just had built. It was about eight feet by eight feet, a perfect square. Inside was his bunk, an army field desk, and one of the most elaborate stereo systems I had ever seen. It completely covered one wall, with speakers aimed at me from every direction around the room. He began to describe in detail all the miracles it could perform. It happens that I have the electrical aptitude of a mud turtle. I didn't understand a thing he was telling me but I did like the beer he handed me. It was ice cold. I took a long pull at it and looked at him in wonder.

He smiled. "We managed to liberate an ice-maker from Lai Khe. Of course, we damned near got our asses shot off driving it up here on Thunder Road at night. Have another one, we've got plenty."

Gratefully, I reached for another can. "I thought you guys were only supposed to eat snakes and drink untreated swamp water."

"That's a rumor started by our own PR men," he said, belching mightily. "Actually, we don't live too bad here. At least it's better than one of those damned A-Team camps. I started coming to this place in '63 and it's been a right steady thing since then. Sometimes it seems that I've spent half my life crawling around in some damned swamp or other. So have most of the men here. I'm perfectly willing to let some of the young bucks earn their decorations and leave me back here with this." He fondly patted the nearest speaker.

"How long before you DEROS?"

"Oh, I've still got a few months to go, but truthfully, I'm not in that much of a hurry. I want to get to Hong Kong or Taipei one more time before I leave. There's still a few components I want to pick up. If you can get the time off I'll be glad to have you go with me."

"Afraid I can't," I said. "I've already used my R and R to meet my wife in Hawaii."

"Hell, that doesn't matter. The agency has a Herky bird that we can use to fly the teams to an R and R city, providing they survive the mission. Give 'em five days there, then they go back to prepping for the next one. It's probably the only reason we can keep the crazy bastards doing it. There's always plenty of room to stow away on the bird."

"You mean CIA? Is that who's running the Hercules?"

"Didn't anybody brief you on all this shit?" Burl asked, looking at me wonderingly, as though I were a bright child who just said something incredibly stupid. "We never use that name. Let's just say that we don't take operational orders from the army. And no matter what the Air Force says, you don't either. They just provide the resources, and if they try to hold out on you in that regard, just let me know and I'll get in contact with somebody who's got the muscle to pull their chain. The army tried to do it with us on the helicopters and crews until MACSOG started whispering sweet nothings into the ears of some folks back in Langley. When somebody tells you that we've got the highest authority behind us, that's exactly what they mean.''

I didn't say anything about how I felt about the highest authority crap. He might have shut off the supply of cold beer.

"I need to get some things straight with you," I told Burl, "on just what we're supposed to be doing up here. Lay it out in simple terms so that even I can understand it. And why are they hiding the operations anyway? I mean, of course it makes sense to tie maximum secrecy to the assigned target area. But that's just a tactical move, not a policy statement. Not that it matters too much anymore because I'm here, but I'd like to get your thinking on it.''

He sighed and reached for two more beers, punched holes in both, and handed one to me.

"I think the assholes do it out of habit as much as anything else. Either that, or they're afraid of losing a few votes from people who wouldn't vote for them anyway. Personally, I've given up trying to reason why they do a lot of things. Maybe the President's or the Defense Secretary's wife is on the rag or something. Who knows? But, that's the way they say to do it, so that's the way we do it. For sure, old Charley knows we're wandering into what used to be his private orchard.''

"OK, I think we're beating a dead horse. Tell me about the missions.''

"The way I see it," he said as he hunched forward, "the OV-10 can be the most flexible thing we've got up here. You people can stay airborne at least twice as long as the Hueys and you've got more than twice the speed. You can carry quite a bit of armament, and you've got a radio setup that would make a command post jealous. One of our biggest problems has been that if and when the team is compromised, we haven't had anything that could react quickly enough to give them immediate help. The army O-1s don't carry shit, and even if we laager the choppers right on the border we've still got a lag time of twenty minutes or so before the first guns can get to them. That's a pretty important twenty minutes. Pretty often it's twenty minutes too late. Now, if we have an OV-10 flying within twenty klicks of the team, he could be there in a couple of minutes with at least enough support to maybe help them hold out until the guns can get on station.''

He paused for another long pull on the beer can. "Then too, we'd like to get some day and night recce out of you folks. There's also a requirement for y'all to do the BDA for the Arc Lights across the border.

A lot of the recce can be done while you're flying radio relay for a team. You may know that even in the chopper alert area we can't hear from the team on the ground; it all has to be passed through you people or the army O-1s if they happen to be on station. We can also use your pilots to give the teams a navigational fix when they need it. They're often in areas so thick that they can't find squat to navigate on, so it's helpful if you can fix their position and pass it to them. You have to be real careful about that though, because flying in a circle over them will sure as hell compromise their position. And everything has to be coded, because the NVA monitors all of our radio transmissions in this area. There may be some other odds and sods, but that's generally what we'd like to get from you and your people. Is there anything else I can tell you?"

"Yeah, something close to my heart. What happens if an aircraft goes down across the border? Is there any plan to get the people out?"

"I give you my word on this," Burl said, looking directly into my eyes. "As long as there's a chance in hell of pulling the pilot or crew out of there, then we'll be doing it. If need be, I can have the Mike Force loaded and airborne in fifteen minutes. It's not big but they're all experienced people. I'm going to be straight with you on this though. If I decide that there's no way we can effect a rescue, I'll order the gunships to fire at you to prevent the enemy from getting their hands on you. I can't risk having any of the teams compromised if they take you alive."

Well, I did ask. I mulled over what he had said as I sipped my beer. I guess it was better than having to tote a cyanide pill with you and forever wonder if that really was an aspirin you just took for your hangover.

"OK," I said. "From what you just told me, I need to ask two things of you."

"What's that?"

"First, I'm going to need at least one more plane and pilot assigned to this mission."

"You've got it," he said immediately. "What's the other thing?"

"You've got to promise to give me time to put on a blindfold before you start shooting rockets at me."

One of the radio operators shook me awake just as the dawn was breaking the next morning, pulling me from a dream that I'd just as soon have continued. The word had been radioed that the division ALO, a bad-tempered lieutenant colonel, would be arriving within the half hour and that I'd better, by God, be on hand to tell him why he was having to deliver one of the division aircraft to me. In addition, where in hell did I get off requisitioning another pilot.

Throwing on my flight suit, I called Burl to explain my predicament. He brushed it aside and told me not to worry. That was fine for him; the ALO didn't write his effectiveness reports. However, by the time he'd arrived there was a message waiting for him to call the group commander immediately. I drove him to our control room to place the call. It was not a pleasant ride. Glancing at him out of the corner of my eye I watched him chew ferociously at his cigar. Why did so many ex-SAC men smoke cigars anyway? To emulate Curt LeMay?

I left the room while he made his call. Emerging, he was more subdued but no more pleasant. You could tell it was like pulling teeth, but he told me that I had the airplane and another pilot, to be drawn from the resources of the local brigade. I saw him off in the backseat of one of the local FACs, whose mission was going to be interrupted by the delivery of his scowling passenger back to division headquarters. The pilot looked decidedly unhappy with the conversation coming over the aircraft's intercom.

One team was to be inserted in midafternoon with Jake scheduled to cover. There wasn't a lot we could do during the immediate insertion; the gun teams were on station and if the ground fire was too heavy they would bring the team back out to try again at another location. If things went well, Jake would remain above them for approximately three hours until relieved. Since we had an additional aircraft now, I decided to launch with Jake and get familiar with the process. Steve would take off in three hours to remain above the team—if they were successfully landed—until they were secured or bedded down for the night.

We gave the aircraft a thorough preflight inspection and then watched as one of the Special Forces NCOs keyed our KY-28 secure radios for the day's frequency. This allowed us to talk between the aircraft and the ground without fear of being monitored. Through some miracle of electronics, the signal was scrambled and then put together again into intelligible speech. Anyone trying to listen in got a weird, static-filled screech in his earphones. We could hear each other very well, although it did sound as if we were talking inside a barrel.

Preflights completed, we sat on the revetment and watched the helicopter crews and team members arriving. I was surrounded by our own ground crew, who made cheerful complaints about the clouds of pipe smoke I was sending up. I was starting to recognize them by the mud patterns they wore.

The team members were all dressed alike—jungle fatigues with no markings, NVA boots to confuse trackers, bush hats, and six canteens. The dominant weapon was AK-47s, though one of the Americans carried a silenced Swedish-K submachine gun. The Americans also carried in shoulder holsters what looked like silenced .22 pistols. Stabo rigs were worn to allow the men to be pulled from the jungle on ropes. One American carried a lightweight model radio; he had a small boom mike and headset to allow his hands to remain free to carry his weapon. I noticed that none had slings on their weapons—this eliminated the temptation to put the weapons on their shoulders rather than in their hands where they could be put to immediate use. Their rigs and rucksacks were festooned with smoke and frag grenades, which looked like Christmas ornaments hanging on a tree. Each team member must have been carrying well over a hundred pounds.

The man with the radio waved at Jake and slowly sauntered toward us. Last night they had referred to him as Baby-san. He looked it, having a smooth baby face and short-cropped blond hair. He looked about twenty, though Jake told me later that he had participated in more than thirty cross-border operations in his three years in Vietnam.

"Hi Jake," he called as he walked up to us, the weight of his gear pushing him down into the mud. "Looks like we got a good day for it."

"You're always the optimist, Baby-san," Jake said in return. "I'd like you to meet the new Pretzel O1." We shook hands. He seemed even younger up close.

He grinned at me. "I ought to let you know what I sound like down there." He lapsed into a slow whisper. "If I don't sound like this, then you'll know something is wrong for sure. If I sound like this," he went into an agitated parody of someone gasping for breath, "then you'll know that we've stepped in some shit for sure, so come a'running."

Assured that we would indeed come a'running if he needed us, Baby-san grinned once more and sauntered back to the loading helicopter. We watched him climb aboard and pull his flop hat down firmly, and returned the brief wave he gave us. Jake stubbed out his cigarette and I knocked the dottle from my pipe against a sandbag. We filled our baby bottles with water from the lister bag and were climbing aboard our aircraft as the helicopters began to spool up. I sat in the cockpit and watched them take off, heading northeast. Because of the speed differential, we would follow in a couple of minutes, in time to regain the formation by the time it reached the border.

Jake and I lined up together but made individual takeoffs rather than going in formation because of the maneuvering required to miss all the holes and ruts. After we were airborne, Jake powered back to let me overtake him in a straight line toward the border rather than circling over the field. We kept the formation loose, allowing me to map read en route. He signaled me to switch our radios to the helicopter command frequency. At the same time we set our other radios to monitor the gunship frequency and the team's FM frequency. On yet another radio I listened to Jake report our position to the control room. It would be our last position report until we were back inside South Vietnam.

We intercepted the helicopter formation just south of the border and climbed to stay out of the way, making lazy circles around them. The team members were already sitting with their legs dangling outside the slick. One of them waved at me as I flew by the helicopter. I wiggled my wings in response. Below us the heavy rain forest rose rapidly in elevation to what would become a mountain chain just over the border. I saw the battle-scarred features of the Bu Dop camp slide below us. It was to be used for the helicopter laager after the insertion. From this point on, we were beyond the might and power of any friendly units.

Past the camp the helicopters swung to a predetermined heading that would take them to the primary LZ. The team-carrying Huey descended until it was flying just above the treetops. The four gunships settled into a loose square around the Huey but a few hundred feet higher. At about a thousand feet the air commander directed the low ship toward its destination with a series of terse orders, calling course corrections and distances to touchdown. He had to be higher to see the tiny LZ, which certainly didn't look like the broad, open areas I was accustomed to seeing in a combat assault.

Ten minutes and three course changes later the air commander said, "Forty-four, this is Six. Right five degrees, slow to fifty, five hundred meters ahead."

"Roger Six. Slow to fifty and right five."

High above them I finally distinguished the tiny LZ they were aiming for. It didn't look large enough for the blades to clear the tree limbs.

"Forty-four, this is Six. On course. Slow to thirty; three hundred meters."

"Roger, slow to thirty. Holding course."

I glanced around to make sure of Jake's position. He was on the opposite side of the circle from me. I eased the stick back to get a little more vertical clearance between us. We hadn't spoken for the entire flight.

"Forty-four, this is Six. Slow to fifteen. Target is directly ahead at fifty meters. Guns, get ready!"

The gunships commenced a slow circle around the slick, which had little forward speed as it now approached the LZ. The team members were standing on the skids, holding onto the helicopter with one hand and their weapons ready to fire in the other. The slick never touched down nor did it come to a hover, but floated slowly over the LZ. First one man, then the remaining five leaped from the skids and disappeared into the foliage below. They would now move as rapidly as possible for half an hour, then go to ground to see if they'd been pursued.

"We're taking fire from the west!" the slick pilot called just as the team jumped.

I saw the twinkle of automatic weapons from the trees on the far side of the tiny LZ. Fortunately, the plan called for the team to depart the LZ toward the east. But they'd been on the ground for only five seconds and already they were compromised.

"We're taking hits!" the slick pilot called as he tried to pull out of the hole in the trees. His speed was very slow and he couldn't continue forward until he had gained enough altitude to clear the large trees to his front. The NVA gunners on the LZ were having a field day. At least three streams of tracers licked their way across his fuselage before the gunships could get in a position to fire without hitting him or the team on the ground. As they started their runs I could see the smoke from their gunfire trailing behind them and the flame as they launched their rockets from their pods.

Explosions in the tree line momentarily silenced the enemy gunners; then they recommenced. Another enemy automatic weapon began to fire from just north of the LZ. The gunship pilots, their voices high with excitement, talked rapidly to one another on their radio frequency, giving directions and calling in points where they saw the guns.

During the assault by the gunships, the slick helicopter had managed to clear the trees. With its nose tucked down, it was racing clear of the area. The pilot called that he had two wounded on board and was heading for Quan Loi. I was astounded that they hadn't been shot from the air.

With the departure there was another problem. Should the team need an immediate extraction, there was no chopper to get them. Over the radio the air commander called for his reserve team, one slick and two guns, to launch from Bu Dop. At the rate the gunships were expending ammunition they wouldn't be effective much longer. However, there was no choice, for they had to attempt to stop the NVA from pursuing the team if at all possible. If they didn't, there was going to be a very messy extraction attempt.

"Pretzels," the air commander called us, "it looks like we're going to need you until the new guns can get on station."

"No sweat, we're ready," Jake replied.

"OK, wait until these guns leave, then work over the western and northern parts of the LZ, but try to save some of your beebees and rockets if you can. The way things are going, we may have to try to pull the team."

Jake called on the interplane frequency and we made a quick plan. We'd set up a pattern, just like at gunnery school, with one of us attacking just as the other pulled off. We'd fire rockets in singles and use only two of the four guns on each pass. The simple plan constructed, we went back to the small war continuing below us.

The ground fire was growing heavier as the little people brought up reinforcements. No one had been able to raise the team yet, which could be bad or good. They may be dead or they may be running under cover of the fight going on behind them.

Another gunship was limping back toward the border after sustaining numerous hits and a wounded copilot. The remaining three birds all reported battle damage and were nearing the end of their ammunition. The reserve team from Bu Dop reported ten minutes out. I glanced at the clock on my instrument panel. Only seven or eight minutes had elapsed since the team had plunged into the rain forest.

"The guns are out of here," announced the gunship leader. "You Pretzels watch the northern part of the LZ. It looks like they're trying to flank it in that direction to go after the team. You might also try to put a few rockets to the south in case they're going that way and we didn't see them. We're heading back to reload. Hold the fort, guys.''

Still nothing from the team. I watched the air commander's helicopter drift westward, still holding his altitude and awaiting the reserves. Jake's roll-in call brought me back to the situation below us.

I watched the rocket leave the aircraft. His right sponson guns began to fire as I rolled my aircraft into a knife edge against the ground and let the nose slide toward the small clearing. As it approached forty degrees below the horizon, I quickly leveled the wings and bumped the rudder to put the lighted sight in the windscreen on the target, the northwest edge of the jungle clearing. I tried to ignore the flickering lights of the automatic weapons coming from the darkness of the foliage. I shoved the rocket-firing button on the control stick, then rapidly placed my index finger on the trigger to the guns.

I saw movement on the ground north of the dark gray smoke where my rocket impacted. Bumping the rudder once more, I swung the nose a few degrees toward the movement and continued the dive toward the trees. After a two-second burst, the tracers converged toward the target. The trees were getting very close. What's the elevation here anyway? I must remember to check that if I'm going to continue to hurl my pink body at the ground this way. With the stick hard back into my lap, the familiar graying of my vision began. I tried to look at the g-meter, but couldn't with tunnel vision and my head too heavy to turn. Slacking off a little on the stick, I could see the lights and colors start to return, enough to see the tracers flashing by my canopy. Then I was back into a tight, climbing turn. The sun glinted off Jake's canopy as he plummeted toward the ground again, this time from another direction.

He was off and down I went again. The ground fire was getting heavier, seeming to come from all around the LZ now. What we really needed were some bombs for this place, but of course that was out. No fighters across the border. Wouldn't want to offend Prince Sihanouk or the League of Women Voters or whomever.

The new gun team called in after we'd made a dozen passes each, and the air commander herded them toward us. They'd need their full load of ordnance if the team had to be extracted. Where the hell was the team anyway? They still hadn't checked in.

Jake and I continued our attacks, more interested in keeping their heads down than in creating casualties. Just keep Charley off the team until they can break loose.

Baby-san's voice broke in on the ground frequency. It sounded like he'd been running hard. His voice was ragged and he was gasping for breath. He was difficult to understand even when we stopped attacking to listen.

"Six, they're right behind us. We're running southeast and not sure exactly where we are, but we've been heading in this direction since launch. At first there were only a couple of them and we thought we could lose them, but now there's a big bunch. Ahh! It sounds like they're about fifty meters to our rear and we're having to move fast. Haven't had a chance to hide. We're going to need help pretty quick. I don't think we're going to be able to stay."

"Roger that," the air commander replied. "Just keep going in that direction and you'll be coming to a dry streambed pretty quick." The command helicopter was already herding the freshly arrived reserves in that direction like a hen with new chicks. "When you hit that streambed," he continued, "drop smoke and turn due east. Go in that direction for about another 150 meters and you'll hit an area where the trees aren't that tall. It looks like secondary growth. We can't get a bird in, but we can get you out on strings if you can get there. As soon as we've got your smoke in the streambed, we're going to start massaging the LZ. Be ready for pickup as soon as you get there because we've only got a light gun team and Pretzel is running short on ordnance. Let's do it right the first time. You got all that, Baby-san?"

"Yeah, I've got it," he gasped. "But, as soon as we hit the streambed we're going to stop and give them about two minutes of all the fire we can put out. That might make them pull their heads down enough to let us make the turn without them seeing us. If we don't, I don't think they're going to give us time to get pulled."

"OK, Baby-san. It's your call."

We followed, for there was little point continuing the attack against the old LZ. Anyone still there was no longer a player in the game. I saw the streambed and due east of it the slight dip in the treetops where the helicopter would try to pluck the hapless team. Jake and I shifted into another wide circle that encompassed the helicopters, the new LZ, and the team somewhere below us running for their lives.

Several minutes passed; then with the sound of rifles firing on automatic in the background came the terse message from Baby-san: "Smoke's away!"

"I've got Goofy Grape," the air commander said.

"That's affirm," responded Baby-san.

I had watched the six figures tumble into the streambed, take up positions, and begin firing back into the bush. As the smoke began to rise, all but one leaped to their feet and began a ground-eating lope on a compass heading of east. The remaining figure continued firing for another minute, then leaped up and followed his comrades.

"Pretzels, you guys want to start cleaning your tubes around the pickup zone? I'd like to save the gunships for the extraction."

"You bet," Jake answered quickly, already rolling in for his first pass.

I was in right behind him, releasing my rockets just as soon as he had started his pullup. We knew we had time for only a couple of passes each. The second time in I watched his remaining rocket salvo, exploding against the tree line opposite the point where the team should emerge. I spaced mine out two at a time, taking the north side of the LZ. Jake made a tight pullout and was quickly firing his machine guns into the foliage. I took the south end and on pullout announced, "Pretzels clear!"

"Here we come!" Baby-san yelled, not trying to keep his voice down anymore.

"We're ready! Twenty-two, start your approach."

The slick pickup ship floated over the slight opening and came to a hover just as the small group of men burst from the jungle. Quickly, they ran beneath the hovering aircraft, which was blowing the smaller trees and grass into a flattened arc. Ropes were thrown through the open hatchway and the men quickly attached them to their rigs while continuing to fire back into the darkness under the trees. One made a waving motion with his hand and the helicopter began to rise. The dangling figures continued to fire into the trees. The gunships darted in frantic circles around the slick, firing their guns and rockets randomly into the undergrowth, trying to keep the enemy's heads down until the slick was clear. The rescue helicopter had barely gained enough height to allow the dangling men to clear the treetops when it stopped its ascent, tucked its nose down, and accelerated toward the border. The guns fired a final salvo into the clearing, then turned to join the slick. Jake and I, now toothless, followed at a reduced speed, but still overtaking the formation.

"Looks like they're going to drag 'em all the way to Bu Dop," Jake said. "Not much need of us staying up here any longer. Besides, I took a few rounds back there and I'd like to get back and check over the bird. OK with you?"

It was plenty OK with me. I was getting the after-action wearies! My arms and legs felt numb, and my brain felt as if it were overloaded and wanted to shut down. I glanced at the clock and saw that we had been airborne just under an hour. Somehow it had seemed much longer than that.

"Will they try to put them in again?" I asked.

"Yeah, but they'll probably wait a day or two. Let 'em have a chance to calm down a little first. There's still the other team that goes in tomorrow, so this bunch will probably go in the day after that. Really a lot of fun, ain't it?"

"Yeah, really a lot of fun."

Jake and I accelerated and moved past the helicopters now approaching the border. Jake took us down to the treetops and we crossed the invisible line; then we aimed at the deserted camp where the first group of helicopters was rearming and refueling at a leisurely pace, having been informed that their services would no longer be required. Following Jake's lead, I did a low aileron roll as we flashed over them. The crews answered the greeting with erect middle fingers jabbed skyward, proving their low-class origins. I swear, if it weren't for the Air Force this war would be nothing but a vulgar brawl!

The base camp was shelled heavily that night and sappers penetrated the perimeter wire in two spots, eventually blowing up a couple of bunkers and destroying one of the cav's helicopters before they were killed. The Soviet-made 122mm rockets would scream in for several minutes; after a pause, they would begin once more. This and the counter-battery fire of our own artillery made sleep in the muddy bunker impossible.

By 0300 most of the enemy rounds had stopped. I called the ground crews to meet the pilots on the strip to inspect the aircraft. One rocket round had impacted about fifty meters from the aircraft, causing significant skin damage to one of them. It was bad enough to keep it from flying missions or for that matter even ferrying it to Bien Hoa for maintenance until it had some repairs. I directed our ops officer to get busy trying to get a new bird up here, for I knew that the brigade FACs were going to be very busy come daylight trying to find the rocket locations. The gunners would surely be gone, but they still had to make the effort.

By dawn we had everything squared away once again. We returned to the hootch just as it was starting to get light in the way that can happen only close to the equator. The predawn darkness is so black, it seems to seep into your pores; then, too quickly to be real, the light is there and a million birds are squawking their heads off. Dawn is the best time in the tropics, before the sultry heat of the day turns you into a mindless thing that wants only to get out of the sun. Mosquitoes and other flying insects seem to take a break in that brief period when the sun is just appearing over the horizon. The peace of that time was marred only by the first sticks of helicopters departing for the day's air assaults.

The Pretzel FACs decided that since we were up anyway, this would be a grand opportunity to beg a breakfast at the Special Forces compound. They ate much better than anyone on the base camp, even the brigade staff with their regimental silver. The air force bunch mooched food wherever we could since we had no regular messing facilities. It was beg or eat C rations, and after a few months of ham and limas everyone would whimper and snivel to get an invitation to a real meal. An invitation to Burl's mess was a coveted experience, for he had a Vietnamese and a Chinese cook, paid for out of God-knows-what funds. They prepared excellent meals from an unlimited store of foodstuffs that the Special Forces always seemed to have available. There was also freshly brewed coffee and cold beer for those with a reason to get inside the compound. We tried not to wear out our welcome, but the food was so good that we shamelessly wheedled every meal we could out of them.

My eyes felt puffy and full of sand as we drove toward CCS. Odd, I thought, most noncombatants never recognized one of the most real dangers in combat—lack of sleep. Most of the men I knew were in a state of chronic exhaustion. I'd seen pilots go to sleep in their ejection seats while waiting for a scramble. As near as I could figure, I'd had about nineteen or twenty hours of rest in the last week. Our last briefings were usually about midnight, when the missions were firmed up for the next day's flying. We usually got to bed about 0200 but were often jarred from our sleep by incoming or outgoing artillery fire. Many nights we got no sleep at all. Everyone was up by 0530 in the morning.

The war, I thought, and all its hard decisions affecting the lives of others, is being run by exhausted men whose judgment had to be questionable under such circumstances. I wondered how much the lack of sleep had played in some of the momentous events in military history. Would there really have been a "Damn the torpedoes. Full speed ahead!" if the old admiral had had his eight hours of z's the night before? Would Henry V have thrown his modest army at the French at Agincourt if he hadn't spent the entire night gabbing with his staff? Would I drift off and fall out of this jeep? I forced my mind to think of the fresh eggs we were going to scrounge at CCS.

We pulled into the guarded gate at the CCS compound and instantly knew that something was wrong. The Nung mercenary guarding the gate was very nervous and swung his carbine at us as we attempted to enter. He knew us all by sight and never had done such a thing before. Looking through the bamboo wall we could see that the compound had taken one of the rocket rounds from last night's attack. I could hear Burl before I saw him.

"Can we come in?" I yelled through the barrier. Burl's curly head peered around the guard shack.

"Well, let 'em in you chuckle-headed idiot!" he yelled at the guard, who probably didn't understand English but quickly got the intent of the message. We drove into the parking area beneath some of the rubber trees. It was immediately apparent what had happened. Only one rocket had fallen within the compound, but it had landed dead center on Burl's new hootch. His pride and joy, newly constructed of tropical hardwoods, was now a gaping crater about six feet deep and already filling with groundwater. The Japanese stereo system with all its woofers and tweeters had been assigned to that sludge pit in the sky. More than five thousand bucks worth of gear gone in an instant.

Trying to keep my face straight, I said: "Burl, there's something different here but I just can't put my finger on it."

Steve stood at the lip of the crater and solemnly peered down into it. "Are you thinking of putting in a fish pond, Major? If you are, why don't you get some of them big shiny ones, with the real bulgy eyes. They've always been favorites of mine."

"Looks like you've been having some trouble with your neighbors," said Jake. "I guess they finally figured they'd have to do something drastic to get you to stop playing all that awful hillbilly music. I knew it would come to this some day."

Burl glared at us, his eyebrows almost touching his nose with the weight of his frown.

"Very goddamned funny, I'm sure. There must be a hundred goddamned hootches in this godforsaken stretch of shit, and that one-lung son of a bitch had to fall on mine. It couldn't have been on the air force hootch, where all it would have done would be to wipe out a bunch of goddamned perverts and drunkards. Oh, no! It had to find the hootch of a poor but honest army officer who wants nothing out of life but to be left alone and is even willing to tolerate social rejects like y'all in order to insure peace and tranquility. Why the hell couldn't it have fallen on the brigade executive officer? I hate that son of a bitch. Or the chaplain? He doesn't do anything but sit around with his thumb up his butt counting missals and telling everybody they're going to hell. Now, I've got to start all over again, and I guess I'll have to turn to outright thievery this time. Or maybe I could start charging freeloaders like you for all the meals you eat here. By the time I DEROS I'd probably have enough money to replace all my gear. Boys, you're looking at a broken man.''

"Uhh, speaking of eating, do you think you could spare three hungry orphans one of your internationally praised breakfasts?" Jake asked.

"You can have my firstborn if you do," Steve added, "provided you name him after me."

Burl grinned. "Get your sorry asses into the mess hall. Let me get some things straightened out and I'll join you. By the way, we've moved the launch time for the insertion up to 1100. I've got a good feeling about this one. I think they're going to stick.''

The breakfast was superb. We each had three fried eggs with French bread to sop up the yolk. Their coffee was brewed, not the C-ration crap we had back at the hootch. The team that was going to be inserted was sitting at one of the other tables, not eating much, mostly drinking coffee and smoking. We waved as we sat down. Three of the six were American, but they were speaking to the Khmers in their own language. They seemed quite proficient and there was a great deal of laughter and arm waving. They all seemed to genuinely like one another, though it may have been the coming danger that was pulling them closer together. A common threat often does that: An *us* versus *them* attitude develops.

After eating we drove back to the hootch and I watched the sky with a critical eye. It was definitely lowering and the clouds looked swollen with moisture. It was time for the monsoon to be over; often, though, it refused to listen to the climatologist's schedule. The weather shouldn't affect our ability to insert the team, but it could hamper operations if we had to pull them.

At the hootch we separated to do our own assigned chores within the TACP: Steve to the flight line, which he oversaw as the maintenance officer; Jake to an ammo box desk and the world's oldest Underwood, on which he tried to stem the flow of paperwork directed at us; I to the enlisted hootch to inspect it, not for cleanliness but to determine if it was still safe to live in after the monsoonal rains. It was, just barely. If it weren't for the rockets and mortars it would really be easier to live in a tent. The enlisted men's hootch was almost as bad as ours, permeated with the smell of mildew and damp earth.

One of the armorers was stretched out on his cot sound asleep as I walked through. Good for him. This wasn't the Boy Scouts. You had to grab sleep when you could. There was no way we could schedule men for a duty period as was done on the larger bases. If something needed to be done, everybody did it.

Back in our hootch, I asked Baby Henry, a huge FAC for the brigade, to wake me in an hour since I was planning on covering the insertion by myself today. I stretched out on my damp poncho liner covering the mattress and was instantly asleep.

I felt I had no more than closed my eyes when Baby Henry awakened me by kicking the foot of the bunk. The midmorning heat was settling in and my fatigues were soaked through with sweat. I stripped to my skivvies, walked to the back of the hootch to take a whore's bath, then dressed again. I buckled on my pistol belt and slipped into my survival vest, first checking it over, paying extra attention to the two survival radios in the front pockets. Satisfied that all was as it should be, I picked up my parachute harness from the nail it was hanging on and partially buckled into it, leaving the leg straps until I actually entered the aircraft. The parachute itself was built into the ejection seat, and the pilot had only to connect his harness to it on boarding.

At the flight line I watched the helicopter group starting engines, then climbed into the cockpit and buckled in. Today's insertion was to be relatively deep inside Cambodia, so I would delay my takeoff for some minutes after the helicopters left. That would give me plenty of time to catch them before reaching the border and also save a little fuel.

After takeoff and going through a thousand feet, I checked in with the control room and reported airborne using my brigade call sign. I would use ''Pretzel'' only after crossing the border. The radio operators never questioned our final position report at Bu Dop though they must have wondered. They probably knew exactly what was going on as well as the other pilots in the TACP.

I shoved the nose over at 1,300 feet to stay below the cloud base. That really wasn't too low unless you were trying to fight an air war beneath it; it could then become terribly confining. Binh Duong province floated away beneath my wings, an almost unbroken expanse of green except for the ugly red bomb craters, now filled with multicolored water from the rains.

Far ahead, the specks I had been watching turned into the helicopter formation. The reserve team peeled away to begin a descent into Bu Dop, where they would laager until needed. I switched to their frequency.

We flew steadily across the border like a small invasion armada, gradually losing altitude. The formation assumed the insertion spread, with the guns spaced around the slick carrying the team, and the air commander overhead. He began his litany, directing the slick toward the LZ.

"Guns Two is taking ground fire!" one of the gunships called. The NVA gunners might have been trying to really bring down one of the choppers or just to alert their comrades farther north of our impending arrival. Probably some of both. The air commander acknowledged with a curt "Roger" and continued giving directions.

I was with the formation by then and had throttled back as much as I could, trying not to overrun them. They turned on the final heading toward the LZ, the team members taking their places on the skids of the helicopter.

"Come right five degrees. Slow to fifty. Target is six hundred meters." The team was so laden with gear, they looked like caricatures of the Michelin Man going to war.

The calls continued until the slick was over the LZ, a clearing that wasn't actually a clearing, just a thinning of the trees. It certainly didn't look large enough to take a helicopter. It didn't matter.

"We're taking fire from all around the perimeter!" the slick pilot yelled over the radio. I could see his door gunners returning the fire and the gunships already rolling in to help out. I tried to stay out of the way until I was needed.

"Pull out straight ahead," the air commander told the slick pilot calmly. Why shouldn't he be calm? No one was shooting at him!

The Huey accelerated and cleared the area. The air commander spoke again: "Come right twenty-five degrees and stay low altitude. Increase your airspeed to sixty. We're going to try for the secondary LZ." The team had swung back inside the Huey, sitting once more on the floor with their legs dangling outside. In only moments the routine began again.

There was no gunfire from this LZ, and I watched the team leap into the green and let it envelop them. Maybe Charley was taking his siesta or had decided he'd had enough of the war. Whatever, the team was on the ground and the chopper was out without a shot being fired. As a diversion, the slick with its accompanying gunships went to yet another LZ on which a mock insertion was attempted. They took heavy fire as they approached the clearing. The slick ship had a gunner killed and most of his windscreen blown away. He slowed to keep the windblast to a minimum and turned toward the border. The reserves back at Bu Dop were directed to intercept him and escort him back to Quan Loi. The air commander and gunships remained in the area with me until we could determine whether we had a successful insertion. We wouldn't know for half an hour or so.

The time passed slowly as we monitored the wounded chopper's flight back to base camp. Eventually, he announced that he had the field in sight. Moments later, I heard a whispered radio call.

"Pretzel, this is Redeye. Do you read me?" It was my first speaking role in the play that had been unfolding.

"Redeye, this is Pretzel. Read you five square." I had to force myself to speak in a normal voice as I answered. Unconsciously, I wanted to copy his hushed tones—not that it made any difference since he was wearing the stethoscope headset.

"Roger, Pretzel. Redeye has gone to ground. Some people went by about ten minutes ago but they didn't see where we left the trail. Haven't heard anything since then. We're pretty secure but we're going to sit tight until first light tomorrow. Are you going to be on station for a while?"

"Roger, Redeye. I'm on station and will be until I'm relieved in a couple of hours. One of us will be up here till dark or as long as you need us. Anything special I can do for you?"

"Naw, we're going to sit tight. I'll check in every hour or if anything happens, but we look pretty solid right now. Out."

"I'll be around if you need me. Out."

Burl's good feeling had been correct. This indeed did look like a good one. The helicopters peeled off and made for their laager across the border at Bu Dop, where they would stay on alert until dark or until I released them. I climbed to 5,000 feet, where it was cooler and where I'd also be out of small arms range. I surveyed the unbroken rain forest stretching to the horizon in every direction, the tall emergents climbing to well over 200 feet in their attempt to beat the competition for the sunlight. Most of the small streambeds of the watershed had already dried up from the lack of rain. Not a sign of any type of movement beneath the trees. No slash-and-burn farm plots; not even animal trails visible in the undergrowth. The team members have told me that it's not difficult to move beneath the trees, for little sunlight seeps below the second and third canopies, discouraging low foliage. The real jungle appears beneath me only where some human has hacked down the trees and later abandoned the plot. It's reclaimed very quickly by tangled, fast-growing bushes and vines.

By extending my lazy circle and squinting really hard I thought I could see a thinning of the forest to the west, way out on the horizon. It was well off the map so I couldn't confirm it, but I knew there were a few towns and some farming areas in that direction. I followed a train pattern of bombs left by a B-52 air strike. I tried to tally the craters but lost track at fifty-odd.

"Pretzel, this is Redeye. Sit-rep normal. No problems. Out."

I clicked the mike twice in acknowledgment and switched frequencies to pass the situation report back to CCS. I didn't call it to the helicopters, for they'd be monitoring my transmission and would hear anything I passed on. If they did miss it they'd automatically make an inquiry in a few minutes.

Back to my explorations. There were two well-traveled dirt roads cutting through the area. Intelligence said they were now used exclusively by the NVA for transshipment of supplies into South Vietnam. They must be busy little beavers, for the roads appeared to be in great shape. I knew that one of the objectives of the team now on the ground was to implant listening devices along both of those roads. It was an odd feeling to know that there were probably hundreds of eyes down there watching every twitch of my aircraft. Idly, I wondered which would be the best way to go if I had to eject. Would I be better off to try to steer the chute toward the rain forest or the road? Some things it's better to not even think about.

I broadened my circle even more, trying to memorize every prominent point I could find on the ground and relate it to my map. There weren't that many of them. I realized just how difficult it was going to be to find a set of coordinates. I ought to check with Steve and Jake and see what fixes they use.

The air was smooth here at 5,000 feet, so I could steer the aircraft using the pressure of my knees on the control stick while I attempted to orient the map using both hands. The aircraft gains and loses several hundred feet with no hand to correct the elevator pressure, but what did I care? There was virtually no chance of running into another aircraft.

The team checked in again and once more I passed the sit-rep to CCS. The radio operator sounded very cool down there, stuck way the hell and gone in a foreign country and surrounded by folks who would like to do him harm.

I stooged around for one more hour, passing on another ops normal report for the team. Boring. Nothing to see except green, and no ground fire to keep the old adrenaline flowing. Finally, I heard Steve checking in airborne with the control room. Within a few moments we were connected on the secure radio and I passed on what I had to him.

Still bored, I climbed into the sun and lurked, awaiting his arrival. Finally, I saw him well below me, head bent toward the ground, studying the terrain. He was dead meat—the Masked Avenger was about to fall all over him.

Rolling inverted, I let the airspeed build up until it was kissing the red line, and came down vertically at him, whipping by his right side, then using the momentum to carry me back into the loop that would put me on his tail again. He was quick to react, though, and broke hard away from me into a climbing turn. Fool! Doesn't he know the Avenger can't be stopped by mortals?

The fight went on for another five minutes before we broke it off by unspoken agreement. I waggled my wings for him to join up on me, and I showed him the LZ that was used for insertion and about where the team thought they were. Then I waved bye-bye and headed for the border. God knows what the NVA would have thought if they'd seen our juvenile antics. Unless there was a pilot down there. He'd understand.

Approaching the border, I pushed the nose down and the throttles forward until they were against the stops. Crossing at treetop level I aimed for the circle of helicopters sitting on the old abandoned airstrip at Bu Dop. Letting the Bronco sag down to twenty feet, I roared over them and yanked the stick hard back into my stomach, raising the nose until it was sixty degrees above the horizon. Then I slammed the stick to the left side of the cockpit and did three aileron rolls before letting the wings come level. Looking back at the troops I saw they were all on their feet, jabbing their middle fingers in the air once again. Peasants!

That team stayed in place for seven of their ten scheduled days before they were discovered and had to be pulled. It was a mad race to find a suitable LZ. They got out four live ones and two bodies after the team had carried their two KIAs over two miles at a dead run. One of the dead was the American radio operator we all had spoken to every day.

Before this team was pulled, another team was already on the ground in a different sector and two more were in the preparation phase. The days began to run together, distinguished only by how badly frightened you were on a particular mission.

A new face showed up in the hootch one day after I returned from an especially bad mission. Five rounds of machine-gun fire had stitched a neat pattern through the rear cockpit, fortunately unoccupied, but it put me in a foul mood. It wasn't improved by the appearance of our visitor, a large, chubby captain on a visit from one of the B-52 bases in Thailand. We introduced ourselves and I found it remarkable that any person could piss me off as quickly as he did. The Strategic Air Command encouraged their crew members to visit in-country, to see how the other half lived, I suppose. Hell, even our *own* people didn't want to come up here and they never spent the night when they did. This guy was to be our guest for three days.

Immediately, he let us know that he couldn't fly with us because his job as a SAC crew member made him privy to entirely too much top secret material to risk his capture. No one had asked him to fly with us—we didn't want this asshole in the rear seat for any reason. One of our ground crew asked him if they didn't risk capture when they flew their missions out of Thailand. He stuttered a bit in his answer, finally conceding that they flew well over the defenses of the targets they bombed.

"Do y'all get credit for a combat mission after one of those?" Steve asked.

"Oh, yeah!" he replied, adjusting his cowboy gunslinger type of holster around his ample stomach. "We get credit just like the F-4 and F-105 crews do flying out of Thailand."

One small difference, I thought. Those guys are flying into the hornets' nests of North Vietnam and Laos.

"I've already completed one combat tour on Guam. The missions out of there run more than ten hours so I ended up with five hundred hours of combat time logged."

"You mean you log all that over-water time as combat?" Jake asked incredulously. He was leaving the next day for out-processing at Bien Hoa before rotating stateside. "Jesus Christ! Five hundred hours and you've never even been shot at!" Jake probably had a bullet hole in his aircraft for every other hour that he'd flown for a year.

"Well, those are the rules," the copilot said defensively, "and we didn't make them."

Jake stomped out of the hootch in disgust. "Well," I said, trying to be the congenial host, "take a look around. There's not much to see but at least most of the mud has dried up and the dust isn't too thick yet. Rocky's on R and R so you can use his bunk. The food isn't much but we've got plenty of C's and they're not too bad if you don't have to eat them for long. Let me know if there's anything I can do for you." With that I turned him over to the acting brigade ALO and tried to forget about him.

That evening he regaled a circle of avid listeners with stories of life in Thailand. It sounded like paradise to the crowd of young pilots and ground crew listening to him with a mixture of awe and disgust on their faces. He was from a different world—one with bars and USO shows and air-conditioned quarters and cold beer and restaurants. But most important, their twenty- and twenty-one-year-old minds wove a tapestry of a land of lascivious, beautiful women who lusted for such magnificent specimens of manhood as themselves. I'm sure there wasn't one of his audience that night who didn't entertain erotic thoughts of life in Bangkok.

Shortly after midnight the rocket and mortar barrage began, and it was quickly apparent that it was not going to be a light one. Incoming mortar rounds exploded in a random pattern around the base camp between the heavier rocket bursts. The rounds were too close and too many to try for the bunker. I regretted kicking away some of the sandbags from around my bunk to allow the air to circulate. I huddled as close to the remaining bags as I could get.

Between explosions, I became aware of a high, keening wail coming from somewhere in the bowels of the hootch. Someone had been hit badly, I thought. "Who is it?" I yelled down the bay. The wail continued, sounding like a wounded dog, then was replaced by a screaming voice that I recognized as belonging to our guest from Thailand.

"Oh, Jesus! What's happening? Somebody help me! What's going on?" The rockets and mortars continued to fall, some of them getting very close now.

"Don!" I yelled to the senior FAC who had the bunk next to our guest. "Can you tell if he's hurt?"

"I'm crawling that way now," he yelled back. Minutes passed. "He's OK," he finally called, "but I'm not staying here with him. He's shit his pants!"

A chorus of jeers and boos filled the hootch. Don's announcement had rung out during a break in both the explosions and the screams, carrying even across the dirt road to the chopper pilot hootch. One of them yelled into the suddenly still night air, "Who shit in his pants? Was it Jake?"

Jake's voice answered out of the darkness: "If it had been, Mulroney, I'd have left it on your bunk to remember me by. I'm too short for all of this crap!"

"If I had as long to go as you did, Jake, I'd cut my throat," another army pilot called. He and Jake were leaving on the same chopper tomorrow. Or rather, later today. The explosions began again.

About 0200 the attack stopped as abruptly as it had begun. We were finally able to lead our Thailand visitor from his cubicle of sandbags and persuade him that it was safe to go outside and clean himself up a bit. We gave him what sympathy we could, which was very little. We remembered his stories of life in Thailand and were secretly delighted that the NVA had chosen this night for one of their attacks. No one mentioned his accident again during his stay, but he knew and he knew that we knew. That was good enough. No doubt there'd be a highly modified story of his visit when he returned to Thailand.

The box for the B-52 Arc Light target was about fifteen klicks over the border into Cambodia. It was my turn to do the bomb damage assessment, and I was trying to orient my map to correspond to the three long strings of craters on the ground.

I'd come to not expect a lot of the strikes. The NVA were there all right, but any damage was either quickly repaired or hidden immediately. As soon as the raid was over, anyone adjacent to the bomb lines converged on the attacked area to help survivors and remove the dead. The BDA had to be done immediately after the dust cleared or all we'd see was footprints. Occasionally, the bombers would uncover a base camp; we would find the collapsed bunkers but seldom any KBAs. The bomb blasts would fling aside the huge trees and leave the soil around the craters looking like freshly plowed ground. Footprints showed up quite easily.

I finally got the map oriented correctly and began the assessment from the relatively high altitude of 3,000 feet, the better to see where each of the three heavy bombers had struck. All bombs appeared to have been inside the box—the heavy bombers were seldom off by more than a few meters. The attack had taken place as I took off from Quan Loi. Dust was still settling now, some twenty minutes later. With my grease pencil, I scribbled on my windscreen that all bombs were on target. I glanced at the darkened tree lines surrounding the bomb craters. I had little fear of ground fire, for the survivors of an Arc Light were too shook to respond.

Shoving the stick to the side of the cockpit and stomping on the right rudder, I started down to complete the BDA. I figured one pass along each of the three bomb trails, then heigh-ho, Silver! and back to Quan Loi. I leveled at 300 feet just in front of the first bomb crater and pulled the throttles back; I wanted to fly as slowly as I could to give the place a first-class eyeballing. I hadn't realized how long a train of one hundred-plus bombs was. From my low altitude, I couldn't see the end of them ahead of me.

About a third of the way up the first train I saw that the bombers had indeed gotten meat on this one. A crumpled, broken figure was sprawled between the blast area and the tree line. I circled slowly over the still figure. A closer look showed other bodies, many partially covered with soil. The bombs had not only killed them but attempted to bury them as well. I tried to squeeze out a tear or two for these people but couldn't. We'd been trying to kill each other far too long for that.

I continued up the crater string adding bodies to my report. Then I was over what had been a bunker complex. The way the bodies lay they'd probably been moving into or out of it when the attack hit them. It wouldn't have made any difference if they'd been in the bunkers, for the log bunker tops had been blown away and most of the walls collapsed.

At the edge of the complex were three trucks, two on their sides and the other on its back. They were probably used to bring supplies or equipment south. One thing for sure, soldiers hadn't ridden in them. Uncle Ho believed that exercise was good for the troops and they would have walked every step of the way. More than likely they were resting here before their last push across the border.

There were at least thirty-five destroyed bunkers. I added to my grisly tally as I continued to work my way up the first train. Passing over the last crater I turned hard left, staying at 300 feet, to intercept the next bomber's train. It was easy to pick up and I started a new column on my windscreen.

There was nothing to see until I came approximately even with the first bunker complex to the east. These people must have been farther from the blast, for the bodies were not nearly as covered as the others had been. It was obviously a continuation of the first group, probably a long column moving through the rain forest when the hell came at them from above. It looked as if a large scythe had harvested them and they were waiting for someone to come along and stack them into neat piles.

I circled and counted. I almost hated to give the B-52s credit for such an outstanding mission, for they flew so high they had no idea what they were bombing and their only danger was from being bored to death. But, fair's fair. Just so long as someone got the enemy. Anyone who felt differently simply had not been shot at enough. I was perfectly willing to be friends with the Viet Cong and the North Vietnamese if they would just stop trying to kill me. The NVA were as much strangers to this part of the world as I was, after all. I was willing to go home if they would.

Tracks led away from the largest pile of bodies near the ragged tree line. The footprints were easy to see on the soft earth; one set looped back and forth like a sailor tacking against a strong wind. The tracks wandered over one of the newly created clearings and ran directly into the trunk of a large jungle tree blown over by the blast. The tracks stopped and made a tight little circle, as if trying to figure out how the obstacle got there. Smoothed patches in the soil indicated that the person had attempted to scale the log but had toppled back onto the soil, there to scrub around for a while before once more regaining his feet. I was beginning to feel like Leatherstockings!

An interesting development. Tracks number one were joined by another set emerging from the western tree line. The second set didn't appear to be too steady either, but it ran an intercept on tracks number one, finally overtaking them and joining up in close formation. The earth was flattened where both people seemed to have sat or lain for a while. The tracks continued westward very close together, as if one was supporting the other. For no apparent reason the tracks turned south along the disturbed ground of the bomb line.

Suddenly, I was over them. Sure enough, there were two soldiers, one with his arms twined about the other. It was hard to determine who was supporting whom. They stopped and sank to the bare earth as I flashed over their heads, still at a very low level. I put the Bronco into a tight, level turn, trying to keep them in sight. One of them had either an AK or a rifle slung over his shoulder; the other appeared unarmed. The one with the weapon unslung it and tried to track me as I continued the turn toward him. Even at my distance I could see he was having problems keeping his assault rifle in place. His partner was flat on his back and didn't appear interested in what was going on.

I gained a few hundred feet of altitude in the turn and flipped the arming switches to my machine guns. I let my finger lightly caress the trigger as if to assure myself that it was still there. As I completed the turn and rolled out heading toward the pair, I quickly adjusted the mill setting on my gun sight and let it settle just beneath them, then neutralized the rudders. There was no way I could miss them.

The NVA soldier aiming his weapon at me suddenly let it fall from his shoulder and slumped forward wearily, keeping his eyes on my fast-approaching aircraft. He reached out with his left hand and put it on the shoulder of his prone comrade.

I swept over them but couldn't bring myself to fire. I pulled up hard to miss the tall trees, then slammed the stick over viciously to reacquire them. They hadn't moved, except the one kept turning his head to follow me with his eyes. I wanted him to get up and run. Or to fire his weapon at me. I could have done it then. But I knew I wouldn't fire as long as they sat there. It was as if he knew it as well. I passed over them twice more but they were motionless, except for the watching eyes. Dammit, I thought to myself, if the positions were reversed he'd burn my ass for sure. There was no way that I was going to kill these two today though. They may already be dying of injuries received during the raid. If so, good enough. But I wasn't going to do it.

I finished my BDA and made a final low pass over the pair. They still hadn't moved—the one prone, the other on his knees watching me. I made a hard pull-up and waggled my wings at them as I started back toward the border. They made no response.

Presentiment had me by the throat as I strapped into the aircraft. For several days a dark feeling had been within me that was as real as the nausea threatening to overflow from my stomach. At least there was a reason for that, for I was still recovering from one of my periodic attacks of low-grade malaria. I shouldn't have been flying, but the schedule was heavy and the other pilots had their plates about as full as they could handle. My temperature still hovered around a hundred degrees— just about the same as the air temperature, I thought giddily. My eyes still had some of the blurring that came with the disease, along with general lassitude. Hell, I wasn't even sure it was malaria although the doc had said it was. It could have been dengue or a host of other tropical critters that seemed to infect most of the people up here.

Finishing up the cockpit check, I glanced over at the other aircraft to see if Steve was ready for engine start. In an unusual move we were going out together today to try to find a jungle road first spotted by one of the ground teams. If we did locate it, we would try to map it. If it were a transshipment road, it would undoubtedly be heavily defended, the reason for the pair of us.

Steve looked up from the cockpit and gave one nod of his head, indicating he was ready for starting. I gave him a quick twirling of my index finger, telling him to start engines. Another quick glance at my instrument panel and I engaged the starter for the left engine, watching the oil pressure come up and the engine temperature peak. Flicking off the switch, I put that generator on the line and went to the other engine. Everything looked fine, but I couldn't shake the feeling that something was not quite right. I felt light-headed and dizzy, as if I were watching my movements over my own shoulder. I seriously considered shutting down and crawling back into my cot in the hootch, but that would leave Steve to fly the mission alone. I couldn't do it to him.

Jesus, I thought, everybody's playing hurt at this part of the season. I giggled. Before I started to taxi I made a motion to the crew chief that I wanted a drink of water. He finally understood my hand signals and brought a dipper of water from the lister bag. I drained most of it and managed to spill the rest into my lap. He looked at me strangely when I asked for another dipper full.

Finally ready to taxi, I gave the other ship a quick nod and pulled out onto the beaten-up strip. Steve's voice came over the radio: "Lead, is your radio working? They're giving us a red light."

Glancing at the makeshift control tower, I saw that they were indeed giving us a red light. It was blinking at me furiously. My God, I thought, I really must be sick if I pull onto a runway without clearance or even looking to see whether a C-123 might be trying to land on top of me.

"Sorry 'bout that, Tower," I transmitted. "Just a little radio problem." His tone indicated what he thought of that. I wondered what Steve was thinking. Probably that he'd be safer flying this sortie by himself. I made an effort to pull myself together and concentrate on matters at hand. The drink of water seemed to make me feel a little better, but I was sweating even more profusely than usual. I sponged my face vigorously with the GI towel I habitually wore around my neck like a scarf.

The takeoff and climb were normal, and as I turned toward the border I glanced over at Steve's aircraft tucked smoothly next to mine in a tight formation. He was so close that I could see every feature of his face quite clearly. I didn't bother to kick him out into a combat spread. He'd do it himself when we approached the border.

A haze and smoke layer had reduced the slant-range visibility to less than three miles. There was no problem seeing the ground below us, but it was difficult to make out the ground's features a short distance in front of the nose when looking forward. There was probably a temperature inversion aloft, for the haze seemed to stop about 2,000 feet above us, trapped by the higher temperatures. This was not good weather for visual recce, but it might not change significantly until the wet season began. Even so, it was better than dodging thunderstorms throughout the flight.

I trimmed the nose down slightly as we started a descent to cross the border. Steve had moved his aircraft out about a hundred meters and taken station slightly aft and above me.

"Pretzel Two, this is Lead. How do you read?" It was our first contact since he'd warned me about taking the runway against the red light.

"Two's got you loud and clear, Lead. The viz is not very good today, is it?"

"It sucks," I responded. I couldn't tell if I was having a little radio trouble or if the malarial fevers were making my ears ring. "When we get to the area, you plan on staying high and I'll go low to try to root out the road. I'll let you worry about plotting it if we do find it and directing me if I stray too far."

"Wilco. Are you feeling OK?"

"Yeah, I'm great. Let's arm 'em up," I said as we scurried across the border, just above the trees.

Good sense, as well as the USAF's SOP, said that weapons shouldn't be armed until you were ready to use them; however, those seconds were too precious for us to waste by taking our eyes away from our adversaries. At low altitude, the one to survive was usually the one who shot first. Like gunfighters of the old west, if you couldn't be the best shot it helped to be the fastest draw.

With the border some kilometers behind us, I made an abrupt pull-up, leveling at 2,500 feet. This would be our base altitude where Steve would fly and plot the road should we discover it. I didn't bother to look back to see if he'd stayed with me in the climb. I knew that he had.

I aimed for a streambed that showed on our map and that the road was supposed to cross some twenty-five klicks across the border. The NVA would probably have more trouble hiding the crossing than the road under the jungle canopy. I scanned the top of the tree mass. It appeared unbroken except for dry streambeds, which showed as sudden red gashes in the surrounding green ocean of trees.

I picked the most likely streambed and checked it against my map. "Does this one look right to you, Steve?"

"As near as I can tell it's the right one," he answered in his slow drawl. "I sure can't see anything that looks like a crossing though."

"Naw, I can't either. But it's supposed to be where those two streams come together and run northeast and southwest from there. I guess I might as well go down and take a look. Where are you going to be?"

"I'll be circling at base altitude. You sure you don't want me to go down? You were still looking a little peaked at takeoff."

"I'm fine," I insisted. In truth, I was feeling much better. The air flowing in from the ventilation ports seemed to have cooled me down a bit, although I was still perspiring heavily. I mopped my face with the towel again as I studied the minute clearing at the juncture of the two streambeds. There were certainly no tracks visible. I would have been very surprised if there had been. If anybody was down there they'd certainly been alerted by our circling. Couldn't be helped though.

Waving bye-bye to Steve, I put the Bronco over into a steep dive, leaving the throttles full forward. This first pass was just to see if anyone was at home. At 1,000 feet I pulled back hard on the stick. I couldn't see much as I bottomed out at 200 feet, having about blacked myself out. Glancing at the accelerometer I saw I had pulled more than six g's.

"I didn't see any shooting," Steve said.

"I didn't either. I'm going to try to follow the streambed up this time until I get to the junction with the other one. There's wing-tip clearance on both sides if I'm careful."

"OK, but watch yourself. That looks like it's going to be mighty close."

Going up to five hundred feet to keep the streambed in sight, I put the Bronco into a lazy turn, giving myself plenty of room to line up exactly with the dry stream before I went below tree level. As it came dead centered on the windscreen, I rolled the aircraft level and started toward the streams' juncture. I leveled off at fifty feet, too low to tear my eyes away from the trees and the stream bank on either side of me. It was like flying up a canyon. I slowed the aircraft as much as I could, but even so I seemed to flash over the suspected crossing. I had time for only a quick look under the trees to my left, but there it was.

Lifting the nose, I rammed the throttles forward and kicked hard right rudder to miss a huge tree that suddenly seemed to have sprung up in front of me. I skidded around the tree, too low to put a wing down for a normal coordinated turn. My mind replayed the snapshot it had taken of the area beneath the trees. The tracks leading from the crossing had been obliterated, but back under the trees some twenty meters, which the NVA probably thought would be safe from observation, a well-defined roadway pointed to the southwest. I hadn't had a chance to look in the other direction, but I was sure we'd find a road on the northern part of the streambed pointing toward the northeast as promised. Now, we'd have to find out where the damned thing went. I leveled off and rolled out on the opposite side of the large invisible circle Steve was flying.

"I didn't see any shooting that time either," he said, "but I thought you were going to try and fly through that big ole' tree. It looked pretty tight to me."

"Yeah, it was. But the road is there, I think. I only got a glimpse, but I'm sure that's it. It runs in the right direction, and back under the trees there are what looks like ruts. I didn't get a chance to look to the north, but about twenty meters toward the south they've got all kinds of bushes and shit piled up trying to hide it. Lemme complete this turn and I'll go down again and peek the other way."

"Let me, I'm already in position," he said.

"Go ahead. I'll cover," I responded.

He immediately put his aircraft up on its wing and started a dive, flying a parabolic curve that allowed him to pull out and roll his wings level at the same moment to descend neatly below the trees into the dry bed. That old Arkansas boy can fly, I thought.

I watched him nudge his aircraft along the curving streambed until he was over the confluence of the two streams. In an instant he had pulled effortlessly over the tree I had skidded around and rejoined me in our airborne circle.

"Yeah, that's it," he said. "It's just like you described on the other side and it goes in the right direction. It looks like it's in better shape than a lot of the streets back in Texarkana. Think we'll be able to see enough of it to be able to map it?"

"Well, we'll get as much of it as we can. MACV will probably get a recce bird up here to take pictures eventually, but Burl may want to get somebody targeted against it before then. Let's give them as much as we can."

Now that we knew the road's approximate location and direction, we'd probably be able to pick it up in the trees below us. We began to quarter the area, staying at 1,500 feet for better observation. Any lower and we wouldn't be able to pick up irregularities in the trees.

The little people were clever, you had to give them that. On close investigation we saw that their road-building teams had tied the treetops together over the road, pulling them tightly to form a natural camouflage net. A few small things gave them away now that we knew the road was there. During the top-tying routine they had broken some of the limbs, which had turned brown and now showed up against the lush green background. It was like a marker proclaiming the route of NVA 87 or whatever this branch of the Ho Chi Minh Trail was called. Also, though the jungle top appeared to be unbroken, it was not. Looking down through the trees, an occasional glimpse of the red earthen road could be discerned. Dust from the trucks traveling the road had also risen to coat the branches of the trees directly overhead. Looking at the dusty boughs from a certain angle helped us pinpoint the general path.

We tracked the road northeast for several klicks until it appeared to cross a wider streambed, this one still containing a small flowing stream of water.

"I'm going down to take a look," I radioed to Steve.

"Roger. Hey! Wait a minute, I thought I saw a truck! It was just pulling under the trees on the south side of the crossing."

I looked closely but couldn't see anything that looked like a truck. The sun was reflecting off something shiny next to the streambed, however, where the trees were the thinnest.

"Look! There's the tracks!" Steve said excitedly. The more excited he got the thicker his southern accent became. "And the water's still muddy."

His eyes were better than mine, but I looked closely and was able to pick up the muddied water.

"OK, I'm going to make a quick pass and see what we've got," I said. "I'll do it the same way I did before."

I lined up on the streambed some distance out and let the aircraft sag down until I was once again below the tree line. This streambed was wider than the first one, so I wasn't that concerned with wrapping a wing around a teak tree.

A slight bend to the left and the aircraft was over the crossing point. I made a quick correction to keep me clear of the trees and pivoted my head to the left, searching for the truck. It was there, along with a group of others—a whole nest of them. We'd stumbled onto a truck park where the NVA convoys hid during the dangerous daylight hours. I don't really know what they were afraid of; except for the odd B-52 strike, the allied forces never hit anything over here.

I stayed at low level until I was clear of the crossing, then raised the nose until I was just clearing the treetops. I pulled the aircraft around in the first movement of a crop-duster 90-270 degree turn, designed to aim me back at the target but on a reciprocal heading. During the turn, I called Steve.

"We've hit a good one, amigo! There are at least twenty-five trucks down there parked about fifty meters south of the stream crossing. I don't know what's north of the stream. Didn't get a chance to look. Get on the radio to the control room and give them this coded set of coordinates and see if there's any way that III DASC can divert an Arc Light over here. I know damned well they won't send any fighters. The B-52s either, more than likely, but we've got to try. If not, you and I will take them on. I'm coming around for another pass in the opposite direction. Hell, with all those trucks parked to the south they may have a Howard Johnson's north of the stream."

"You watch your ass, Lead. They know we see 'em so they're going to start shooting."

"Roger that!" I was in the final part of the turn that would line me up for the next pass, my down wing tip just clearing the treetops. A little aileron pressure rolled the Bronco upright and I nudged its nose into the streambed once again. A little forward pressure on the elevators and I was below the tree line. The sun was directly in my eyes now, and even though I had the tinted visor of my helmet down over my face, it was still difficult to see the trucks. That delayed me in turning my head to look north of the stream.

I shouldn't have waited. As I turned my head to the left I looked down the barrel of an antiaircraft gun. I pulled the stick back hard into my belly, knowing even then it was too late. There was no way for them to miss at that range. They'd probably been tracking my engine noise throughout the turn after I made the first pass, and they were lined up and ready. Oddly detached from the scene of impending doom, my mind considered the fact that the gun was probably a 37mm.

In the two or three seconds it had taken me to recognize the gun and get the stick back, the aircraft had barely started to respond to the climb command before an orange blossom grew out of the barrel of the weapon.

Things happened. I didn't know what. I wasn't in the aircraft anymore but dangling from the straps of a parachute. I didn't think that I had time to pull the ejection handle, yet here I was. I was conscious of a high-pitched, screaming roar behind me and tiny pieces of hot metal burning my clothing. The trees were just below me and I twisted my head in time to see my aircraft impact into the rain forest, shedding pieces as it went. It was the source of the roaring sound I'd heard. I hadn't realized how loud the Bronco engines were. A loud explosion and then a ball of flames marked its grave. The tops of the trees were coming up much too rapidly. It's not fair. I haven't had time to get things sorted out properly.

I drifted below the highest tree canopy just as additional explosions began in the direction of my wrecked Bronco. Probably the rockets cooking off. Training and instinct took over, for it certainly wasn't rational thought that made me cover my face with one arm and cross my legs at the ankles to keep from straddling a tree limb on the way down. I was trying to remember the correct position for landing in a parachute as they taught it in the survival school. Then I hit. Very hard.

The transition to earth was almost more than my befuddled brain could take in. One moment I'd been sitting in a very familiar airplane; seconds later I was dangling from a parachute; in another few moments I was sitting on my backside on the floor of a jungle with my legs splayed out in front of me like a little girl playing jacks. I wasn't handling it at all well.

I continued to sit, turning my head slowly to look around me, only there was nothing to see. It was as if I'd been dropped into a green barrel. My detached frontal lobe noted, however, that my eyesight seemed sharper. It was as if I suddenly had increased my perceptive powers. The shadows seemed darker and more crisp; the contrast between them and the filtered sunlight seemed heightened. My mind dwelt on the trivia—the trees, the bushes, and lianas. They weren't just green, but many shades of wonderful green. I became increasingly aware of the contrasts around me.

It was the shout that brought me back to reality. First one voice, then the answer by another. In Vietnamese. What did I expect, Swahili? Of course it would be Vietnamese. They weren't too close but not so far away that I couldn't hear the voices distinctly. I spoke no Vietnamese but I was sure what they were saying: "Nguyen, you go that way and I'll go this way and we'll blast the running dog as soon as we flush him from his hidey-hole."

Steve discouraged this strategy by unloosing a pair of rockets in their general direction. I doubt that he'd seen them but he must have seen something. Steve! I'd forgotten all about him. I clawed frantically at one of the two emergency radios we all carried in our survival vest. Ripping one of them from its pocket I hurriedly raised the small antenna and switched on the set. Oh God! I thought. If only I've remembered to keep the batteries fresh. I didn't dare look, for I'd have wept if they were out of date. I waited anxiously for the set to warm up, plugging the small earpiece into my ear. No, that didn't fit. Maybe it'd be better if I took off my helmet *before* I tried to insert the earpiece. That's better.

Mentally, I grabbed myself by the jacket front and gave myself a good shaking. Steady down, man. You're not dead yet. But here you sit thrashing around and there could be someone five yards away staring at you right now. Think! Sit and listen quietly for a while. Steve's not going to run off and leave you. He knows what it's like because he was on the ground like this himself not very long ago. What was it he said? The last thing you want to do is to move around because it's the movement that attracts attention against the wild backdrop of the jungle. That's why I'm wearing these camouflage clothes, isn't it?

Oh my God! The chute! All they have to do is look for the chute and they'll find me at the end of it. Looking up, I saw it was snagged on some branches about ten feet over my head. I became aware that I was still connected to that nylon anchor and slowly began to unbuckle the harness. Five buckles and clips and I was free to slide the harness from my body. The chute still hung there though, in plain sight, a beacon to anyone looking for me. I didn't know what to do about it, for sooner or later they were bound to discover it and, consequently, me. But if I tried to pull it down now, the noise would surely give away my position. I solved the problem for the immediate future by ignoring it. There were plenty of other things to worry about anyway.

My landing impact had cleared a body-sized area in the undergrowth. I cautiously got to my knees and pried apart some of the foliage wall to peer out. More foliage peered back. Three sides of my burrow were walled with various sizes of bamboo mixed with other dense jungle growth. The remaining side was more open but the obstacles were thicker. I could see perhaps twenty meters in that direction but less than ten any other way.

Steve's airplane roared directly over me, probably seeking some kind of life around the clearly visible parachute. I hadn't heard him coming when he overflew me, so I had made no movement. I knew that he'd go over another area so as not to give away my position, then come back. I decided to call him, using the noise of his engines to cover it, when he made his next pass.

My earpiece had fallen out, but I managed to find it and get it back into my ear after fumbling the attempt several times. My gloves were covered with the damp soil of the rain forest, which I managed to get into my ear along with the earpiece.

I rehearsed what I was going to say. I couldn't say what I really wanted to: "*Get me out of here!*" The aircraft sounded as if it were on the far side of the circle, away from my location. Fear had dried my saliva to the point that my tongue was sticking to the roof of my mouth. My God, I won't be able to talk. Frantically, I fumbled in my baggy side pocket where I normally carried three baby bottles of water, but I must have lost them when I was blown from the aircraft. I remembered the two soda-sized cans of water in the survival vest. I tore one out and opened it with the small can opener I carried on my dog-tag chain around my neck. I took a tiny sip and rinsed it around my mouth before I let myself swallow. It was torture not to gulp it down.

Listening carefully for the aircraft engines to head my way, I realized Steve was stooging around another area, trying to distract the NVA from my real position. It would still be a few minutes before he would again overfly me. I decided to do a hurried inventory of what had survived the parachute descent. I didn't bother to check the survival vest; it could wait. Besides, it was designed to stay intact on bailout.

Immediately, I noticed that my pistol was gone. The strap holding it into the holster had broken, probably when the chute opened, and allowed it to slip free. It was a small loss. My eleven-inch K-Bar knife was still in its leather sheath on my web belt. My wallet with my ID card, family pictures, and a handful of MPC and piasters was still intact. There were my dog tags, wedding ring, and can opener on the chain around my neck. I had my pipe and tobacco pouch but was missing my Zippo lighter. There were also about twenty bullets for my missing pistol in a leather pouch on my belt. All in all, the inventory pointed to a pretty empty life.

I also checked my rapidly aging body for cuts and contusions. I couldn't find any blood on me, a remarkable fact after having been blown out of an aircraft and landing in a jungle. Only my tailbone seemed sore from the impact. I thought about looking around for the pistol but quickly discarded that as a foolish idea. I sure as hell didn't plan on engaging in a shoot-out with these people. If I had a weapon, there would be that much more reason for them to shoot me on the spot in the event of capture. That made me think unwillingly of the reports that had been circulating of captured pilots in the south being shot rather than marched the long way north for imprisonment.

Cheered by that thought, I began casting my eyes around for the missing pistol after all. I didn't find it and the chances of doing so were small, given the nature of the foliage around me and the fact that it could have fallen out of the holster anywhere. I took another tiny sip of water as the aircraft engines began to grow louder. It sounded as though he'd throttled them back to conserve fuel, regardless of the occasional shots being fired at him.

I could see his features quite clearly as he passed over me, peering down at the collapsed chute. The engines seemed unbelievably loud. I remained on my knees but waved both arms at him, then pressed the transmit switch on the radio.

"Pretzel Two, this is Lead. Do you read?" I held the small radio as close to my lips as I could and barely breathed the words.

"Rog, Lead. I read you. A little weak, but clear. Are you OK?" I could have wept with joy. The thing really worked. It was as if a lifeline had been thrown to me.

"Yeah, Steve, I think I'm all right. I heard people pretty close to me just a few minutes ago, but I haven't heard anything since you fired the rockets. I'm pretty well covered here except for that damned chute hanging in the tree. Think you guys can get me out of here?'' There it was—blatant pleading. Like a child who needs to be reassured after a nightmare. I knew he would be doing everything he could to effect a rescue, but I had to hear him say it.

"I'm working on it now," he said immediately. Maybe the memories of his own shoot-down and rescue made him more sensitive to my plight.

"If I make a pass," he continued, "and let go a couple of rockets, do you think you could get that chute down without them hearing you? It stands out like a baboon's ass right now."

I thought for a moment about the noise of his engines and how loud the rocket explosions had seemed.

"Yeah, it's worth a try. They're sure as hell going to find me if it stays up there."

"OK, I'm going to come in from north to south and I'll fire two rockets, one at a time, and try to make a little noise with my guns. Give me a couple of minutes to get into position and don't move away from your chute because I'm going to be cutting it a little fine."

I clicked the mike button twice in acknowledgment and kneeled over into a sprinter's crouch. I listened carefully for any movement around me but could hear nothing. Even the insects seemed still. There was only the distant whine of the turboprop engines as Steve maneuvered his aircraft into position. The engines' intensity increased and I realized he'd turned in. Suddenly, there was a whooshing sound followed shortly by an explosion as the first rocket impacted. Automatic weapons began to immediately return fire. I heard the other rocket leave its tube. I suddenly had more noise than I needed or wanted. Spent rounds began to fall about my head. I grabbed my helmet and thrust it back on, then scrambled quickly to my feet and lurched to the dangling shroud lines. I hurled all my weight downward against them. They sagged, but nothing gave. Almost sobbing, I heard the Bronco firing its machine guns, getting ground fire in return. I hung from the shroud lines and swung my legs back and forth like a demented puppet. Then it was free and I fell the several feet back to earth, landing flat on my back. I lay for a moment trying to get my breath, the parachute draped over me like a shroud. General Giap and his entire staff could have strolled by me unheard because of the pulse pounding in my ears.

Finally pulling myself together, I began to roll the nylon into a ball. I became aware of a squeaking sound coming from somewhere beneath me. My earpiece had pulled loose again after my fight with the parachute and Steve was trying to raise me on the radio. When I called him, my voice sounded strange even to me.

"Pretzel Two, this is Lead. I've got the chute down but I don't know if anyone heard me or not. Do you think I ought to move or stay put?"

"I think you ought to stay right where you are if you've got cover," he said immediately. "There are a lot of people down there and if you start moving around they'll spot you for sure."

I sat back to mull that over after I acknowledged his transmission. I glanced at my watch and was dismayed to find that it was already 1630. Only about an hour and a half until dark. Night rescues were difficult even when all the conditions were right. Sometimes they're just plain impossible. I figured that Steve had about another forty-five minutes of fuel left. Anything longer and he'd be joining me in the jungle. He probably had relief coming to take his place.

"Lead," he broke in on my thoughts, "I'm going to move out to a wider circle so I don't give away your position. If you hear anyone coming, give me a call and I'll be right back. I've already alerted the control room and CCS. They're trying to get clearance to scramble fighters across the border. Honestly, I don't think they'll get it. But, whether they do or not, ole' Burl is cranking up the Mike Force and has all the CCS choppers on alert. Don't worry, we're going to get you out. But you know we don't have much daylight left and it's going to be the best part of an hour before everything's ready. It's going to have to be your call whether we try it tonight or wait till first light. Let me know what you decide and I'll pass it on. Rocky's on his way to relieve me, and if you decide to wait until morning either he or I will be on station all night."

"Rog," I whispered back. I wanted out right now, but I forced myself to sit quietly and think. I wiped my face with the bundled-up parachute I was still holding. The chances for a successful rescue would be better in the morning. But, that was assuming they didn't shoot off my sorry ass tonight! There was no way an aircraft, or a fleet of aircraft for that matter, could protect me from the little people once the sun went down. On the other hand, if they attempted the rescue tonight there was a good chance they'd lose additional aircraft or I might even be hit by friendly fire. Of course, if everything went smoothly I could be drinking beer in the hootch in three hours.

"OK, Steve, I'll sit it out for the night, but don't you peckerheads get too far away from me."

"We'll be within ten miles of you all night," he said soothingly.

"Just don't go blundering around the woods. Remember, they can't see at night either, so stay as quiet as you can, even if it looks like they're about to step on you. One of us will give you a call every hour all night. If you're doing OK, just click your mike twice. How are you fixed for water, by the way?"

He knew what was important. I must have already lost half my body's fluid through my pores. My clothing was black with sweat and my tongue was sticking to the roof of my mouth.

"I'm afraid I've lost most of it. I had the two cans in the vest but I've already drunk one of them."

"Just think good thoughts and hang on. You'll make it. I'm moving out now. Rocky will check in with you when he gets here and then I'd suggest that you turn off your radios to conserve your batteries. Take care. Out."

I listened to his aircraft drone away until I could no longer hear the engines. I wanted to pick up the radio and scream for him to come back, that I'd made a mistake and wanted him to get the rescue cranked up immediately. A mosquito flew up my nose and brought me back to the real world. There seemed to be thousands of them coming out of the rustling bamboo. Normally, they didn't bother me too much, but these were coming at me in squadron attack. Cautiously, I brushed some away from where they were trying to crawl inside my eye sockets. Under my breath I hummed a few bars of the "Dead March."

OK, what else could happen? I was sure that I'd seen the worst case and I was still alive. The answer came in a flash. They could kill you, you stupid jerk! Or they could capture you and tie you to a tree and leave you there forever. They could catch you and keep you in a cage in this jungle for the rest of your natural life and no one would know. The possibilities seemed endless. OK, think more positively. More than likely I would pass an uneventful night and be rescued at first light and have a great war story to tell for the rest of my life.

The idea of having something to boast about brightened me considerably. I began to look at my hiding place a little more critically. My fight with the parachute had enlarged my lair by quite a bit. I now had an irregular circle about six feet in diameter that had been flattened by my thrashings. The bamboo growing on three sides was so thick as to be impenetrable without a machete or a Rome plow. Some of the joints were as large as my upper arm and went up fifteen or twenty feet. The stuff was terribly noisy. Merely touching it sent rustling sounds all over the place. If there had been any sort of breeze I would have been able to have a sing-along under the cover of its noise. Unfortunately, not a breath of air was moving under the tall trees. At least no one would be able to sneak up on me from any of those three sides. On the other hand, there was no way I could sneak out should someone come in the fourth side. Some things you're better off not thinking about.

There was some bamboo growth on the fourth side, but it was much smaller—fishing pole–sized. It was clear that I had landed on the edge of a large grove of the stuff. The smaller joints were just taking over the scruffy undergrowth of what I was beginning to think of as my front door.

Crawling on my belly toward that undergrowth, I could see about twenty-five meters once I was clear of the bamboo. That meant, of course, that the enemy would be able to see me by the same distance. Crawling under one of the low-lying plants, I scraped the leaves aside from a spot on the soil and began to dig a shallow hole with my knife and hands. I had to get the chute out of sight. Glancing at my watch after the offending bundle had been buried, I saw it was now 1710. Perhaps another hour until darkness.

A voice called out, surprisingly close. I froze on my belly, heart pounding and breathing so loudly that it sounded like a waterfall in my ears. There was no doubt they were hunting me. They must have seen my chute coming down and then had it confirmed by the aircraft circling the area. I was too far from the bamboo to attempt hiding in it. I peered down the slight slope, eyeballs stinging with sweat that somehow continued to be manufactured by my body. Raising one hand I cautiously rubbed dirt from the jungle floor onto my shiny red face. Mixed with the sweat it immediately turned into mud.

I don't know how long he'd been there when I saw him. I hadn't noticed any movement; he was just suddenly there, about fifteen meters away, standing quietly at the edge of the clearest area. He carried his AK-47 at the ready and was dressed in a drab uniform with a small pith helmet. He looked quite young, but most of the Vietnamese did. He was looking at an area ninety degrees away from me, showing me his profile. As I watched he took a cautious step, looking carefully before he moved his feet. My God, he's a trained tracker, I thought. He'll notice this bamboo and know immediately that it's probably the logical place for me to be hiding.

He took two more steps, brow furrowing as he studied the ground.

It came to me suddenly. I had seen that look before. It was like the expression on the face of my son the first time he'd waded in the ocean and crabs had nibbled his toes. That look of caution and wariness was unmistakable. This was no skilled woodsman but more likely a city boy who was no more at home here than I was. He was probably right off the streets of Hanoi and would rather be anywhere else than in this vermin-infested place.

I watched carefully as he leaned against the boles of a huge jungle tree and dug an index finger into his nostril. He brought up the fruits of his labor for a closer inspection and, apparently dissatisfied with it, flung it away and tried the other. Finally satisfied, he glanced casually about the undergrowth, looking but not seeing. He gave a guilty start at the shout of an unseen person farther down the slope, then began to move on cautiously, watching his feet. He was out of sight in moments but for some time I could hear his clumsy progress and that of the rest of the search party.

My relief was enormous but I remained quiet, watching for any additional movement. It was well that I had, for another wave of searchers moved into view within minutes. These were closer together, three of them line abreast moving in the same direction the first group had taken.

I slowly curled my legs under my bush and mashed my face flat against the earth. Surely they'd be able to hear my heart pounding. But they moved on silently and steadily, the one on the flank passing within ten meters of my position. By this time I was so covered by dirt and detritus from the jungle floor that I must have resembled nothing more than another lump awaiting decay. They moved away and my heart slowed again. Jeez, you can take only so much fun at once. More movement, and I cautiously raised my face enough to peer in its direction. Yet another line of searchers moving wraithlike through the forest. These guys looked like they knew exactly what they were doing.

The whine of turboprop engines filled the air and the double line of soldiers began at once to jog rapidly away from the small clearing. It was an unmistakable sound; it was a Bronco. I made certain that there were no other surprises coming through the undergrowth, then scurried back to my bamboo lair and picked up the radio. As it warmed up I stuck the earpiece into place again.

"Pretzel, this is Pretzel 01," I wheezed.

"Roger, 01, this is Pretzel Three. Are you OK?" It was Rocky, who must have relieved Steve on station.

"Yeah, I think so. They've been crawling all over me for the last few minutes, but when they heard you coming they didied back to the bunkers, I guess. Is there anything the matter?"

"Negative, it's just that you missed the check-in and I haven't been able to raise you, so I thought I'd better come over and find out what was happening. But, if you're OK I'll go ahead and move on out of the area."

"Yeah, I guess everything is all right, Rocky. Talk to me in an hour, OK?"

"You bet. See you in an hour. Stay cool, boss. Out."

Yeah, stay cool. It was a good thing they couldn't see me, because it might have destroyed my image. I hunkered in my tiny clearing and tried to turn my mind to the exigencies of survival. The shadows were getting very deep now; it was already dusk on the forest floor. My watch showed almost 1800 and the equatorial darkness would soon fall suddenly. Perhaps another ten minutes of usable light. There didn't seem to be a lot I could do to prepare for the night. I couldn't think of any reason to leave my hole and venture into the coming darkness; my people knew where I was and that should be the biggest advantage in the rescue attempt.

I felt light-headed and dizzy, possibly either dehydration or the malarial bug I'd brought with me. I desperately wanted that last can of water to replace the fluids still being pumped out through my pores. I promised myself that if I waited I could drink the entire can at midnight. I pulled a large green leaf from one of the bushes, folded it, and put it in my mouth. Maybe I could suck a little moisture out of it. A tentative chew or two and I quickly spat it from my mouth, lips stinging. That sure wasn't the answer. Now I needed something to put out the fire that spread to my gums and tongue. To get my mind off my raging thirst and stinging mouth, I pulled the survival vest over to me and began an inventory. Fishhooks. Very useful. Pencil flares. All right! A keeper. A pulley and strap device to help you get down out of tall trees should your chute hang up. Tracer ammo for my .38 Special revolver. The two survival radios. A whistle, in case I felt like directing traffic on the Ho Chi Minh Trail, I guess. Concentrated food in foil packs, which I knew I'd never get down without water. The one can of drinking water, which I carefully set aside. I didn't trust myself to have it in my hand for too long. A red marker panel. A mirror. Two lemon drops. Two lemon drops! At least they looked and smelled like lemon drops, for they were stuck together and had melted and remelted so many times that they looked like little lumps of lava. They'd probably been tucked away by the previous owner of the vest some ten or twelve months ago. Bless his little chowhound heart. I popped them both in my mouth and almost immediately the saliva began to flow.

Rummaging further, I was delighted to find a small vial of insect repellant. I was about to douse my face when I remembered the stories that the grunts told of old Charley being able to smell the stuff in the jungle. Even though the mosquitoes had begun their attacks in earnest, I replaced the bottle in the vest. I also put back the other items I knew I wouldn't need during the night and slipped the vest back on. I placed my dog-tag chain with the tags, wedding ring, and can opener in one of the empty pockets for safekeeping and to reduce the chance of additional noise.

Looking at the bamboo, I vaguely remembered one of the jungle survival school instructors saying something about being able to get water from the plant. Well, I had a good supply of bamboo! I couldn't remember the technique you were supposed to use though. Using my K-Bar I cut off a section of thumb-sized stalk. Every movement made the damned stuff rustle like dry corn. I was a little disappointed when nothing ran out of the severed end. Maybe you were supposed to chew it, but after my experience with the leaf I was wary. Just a cautious lick or two.

Even through the numbness of my tongue the pain almost caused me to yell aloud as the bamboo splinter embedded itself. I carefully put my knife back into its sheath so I wouldn't lose it in the darkness, then removed the gloves I'd been wearing to discourage the mosquitoes. Grasping the offending sliver of wood, I tried to ease it out of my tongue, but it seemed to have grown barbs. No other way. I pulled and immediately clamped my teeth together to stop the ensuing scream, which came out as more of a grunt. Jesus, how do I get myself into these situations. Just forget about the damned thirst. You know you're not going to die of it before morning.

It was pitch black now and the luminous dial of my watch told me it was nearing check-in time. I inserted the earpiece again and turned on the radio. Why hadn't I heard my emergency beeper when my parachute opened, I wondered. As the parachute opened a small transmitter was supposed to send an emergency signal for use in homing in on downed pilots. I hadn't heard a thing, nor had Steve or Rocky mentioned it.

Too late to worry about it now. I replayed the scenario that had ended with me landing on the floor of the Cambodian rain forest. No matter how I tried, I couldn't remember a thing after seeing the gun fire until I was dangling in my chute.

"Pretzel Lead, this is 03. Sit-rep please."

The voice suddenly blaring through the earpiece startled me so much I actually lurched backward. Before I answered I peered quickly out into the darkness to see if my movements had attracted any attention. It seemed quiet enough.

"Yeah, Rocky. I read you loud and clear. Is anything happening?" I felt like a fool as soon as the words were out of my mouth. I knew it was too soon for the morning's plans to be firmed.

"No problems, Lead," he answered cheerfully. "I think we'll be on top of everything by the time we're ready to go. How are you doing?"

"Not too bad, all things considered," I whispered. "I'm sure getting thirsty down here."

"Yeah, I can imagine. By the way, Flagpole [CCS] wants to know if you have any injuries that could keep you from moving real smartlike tomorrow? Will you need any assistance in getting to and on the chopper?"

"Naw, I'm in good shape. Just tell 'em to get the bird here and I'll get on it. Can you tell me anything about what they're going to try?"

"Nothing's really firm yet," he said, sounding evasive. "Just get through the night and don't worry about it. Anything else?"

"I guess not. I'll talk to someone in an hour."

I turned off the radio and thought about the rescue. I shouldn't have asked what was going to happen in the morning. There was a good chance that the NVA were monitoring our frequency since it was not on a secure radio. They needed to hold their cards as close to the vest as possible. They'd let me know my role in plenty of time. Rocky was right. My job was just to get through the night.

If I listened carefully I could hear the hum of Rocky's aircraft, but it may have been my imagination. There was only a tiny sliver of moon to be seen through the tree canopy, accentuating the darkness below the boughs. Stentorian rumblings came from the undergrowth as the nocturnal predators and their victims fought for their lives in the darkness. Huge flying foxes were briefly silhouetted against the pale light of the moon before dipping into the darkness once more. A faint night breeze began to tug at the bamboo, effectively blocking out most of the nocturnal sounds. The air was moisture laden although the wet season was still weeks away. It was an ominous world and I thought of the survival school instructor who insisted that the jungle was our friend. Maybe to him, but to me it was a dark hell. I couldn't have felt more isolated on the moon.

The gunfire began about half an hour later, shortly after I heard the trucks starting up and beginning to move down the road. First, there was an occasional single shot, then bursts of automatic weapon fire. Again on my belly, I crawled to my observation point beneath the bush, mostly by feel, and cautiously raised my head. The firing sounded as if it were about 100 meters from my position. Voices raised in shouts joined the sound of the gunfire. I had no idea what was happening, but they seemed to be getting closer. Soon I was able to distinguish flashlights through the heavy foliage, then the muzzle blasts of the AK-47s. Then it dawned on me. They were using "recon by fire" in an attempt to flush me. They'd probably been monitoring the radio conversations all the time and knew that I was still alive somewhere in the surrounding bushes.

I scurried crablike backward into my hiding hole, then pressed as far back into the mature bamboo as I could before the stalks refused to bend. With my K-Bar I began to slash frantically at the ground in front of me, trying to build up a barrier between me and any gunfire that could come in my direction. In moments the jungle humus had yielded a shallow depression, which I crawled into. The loose soil I pushed in front of me.

I curled into the fetal position as the searchers moved toward me, shooting random bursts into the foliage in an apparent attempt to make me bolt. I might have done so if I'd had any place to go.

Again the searchers moved by me, coming within ten meters of my hiding hole. One burst of fire cut down a swath of bamboo over my head, almost causing my heart to stop. The yells grew fainter as they moved down the slope, and they were soon out of earshot. Having learned from the previous episode that there might be trailers, I remained curled on the ground, listening to my heart race. The gunfire was becoming muted by the damp air and heavy foliage when I heard the sound of aircraft engines again. I glanced at my watch, saw I had missed another check-in, and quickly pulled the radio from its pocket.

"Pretzel 01, this is Pretzel 03. Do you read?" I was afraid to answer aloud this time, even in a whisper. I squeezed the transmit button twice, the universal aviation signal to acknowledge that I was hearing him.

"Pretzel 01, I copy your answer. If you're all right, give me a signal."
Again, I squeezed the button twice.

"Pretzel 01, if you're unable to answer voice, let me know." Two more clicks of the button. "Do you wish me to leave the area?" Click, click.

"Roger, this is Pretzel 03, returning to orbit."

His engines began to fade and I crept from the bamboo on my hands and knees.

At 2200 another truck convoy began to motor along the road south toward the border. I wondered if my presence would make them reroute the vehicles. I doubted it.

My watch stopped sometime after midnight, probably due to the abuse it had received in the last few hours. Then I remembered to wind it and the second hand began its tireless circular journey once more. My nerves were getting frayed, for I'd almost panicked when I thought it was broken. My terrible thirst was making me devise ill-conceived schemes to get water. I thought of trying to slip from my hiding place and attempt to locate the stream over which the crossing ran, fill my belly, and slide back to my hidey-hole. I knew it was unworkable. Even if I weren't discovered, I'd never be able to find my bamboo grove again in the darkness. I tried to drain a few more drops from the two empty water cans, for I had long succumbed to and finished off the other ten ounces I'd been hoarding. It hardly seemed to get to my throat, for the tissues in my mouth absorbed it. I badly needed to replace some of the fluid I had lost through perspiration from my exertions, the heat and humidity, and the low-grade malarial fever still raging in my body. If, for some reason that I didn't even want to contemplate now, I was not rescued in the morning, I would have to get water from somewhere. There was no alternative.

Steve had replaced Rocky and was circling someplace out in the darkness. The check-in times had been reduced to every thirty minutes, in deference, I'm sure, to my slowly sinking morale. Even the tiny sliver of moon was gone now; the darkness bulged out around me but didn't allow me in on any of its secrets. Crawling things went about their nocturnal business and I scarcely gave a thought to their passage. My capacity to be terrorized by unseen varmints and reptiles had long since been exceeded and I scarcely flicked a glance when some night creature made his way past me.

In the distance my real enemy motored by in a steady stream of trucks. I needed human contact, not some disembodied voice coming out of the ether. Now I knew why most suicides take place in the ebb of darkness. I couldn't get any lower than this.

I was wrong. The leeches found me after midnight. Or more properly, I found them. Maybe they'd been there all along and I hadn't noticed. I reached behind my neck to brush away a particularly nasty mosquito when my fingers came in contact with a sluglike body hanging there. I knew immediately what it was and that I must be covered with them. If they were pulled from their supper the wound would invariably become infected. I didn't care. With my knife and fingers I tore loose every slimy shape I could find fastened to me. I even stood up and took down my trousers and opened my shirt. Having cleansed myself of them as best I could, I crawled under the bush where I had buried my parachute and felt around carefully until I found the mound of earth covering it.

Resurrecting the parachute, I folded it into a baglike shape and crawled into the middle, pulling it up around my waist; then I resumed my wait. I tried to think of my family, but that only filled me with more despair. I was almost ready to weep when Steve called for a sit-rep. He surely noticed my despondency, for rather than breaking contact as we had done before, he stayed on the air, chatting as if we were sitting next to each other in the hootch. He launched into a long, complicated story involving his hillbilly uncle and his mule, explaining the coexistence of a one-legged owner and his three-legged mule in his normal deadpan fashion. I didn't understand half of it but found myself chuckling silently. When he did sign off I felt much more cheerful and reasonably confident that I could see the night through.

Somehow the night passed. The first smudge of light of the false dawn came and with it a warm, moist wind blowing lethargically from the south. One way or the other my ordeal would soon be over. Steve and Rocky were both airborne now.

"Pretzel 01, this is 02," Steve called. "How ya' doin' down there?"

"02, I'm still here and that's about all I can say at this point. I'm ready to go home."

"Rog. We're about ready to go I think, or will be in a couple of minutes. As soon as you hear me getting close to you, I want you to shoot one of your pencil flares. It's still pretty dark under the trees and we want to make sure we've got your location. As soon as we've got you pinpointed, Rocky and I are going to start beating up the area around you, so keep down and put your helmet on if you've still got it. After we've worked out, the helicopter gunships will be coming in to work the area at low level. When they get through I'm going to put in a willie pete rocket right close to your position, something for the pickup slick to aim toward. He'll be coming in while the guns are working and will be directed by the air commander, just like in a team pickup. They won't be able to sit down because of the foliage, so they're going to hover and drop you a rope. Since you don't have a rig, you're going to have to tie that rope real good for the lift out. Remember that, tie the rope right and make it tight. It'll already have a noose in it. We'd sure hate to go to all this trouble and then have you fall out of the sling. They're going to have to drag you for three or four klicks to an LZ, where they can sit down long enough to get you inside, and then it's home again. The LZ has already been secured by half of the Mike Force; the other half is on board the other slicks and will be hanging around in case we need them. Any questions?''

"So, there aren't going to be any fighters, huh?''

"Negative.'' That one word told the story. Saigon had disapproved the use of American fighters to aid in the rescue attempt. Assholes! "Here we go!''

The pickup was almost anticlimactic, for it went just the way they'd planned. As soon as I heard the familiar whine of the OV-10s' engines heading toward me, I cocked and fired one of the small pencil flares. It must have made a highly visible target against the still-dark western sky. In moments both Broncos were overhead and circling and diving in the classic gunnery pattern, one diving and firing as the other pulled out from his run. They concentrated most of their fire on the area toward the road, though they worked over the entire perimeter. The sporadic ground fire directed toward them increased in volume as the helicopter gunships began their attack.

At Steve's command I fired another flare, then ducked to the earth as he placed a well-directed marking round within thirty meters of my position. The smell of the willie pete was strong. The clatter of the pickup slick was almost unnoticed in the bedlam around me, but suddenly it was there, hovering over an impossibly small clearing in the trees. Its rotors were clipping small limbs from the large trees as it jockeyed into position.

I had one arm over my face, shielding it from the downblast of the blades, when I saw the rope flung out the open hatch to dangle tantalizingly

out of my reach over the trees. The door gunner made motions for me
to hold my position. I could see his lips moving as he talked into the
boom mike, directing the pilot toward me. Then the rope was there as
the Huey pilot skillfully backed his aircraft toward me.

As calmly as I could I knotted the rope around my waist, distracted
by the guns working on the positions around me. I was finally able to
secure it and looked upward to see the gunner making wild motions,
pointing toward the rope. Following his directions I slipped the noose
from around my middle to under my arms. If they'd dragged me out
with it in the original position, I would have doubled over like a hairpin
as soon as the helicopter took my weight off the ground.

It was bad enough, anyway. The strain under my arms became almost
unbearable as the pilot pulled pitch and ascended. He lowered the nose
and started for the other LZ, dragging my lower legs through the top
tree limbs. The next few minutes were a blur as the windblast forced
my eyes closed.

The windblast slackened and before I was expecting contact my feet
hit the ground. Taken by surprise, I collapsed in a heap. Someone hit
the earth next to me and helped slide the rope from under my arms,
then boosted me in through the open hatch. Immediately, we were airborne
again and I watched as the green-clad figures of the securing Mike
Force ran into the clearing to board the other assault helicopters just
now touching down. They were airborne before we were out of sight.

We crossed the border at Bu Dop and only then did the door gunner
relax his vigil and grin at me sprawled in the canvas seat. He pointed
toward a five-gallon water bladder lying against the aft bulkhead. I went
for it greedily, trying to limit myself to small sips but finally giving
way and taking great drafts.

Burl and his medic were waiting for us at the helicopter pad. The
medic, a huge black man, leaped through the hatch as soon as the skids
touched.

"How ya' doing, Major?" he shouted over the rotor noise. "You
got any problems?" As he spoke he was running his eyes and hands
over my limbs and body.

I shook my head. "Just real tired and thirsty."

He helped me through the hatch and, joined by Burl, assisted me to
a jeep.

"You sure screwed up my schedule," Burl said with a huge grin.

I grinned back. I felt wonderful. My fever seemed to be gone and my skin felt reasonably cool and dry. My only problem was that my legs didn't want to support me as we walked into the command post at CCS. Another Special Forces sergeant came in with a new set of jungle fatigues and led me to the shower stall. There, one of the Nung mercenaries filled a tank with water and I was allowed to sluice my body. Dressed in my new fatigues I returned to the command post, where Burl kept the debriefing mercifully short since I kept nodding off in my chair. A general lassitude had overpowered the adrenaline I'd been living on for the last twelve hours.

My appetite still hadn't returned, so I only nibbled at the huge breakfast set in front of me, then dozed as one of the sergeants ran me back to my hootch in his jeep.

I staggered into the dayroom just as Baby Henry came in from the door leading to the sleeping quarters, scratching his ponderous, hairy belly. He was modishly clad in a huge pair of green GI undershorts and a pair of untied jungle boots. He was alternating sips of C-rat coffee with gnaws on a hard cracker from the same ration. He was also unaware of what had been going on all night.

"Jeez, Major. You ought to start trying to get a little more sleep," he said. "You really look like hell today."

"Yeah, you're probably right. I think I'll try to catch a couple of hours right now. Tell everybody to keep it down to a dull roar, won't you?"

"Sure thing. You want somebody to wake you up later?"

"If I haven't stirred by noon, ask the duty pilot to give me a shake. See you later."

I didn't bother undressing; I collapsed on the bunk and was instantly asleep.

No one had to wake me; the heat did that. I sat on the edge of the bunk and scrubbed my face with my hands. The singsong voices of the hootch girls were strident in the rear as they scrubbed clothes and called back and forth to one another. It was only 1030 but I felt refreshed. All traces of the malarial fever had gone and I was ravenous. I ripped open a fresh C ration and was heating water for the coffee when the field phone rang. The radio operator said that the group commander was inbound and had requested that I meet him at the strip.

We sat in my jeep in the shade of a huge rubber tree, watching the ground crew refuel the aircraft he had brought to replace the one I'd lost. The duty pilot would fly him back later. I wasn't happy and he knew it.

"First of all," he said, "I'm damned glad you're all right. That must have been a hell of a night."

"Yes, sir. It's not the kind of thing I want to do too often. I'd like very much for you to approve some citations for everyone involved in the rescue. They did great work."

"I know they did but I'm afraid it's not on. We can't even acknowledge that you were across the fence, much less that you lost a bird over there. Cambodia is still neutral, and we're not supposed to rub their nose in the fact that we and the NVA operate there at will. I'm sorry, but it's policy and we're stuck with it."

"Is that why I had to depend on the army to pull me out? Was it official policy not to send fighters to help? I seem to remember that when I took this job you said I'd be working for you and the U.S. Air Force. I had the distinct impression that you told me if anything went wrong over the fence, you'd do everything possible to help straighten it out."

"I know I said that and at the time I thought I could honor it or I wouldn't have said it. I think you know me that well. Right now, it all depends on the specific situation, and in your case I guess they figured the army could handle it best. And it seems like they did, didn't they?"

"Colonel, if you don't mind me being frank for a few minutes, I'd like to say that's the most chicken-shit explanation that anyone could come up with. It doesn't hold water at all. No one in the entire USAF except me and the two forward air controllers involved knew what my situation was. The only reason I'm alive today is my good luck in falling into a bamboo grove and the guts my people and the U.S. Army showed in getting me out."

He looked at me sadly. I knew that it hadn't been his decision, but he was handiest. "Do you want a transfer to headquarters to finish up the few weeks you've got left? I can find a place for you on the group staff. You deserve it. You've flown more missions than any field grade officer in the group, you know. It'd probably do you some good to get fattened up and dewormed before you go home. Your new duty is going to be at the Pentagon, isn't it?"

"Yes, sir. But if it's OK with you I'd just as soon finish up here. Right now I'm not feeling too kindly about any headquarters."

"That's it then. Well, I'd better be getting back to my desk. I've also brought up a new chute harness to replace the one you lost." He smiled. "Maybe I can even keep supply from charging you for it."

We walked back to his airplane that the duty pilot had finished preflighting.

"Colonel," I said before we got within hearing range of the others. "I want you to know that if this happens again, I'm going to do whatever I think is necessary to take care of the situation. And if that means scrambling fighters and leading them across the border, then that's what I'll do. If you think our foreign policy can't stand that, then you'd better relieve me now."

He looked at me silently for a long time before he spoke. "I wish to God somebody had done that this time. I hate this kind of shit and I wish somebody would blow the whole thing wide open."

The plane taxied out with him in the rear cockpit. I saluted as he passed and he returned it, then gave me a wink and a nod. How had things gotten so screwed up? I meant what I'd told him. I resolved that I'd do anything to get any of our people out of Cambodia and to hell with the consequences.

The point was moot though. Ten days later U.S. and South Vietnamese forces invaded Cambodia.

"You've got what?" I stared incredulously at Chicken Little. There were about twelve long hairs on his upper lip trying to pass as a mustache. He looked even younger than the eighteen claimed in his service record.

"Maybe I didn't say it right. Here sir, look at this. I had that army doc write it down for me. See? Satyriasis."

Turning my head to hide a smile, I said, "Yeah, that's what it says all right. Did the doctor say how he reached this rather unique diagnosis?"

"Well. I went to see him because I've been having trouble sleeping. Real restless, you know? And these crazy dreams I've been having." He blushed and turned to stare into the rubber trees as if he'd found something of real interest there. "Some of them have been getting pretty wild."

"And what did he tell you?"

"He just said that a few days in the world with the right kinda' professional help would fix me up. I told him that I thought I was going crazy or something because I've always been a real good sleeper and now all I can think of is pu . . . uh, women. Then, he said that most of the men stationed out here seem to have the same thing and not to worry about it. Jeez, do ya' think it's contagious?''

"Yeah, and I expect the rest of us have it to some degree. Don't worry about it."

"You don't think this could get me an early Date of Return then?" He looked disappointed.

"I doubt it, Chicken. If it could I don't think there'd be anybody left to fight the war. It's probably best to wait till your regular DEROS comes up. That's not long from now, is it?"

"No, sir. I've got twenty-eight and a wake-up!"

"Well, it would probably be best if you just soldiered on until then. You know, if you mentioned it to headquarters it'd probably take them twenty-eight days to get anything done so you could leave early, and by then what would be the point?"

"Yeah, you're probably right, Major. You don't think I could pass it on to my girl, do you? I've got some pretty good plans for her." He tried to leer but it came out as a boyish grin.

"No, I'm almost positive that particular disease only infects men and my limited experience has shown that women, while unaffected by it, have their own special variant when the proper setting is provided."

He pondered this for a moment, brow furrowed in thought. "Well, I'm going to write Mom and tell her. I've been here durned near a year and never had a scratch, so at least I can tell them that I've caught some fancy foreign disease. I don't have to tell her what I went to see the doctor about."

"If I were you, Chicken, I don't think I'd worry them about it. You know how mothers are. It's probably turning her hair gray just you being over here. If you mention some foreign disease you've contracted, I'm sure it would really bother her. Like the doc says, just wait till you're home and it'll probably cure itself."

"I guess you're right. She worries enough as it is. Do you think it'd be OK to tell my girl about it? Naw, I guess not."

"I think you're doing the right thing. And don't you worry about it either. Trust me, a few days after you get home you'll be sleeping like a baby again."

"OK, Major. Thanks a lot. You be real careful up there today. You're getting real short too, ain't you?"

"Yep. We're both pretty short now. And Chicken, I don't want you or the other guys worrying too much about what doc tells you, 'cause he's got a pretty bad problem himself, you know."

"What's that?" he asked, eyes widening in anticipation of some scandal to pass on about the officer corps.

"Well, it's not general knowledge, but I think I can trust you to keep it to yourself. I'm afraid the doc has picked up one of these new strains of social disease; you know, one of the real bad ones."

"You mean the doc has got the 'Black Siff'?" This was almost too good to be true, his eyes told me.

"Looks that way. I understand he may even have to go to 'the Island' and you know what that means."

Chicken was silent as he thought on the ramifications of the poxed doctor being banished to that mythical island where victims of a VD strain too virulent to be unleashed on the American public were languishing their lives away while watching their limbs drop off, one by one.

This information was almost too delicious to contain. Chicken Little almost pushed me into the cockpit and he fastened my harness to the chute in record time. As I taxied to the strip I saw him running toward his hootch, anxious to spread the word of the doc's banishment from civilization forevermore. Laughing aloud, I figured this might help even the score in the fight that had begun when the doctor announced in the staff meeting that one of the FACs had contracted a disease that was normally acquired from buggering goats. Mess with the Air Force, would he!

The team had been running for almost six hours. It was Baby-san and his group again, and his voice was showing the exhaustion he must have felt. A real problem had developed since they'd been ambushed. They were now almost entirely surrounded and had not had the chance to stop long enough to locate themselves on the map. If they dropped a smoke grenade to get some airborne help and directions, the NVA, only steps behind them, would have them pinpointed. The triple-canopy jungle was too dense to use the normal methods of identifying them— mirrors or colored panels. In short, we didn't know where the hell they were.

Everything had been going very well. There had been no opposition to their insertion the previous day; their objective was to snatch a prisoner and get him aboard the pickup chopper and back into South Vietnam for interrogation. The team was all highly experienced and led by Baby-san, who had more trips across the fence than anyone in CCS.

Shortly after insertion they took their positions alongside a much-traveled trail and waited for a suitable candidate. The snatch had gone perfectly. Using tried-and-true techniques the team had pounced on an unsuspecting NVA soldier walking alone on the trail, injecting him with a sedative to insure his placidity. Experience had shown the folly of trying to get an unwilling man aboard a helicopter. With the prisoner in a pleasant fugue, they were walking and carrying him to the pickup zone.

I had already alerted the pickup ship, which was only moments from the small clearing, when the gods of war decided things were going too smoothly. The team walked right into the middle of a returning NVA patrol. Both sides had been surprised, but the team reacted first by opening fire, then conking their prisoner over the head and taking to their heels in the opposite direction. They'd been running ever since, with the size of the hunting force growing larger by the moment.

The helicopters had long since returned to refuel and sit alert across the border. Steve had relieved me once and I had just retaken his place.

"Pretzel 01, we're going to have to make a stand pretty soon," Baby-san panted over the radio. "Everybody is just about out of steam."

"I understand. Do you want me to launch the birds?" I hated to ask him that, but it was his decision to make. If the helicopters were launched and the team could reach no usable LZ, they would soon have to return for more fuel, leaving those on the ground with few aerial resources while they made the thirty-minute round trip. A lot could happen down there in thirty minutes.

"Look," I said before he could answer. "I've got an idea if you want to try it."

"Go ahead, Pretzel. We're plumb out of ideas down here."

"It may sound a little dangerous but I can't think of anything else. You say you can hear me circling pretty close overhead, so what I can do is to fire a rocket into the trees and hope that it doesn't hit you. When you hear its explosion, take a bearing on it and guess at the distance. At least it's something to work with because we honestly don't have the foggiest idea of where you are now. It's your call though."

"Let's do it, 'cause we can't go much farther."

"OK, Baby-san. I'm rolling in now so listen up for the impact. Good luck."

I lifted the nose of the aircraft high above the horizon, gave the ailerons a little pressure toward the left side of the cockpit, and watched the ground swing around until it was over my head. Holding the aircraft inverted for a few moments, I searched the green canopy for some distinctive target. One particularly bushy emergent caught my eye and I nudged the nose of the aircraft toward it with the rudder and aileron. Pulling the nose through the horizon I centered the gun sight on the tree and rolled the aircraft upright, then punched the firing button on the stick and watched the rocket wing away.

"Not too far away, Pretzel!" Baby-san said excitedly. "My bearing to the explosion was about 280 degrees from our position. I'd estimate the distance to be about 150 meters."

OK, if the team is 280 degrees *to* the explosion, then it should be 100 degrees *from* the explosion to the team. Elementary, my dear Watson. I flew directly over the smoke of the rocket hanging in the bushy treetop and banked hard left to put the aircraft's directional indicator on to a heading of 100 degrees. Then I began peering hard into the forest below me.

"You're right over us," Baby-san called, "but they're right behind us!"

"OK, your best bet for a pickup is almost due north, partner. There's a string of Arc Light craters running east to west about a hundred meters or so due north. Do you want to try that?"

"Hell, yes! Anything is better than this."

"Right. I'll get the choppers launched and heading this way. Hang in there, Babe!"

I quickly switched to the helicopter alert frequency and found that they were already starting engines. They'd been monitoring the radio, and although they'd heard only my side of the conversation, they realized that a pickup attempt was about to be made. The air commander said they'd be on station within fifteen minutes.

In moments the team burst from the jungle and ran toward one of the bomb craters, staggering with fatigue. One waved a hand at me before they started preparing their defensive positions. Each laid his red marker panel on the lip of the crater in front of him, identifying their position for the airborne forces. With their backs to one another and weapons pointing toward the hostile jungle, they looked like very lonely and defiant little figures.

The six of them had spaced themselves evenly around the crater, which was an old one with crumbling and eroded walls. The jungle had reclaimed most of the blast-cleared area around it. I stayed at 800 feet and circled well away from them on the off chance they hadn't been seen moving into their defensive position. They had.

"They've found us, Pretzel! We're taking fire from the south and southwest. It looks like they're trying to flank to the west. How long before the birds get here?"

"Any moment now." I didn't have the heart to tell them they were still fifteen minutes away. I had all my rockets except the one I'd fired at the tree, and a full load of machine gun ammo. But it would go very quickly. I'd have to try to conserve what I had until the guns arrived.

"Where do you want my fire, Baby-san?"

"Anywhere south. Work the whole quadrant."

"Rog. Here I come."

Flicking my arming switches to fire the rockets in singles, I made a hard diving turn to allow me to strafe parallel to the team's position in the event that one of the rockets strayed. I punched the firing button three times, raising the nose a little between each to walk the missiles across the enemy's front. All I could see was the team in their crater and the treetops.

"How did those look?" I asked.

"Just right!" he answered, the rifle fire in the background almost drowning out his transmission. "But they're closing the noose pretty quickly. You can work it around us on either side now. Don't worry about the north yet. We haven't received any fire from there. Concentrate on the south. That's where the heaviest stuff is coming from. Where are those damned choppers? We've already got two WIAs down here."

"We hear you Baby-san," the air commander called. "We're about ten minutes out. Hang on, Buddy!"

I went back to work, making passes on either side of the crater. My ammunitions were disappearing at an alarming rate.

"We're about two minutes out, Pretzel. We've got you and the team's location in sight," the gun team leader called me. "Where's the best place to put our ordnance?"

"Just about anywhere you want to," I answered. "They look like they're all around the crater now. I'm going to pull up and get out of your way and let you people work. I've been receiving ground fire primarily from the south side, but they've also moved around the crater, I guess, because there was at least one gun shooting at me from there on the last pass.''

"Rog," he replied tensely.

I perched at 1,000 feet and watched the fight continue below me. Taking advantage of the substitution, I drained one of my baby bottles and listened to the guns calling ground fire locations to one another. They were using their loads at a prodigious rate. I saw that one of the team members below was now lying in the bottom of the crater. There had been no contact with them for several minutes. All too soon the gun leader called me.

"Pretzel, we're out of ammo. Can you take over?''

"Yeah, I've still got about half a load left.''

The air commander broke in. He and the pickup slick had been orbiting outside the battle area, waiting for the gunships to subdue the ground fire sufficiently to permit the extraction.

"Pretzel, we've got three more gun birds en route. They should be here within fifteen minutes.''

"OK, but I'm going to be reduced to firing single rockets and only two guns at a time,'' I told him.

"We've got no choice.'' How true.

The quarter hour that followed turned bizarre. I alternated firing passes with dry passes in which I didn't trigger off a rocket or gunfire. I felt silly when I found myself making ''brrrring'' noises in an inadequate imitation of machine-gun fire.

"Pretzel, bring your fire in to twenty meters and give us 360 degree coverage,'' Baby-san said resignedly. "They're right on top of us.''

Twenty meters! My God! I can't shoot that well. Nobody can. But I knew they had to be desperate or they wouldn't have made the request. I looked at the crater closely. It would have to be with the guns; no telling where one of the rockets might head. And it would have to be *low!* Can't take a chance shooting from a normal altitude. Well, shit!

Down lower, I could see the NVA firing from the foliage. My first pass was dry. I wanted to look the place over closely from low level. Pulling out just above the treetops, I made a low-level turn, nudging the top rudder enough to keep the low wing out of the branches, and aligned myself for the first firing pass.

An explosion tore a hole in the leading edge of my right wing. I barely glanced at it, concentrating instead on aiming the quick burst of fire from two of my guns. I was close enough to watch the bullets walk over the forward rank of NVA troopers crouching in the thin foliage of the blast area around the bomb crater. Jesus, they were close to the team! As the 7.62 rounds waded among them, some turned their weapons away from the bomb crater and aimed them at me. Little sparkles of fire came from their barrels. I watched in a detached sort of way, concentrating on my own stream of death licking the ground.

The attacks blurred and ran together. I seemed to be in a constant turn trying to keep the bomb crater in sight. My own sense of vulnerability returned when I delayed one attack a moment too long to pursue a group of running figures and consequently flew into a treetop. It filled the windscreen and just as suddenly I was through it, the turboprops chewing at the foliage like a hungry caterpillar. One of the two engines began to run rough and out of sync with the other. But the Bronco was still flying.

"Pretzel," the air commander called, "the new gunnies are coming on station. How ya' doing?"

"I'm dry, completely out of everything. I'm going to perch upstairs again."

The drama continued to unfold as the fresh gunships took over the team's defense. They were firing furiously, closer and closer to the bomb crater. At the radioed command, the pickup bird began moving toward the beleaguered team. The ground fire had slackened somewhat after the air attacks but was far from suppressed. The guns swarmed around the slick like angry wasps. With ropes trailing from it, the slick approached the pickup zone, then nestled over the crater like a brooding hen, still some ten feet in the air. Some of the figures in the crater moved sluggishly about, connecting the ropes to those showing no life. The radio frequency was filled with the staccato voices of the pilots calling hot spots to one another.

After an eternity the slick began to rise slowly from the green prison, ropes tightening with the strain of lifting the team members from the crater. I could see pieces of the fuselage being blown from the helicopter, yet it continued its methodical withdrawal.

"Coming out," the pilot announced calmly. Thuds of weapon fire were audible in the background of his transmission as rounds continued to gouge his fuselage. I counted the bundles hanging beneath the slick. All six team members were there.

One was dead and the remaining five were seriously wounded.

The allied forces were out of Cambodia and the rains were starting again. My year was almost completed, just two weeks and, heigh-ho, the World. I was one of the few who had refused to keep a short-timer's calendar, for counting every day of a year seemed a sure way to make it seem longer than it actually was. But I had succumbed at last and would find myself idly doodling the number of days remaining when I should have been writing effectiveness reports. We normally tried to cut some slack for those rotating home in two weeks or so, but we were too undermanned for me to quit flying early. Steve had departed, and though his replacement had arrived he was still untrained.

And I had another problem. Those madmen in the green beanies were cooking up something new. The Cambodian invasion had revealed an even more extensive road network than previously supposed. We had thought that the covert highways were contained within twenty klicks or so of the border. The evidence now showed that the NVA were active on roads much deeper than that and in areas uncleared for B-52 strikes.

CCS had planned a night parachute drop from one of the agency C-130s; the team would complete its recce mission, then walk back toward the border far enough so that the pickup helicopters would attract only the normal amount of attention. At the last moment, however, someone higher up had scrubbed the use of the transport aircraft. Burl was trying to convince me that they could complete the mission by having the team jump from the rear of our OV-10s.

"You said yourself that those things were built to carry three men in the back, didn't you?" he said.

"I know I said that," I snapped, "but there are a lot of problems with jumping people from back there that you don't know about."

"Like what?"

"Like the fact that the way the teams go out, they weigh twice as much as a regular jumper. Like all we've got to communicate with them when they're back there is one light that I can turn on to let them know when to jump. The rest of the time they wouldn't have the foggiest idea what's going on. Like you're talking about a night jump, and how in hell are we going to be able to navigate accurately enough over strange country to put 'em on the target. Like none of our pilots have any experience as a jumpmaster who can decide on winds and crap like that. I could go on for the rest of the night.''

"Well," he said, "I don't see any insurmountable problems so far. We can work out something. Like why do you want to talk to them anyway? Hell, they ain't that good at it. I'd just as soon try to talk to a rock ape. Besides, only half of them can speak English. And we can pare 'em down on the weight they'll carry; those little indig people weigh only about ninety pounds. We can put one of our sergeants in the backseat of each aircraft to act as jumpmaster and they can help you navigate. Hitting the target exactly isn't really that important, just as long as they can all get together once they're on the ground. We can choose a general area where there's not too much chance of them going into the trees.''

"Why can't you just drop them from the Hueys or insert them in the normal way?" I asked. "These guys are all used to being toted in choppers, and besides choppers have the advantage of being able to pick them up right away if something goes wrong.''

"You know as well as I do that the minute a helicopter crosses the border the dinks are tracking it the entire time it's over there. Now, you guys with your bright, shiny Broncos could go up to, say, ten, twelve thousand feet and nobody would pay you the slightest bit of attention. You could be at the DZ in half the time it would take the choppers and could just ease down, shove 'em out, and nobody'd be the wiser.''

"Nobody but the Cambodian Air Force. They do have fighter planes over there, you know.''

"Don't sweat that. Those Buddha-heads ain't going to launch after you at night.''

"OK, just for argument's sake, let's say we did it. How do you expect to cover them all to hell and gone out there. Your gunships would have about six seconds on station before they'd have to get out of the area with low fuel. It'd take them the best part of an hour, and they'd be able to make about one pass. And who would the team let know if they did have trouble? You know we can't sit out there and fly radio relay for them the way we do closer to the border. Over here we can say that we're sorry we strayed across, but that's not going to sell way over there. Besides, we'd have a SAM up our ass before the first hour had gone by."

"Our commo people in Saigon say that if you guys were to fly in our regular areas just over the border, but up at about eight thousand or so, you probably wouldn't have much trouble picking them up. And as far as covering them, we won't. The team knows what the situation is. Maybe it'll make them be just a little bit more careful if they know that Wyatt Earp and his gunships ain't gonna come riding over the hill to rescue their sorry asses."

"That's what I like about you, Burl, you're a real humanitarian."

"Don't sweat it, kid. It'll go like clockwork." He sat back and grinned.

"Yeah, just like clockwork. Like all of them do."

The team was on the flight line, and we were trying to show them how it was possible to fit three loaded men into the back of the OV-10. The planes had been designed to carry three people but only if you went about it properly. The cargo doors had been taken off the two aircraft that we were going to use for the mission and Rocky was trying to explain the arrangement.

"What you're going to have to do is crawl in backward and scrooch up all the way to the forward bulkhead, then spread your legs as far apart as you can so the next guy can crawl in and shove his butt up close to your crotch. Then, he spreads his legs and the last guy snuggles up to him the same way, and you're all wedged in as close as peas in a pod. To get out, you hook up to this cable that runs along the bulkhead and use it as the anchor static line. When the light comes on, you're going to have to kinda' duck-walk on the balls of your ass and push off at the edge of the hatchway. We can help you out by raising the nose of the airplane kinda' sharplike so you can slide. Any questions?"

The Americans repeated the explanation to the little Khmers, and amid much giggling we had a couple of dry runs. We assigned spots after considering their weights. The launch was set for the next day and the spirit of the team members was high. I doubted if the Khmers had ever jumped from an aircraft, but they didn't seem particularly worried.

"Let me add one thing," I said. "We're not going to have any belts to hold you in back here, so tomorrow on takeoff be sure you're holding onto the sides real tight. We'll see if the crew chief can't come up with some kind of strap over the door to keep you from falling out, but even if you slide a few inches you're going to have a hell of a time getting back into position."

The team leader explained to his indig team members what I had said. We went over the light drill once more; I decided it wasn't going to get any better by beating it to death, so I waved so long and left. Rocky and I had some hard planning to do if we didn't want to drop them all in downtown Phnom Penh.

We found an unused corner of the command post and spread out the maps that would cover our flight. We knew that many of the night checkpoints available to most fliers would not be available for our use. In a world of small villages and few towns, the lights may or may not be visible. It depended on the time and the amount of foliage absorbing the pale glow from small lamps. Rivers were good if there was enough moonlight to pick up their reflection. There was virtually no night road traffic with headlights to identify the scant highways—unless the NVA turned on their lamps. For most of the route there would be nothing but unbroken jungle beneath us, as dark and featureless at night as the ocean.

We eventually planned a series of four legs designed to aid navigation as well as disguise our true destination. Maybe the NVA would think we were a pair of recce birds making nocturnal flights over the countryside. The chosen drop zone (DZ) was a flat-appearing piece of land almost a kilometer square in size. We plotted the heading and distance from our last checkpoint, the confluence of two streams some two klicks away from the DZ. The map showed no population areas for some distance, provided the NVA hadn't moved in, in strength.

The map work completed, we discussed some of the technical problems we might encounter, like how to get the aircraft off the ground with that much weight on board. The center of gravity would be altered a great deal by the addition of the three men and their gear. Neither of us had ever flown the aircraft with any significant weight in the cargo bay, so it was going to be guesswork. We would also have to carry maximum fuel; not only was the trip long, but one of the aircraft would stop at the border on the return to act as radio relay until the team gave the secure signal. It should work.

Everyone was at the flight line before dusk, the team hyper and full of jokes, the support crew fussing over them like broody hens. The air force ground crew watched the strange goings-on from a prudent distance as if they might catch something if they got too close. The brigade FACs had turned out to see the departure, alerted in some unspoken manner that something unusual was happening.

Our ground crews, assisted by the CCS cadre, literally lifted the team members into the cargo bays, where they faced aft and squirmed backward until they fit spoon fashion against one another. Their youth was striking, the oldest being perhaps twenty-four. Their loads had been pared but still just managed to fit inside. They wore no reserve chutes.

Rocky and I each checked the three we would be carrying and crawled into the cockpit. I was leading and, after the start, made the radio call and began to taxi onto the runway. Night was falling rapidly. Rocky aligned his aircraft slightly behind me and to my right. It was too dark to see his face, so I turned off my wing lights. He responded that he was ready by turning his off, then back on. I flicked my light switch back on and advanced power to begin the takeoff run.

As the aircraft gained speed the nose began to rise of its own volition, long before I wanted it to, although I had cranked in almost full nose-down trim before starting the roll. The stall-warning horn was screaming at me as the aircraft left the ground, despite the fact that I had the control stick full forward. I wrestled it for a few moments until I had enough flying speed to get it back under control.

"Rocky, give yourself full nose-down trim," I radioed. "It flies like a tub of shit with those people back there."

I adjusted my cockpit lighting until it was so dim I could barely see my instruments, then I turned to a heading that was aimed for our first checkpoint, just over the border. A half moon was rising, its glow still too weak to help us recognize features on the ground. Odd, I thought, that most people think all modern warplanes have myriad modern navigational systems that could take them anywhere in the world. Would they believe that we were sitting here using techniques that went back to Lindbergh?

"Pretzel 03 is in position," Rocky called. I saw him about half a mile behind me and 500 feet low, as we planned.

"Rog, 03. You can turn off your lights. Let's go secure."

We switched into the secure radio mode, coming up to the first checkpoint at 10,000 feet. The small village slid beneath us. I turned to our new heading, then started the stopwatch for a dead-reckoning time check to our next fix. I flicked on my wing lights to let Rocky know I was turning and watched as he turned on his own briefly in acknowledgment.

Mine came back off then. We'd be doing without them now except for a quick flash at each turn point. Not the healthiest situation with another aircraft in close proximity, but better than letting someone watch us all the way in.

Occasionally, I could see the moonlight reflect off the other aircraft's canopy. The night air was incredibly smooth, and even with its extra weight the aircraft seemed to float effortlessly. Away to the south, lightning flashes darted from the huge billowing cumulonimbus clouds of the southwestern monsoon, creeping closer every day. South toward Tay Ninh, I could see one of the air force gunships firing on some target, its Gatling guns pouring out rounds so rapidly that the stream looked like incandescent water from a hose. Straight ahead, nothing but darkness. You could write a poem about a night like this.

"I gotta' take a piss!" So much for poetry. I'd forgotten about the CCS sergeant in the backseat. His simian build had inspired the nickname "Monk." He had further assured himself of notice by tastefully shaving his head, leaving only a single strip of hair in the middle in Mohawk fashion. Behind the appearance and vocabulary was one of the most knowledgeable men I had ever known on the subject of Southeast Asia.

"Well, Sarge," I said, brought back to reality by his pithy remark, "you can do it in your pants in the Special Forces manner, or if you don't care whether your friends think you're a sissy, you can do what we in the Air Force do and use the relief tube. It's in a bracket on the left bulkhead, by your left knee."

"Hmmm, knowing the Air Force, I thought they'd probably equip these things with little thunder mugs with little pink flowers painted on them."

Ignoring that tasteless bit of interservice jealousy, I checked the time and saw that we should be over our next checkpoint in four minutes, provided the winds were anything like predicted.

On schedule, the small lake appeared. The wind estimates they gave us must have been pretty good. I flashed my lights and started my turn, looking for Rocky over my shoulder and catching the briefest flicker of his wing lights. He was still in position.

The remaining checkpoints appeared on time, and where they should have been, and we were soon bearing on the drop zone. I had purposely aimed a few degrees to the left on our last heading so that I'd be sure to know which way to turn when I hit the river. The moon was up higher now, which made identification of the river very easy. I called Rocky this time instead of using my lights.

"Pretzel 03, I show us coming up to the final checkpoint. Do you concur?"

"Rog, Lead. I'm sure this is the right river. If we turn right and follow it for a couple of klicks we ought to be right there."

"OK, you'd better take up drop position."

He would stay about a mile behind me in order to make sure my jumpers had cleared the area before he came ramming through. He'd also climb 500 feet above my altitude. During the flight he'd stayed low so he could watch me against the sky rather than the dark jungle.

"OK, Sarge. The DZ is coming up," I said over the intercom. "Do you want to circle or just fly right over it?"

"How have the predicted winds been holding at altitude?"

"Just as forecast—light and variable. I don't think there's really enough to worry about."

"OK. Alert 'em and let's fly right over the middle of this mother."

I triggered the switch for the cargo bay light. The next time it came on would be the signal to jump. We peered into the darkness below us, broken only by the ripply light reflecting from the sluggish river. Directly over the final checkpoint I turned quickly to the preplanned heading and started the stopwatch for the final countdown.

"We should be over the leading edge of the DZ right now!" I said as the clock swept around.

"Hold it steady and drop in ten seconds," Monk said from the rear cockpit.

I watched the sweep second hand closely, and as it neared ten seconds I flicked the light switch again. Almost immediately I felt the aircraft respond as the load began to fall away. I helped them out by jerking the nose of the aircraft suddenly into a thirty-degree climb. It was flying like an OV-10 again.

"Jumpers away!" I called over the secure radio. I didn't expect an answer and I didn't get one. Rocky would be too busy with his own job at the moment. I turned to a southerly heading, which would put us on the first leg back to the border.

"All jumpers away, Lead," Rocky called.

The flight back to South Vietnam was nice. The air remained good and in the distance I could see the soft glow of some of the larger Cambodian towns. We didn't have to worry much about the navigation, and at this altitude there was little danger of ground fire. Soon we were able to pick up some of the radio navigational systems from South Vietnam. We monitored the team's frequency, and in a much shorter time than I would have thought possible they called to report that they were all together with no incapacitating injuries. Good news, for night jumps usually had casualties.

Rocky broke away at the border to act as radio relay for the team until they called secure, while I headed directly for Quan Loi. Burl and his NCOs met us at the strip, anxious to hear in detail about the drop. I let Monk do most of the talking, and it was apparent he'd kept a very detailed log in his head. A couple of beers and then to bed.

By noon the next day the team was sending a steady stream of information back to CCS through the radio relay ships. Convoys of NVA were barreling down the roads, day and night, and long columns of troops passed with little fear of observation or attack. Within seven days the team had mapped a good portion of the newly discovered road net. Everyone was in good spirits and Burl happily plotted coordinates for B-52 strikes once his team was clear. Then the gods of war stepped into the game again.

The team had been relocating to a new observation position and the men were crossing a road, one at a time, during the night. One of the Khmers stepped to the tree line on the far side of the road and right into a North Vietnamese patrol. When challenged, the Khmer answered in his native tongue while pulling the pin on two frag grenades; he hurled them and dived to the ground. After the explosions, the team opened fire, then turned on their heels and fled. The NVA patrol had probably been sent to investigate the radio signals that shouldn't have been there.

Rocky had just returned from his airborne stint as radio relay when I got to the flight line with the news. My aircraft was ready and a hurried job of refueling put him on the line as well. We launched together, passing over the border at high speed. The alert helicopters were just getting off the ground and would be almost an hour en route. We tuned in the team's frequency and monitored the conversation between Blue-bird—the team's call sign—and the army 0-1 aircraft relaying for them.

We kept the aircraft at full throttle until we approached their position. I recognized the confluence of the two rivers from the week before when we had dropped the team.

"Bluebird, this is Pretzel 01. I'm about two minutes out and I've got Pretzel 03 with me. How can we help?"

"Ah, roger, Pretzel. We're about a klick west of the road we gave you in the last position. We've just crossed a little stream that runs north and south. Wait, I think I can hear you. Yeah, steer a little north and it sounds like you'll pass right over us. We're heading southwest. I don't think you're going to be able to see us in all this foliage."

He was panting hard over the radio. They'd been running for several hours before they were able to get a message through.

"Most of the pursuit," he continued, "seems to be north of us, but getting closer. OK, you just passed in front of us about half a klick from the sound of it. Can you give us some idea which way to go?"

"One thing's for sure," Rocky transmitted, "if you keep going in that direction the choppers are going to have a hell of a time picking you up. The trees only get thicker, and I don't see anything for seven or eight klicks clear enough to even pull you on strings."

"I agree," I said. "There's a good-sized dirt road that's open on both sides almost due west of where I think you are. Looks to be about two, maybe three hundred meters away. The only problem is that the gomers could be there too."

"I guess we'll just have to go and see," Bluebird said.

I called Rocky on the interplane frequency, the team unable to hear it. "03 this is 01. You got any ideas? The helicopters won't be here for half an hour or so and that could be too late."

"I'm fresh out," he said. "I'm afraid that by the time the choppers get to the road the NVA will already be there if they're not there now. But there just isn't any other place to send them that I can see."

Looking around the area I had to agree with him. The rain forest was as thick as any I had seen. "I sure wish they'd picked some other direction to run."

We continued to circle helplessly over the tree canopy. A large flock of parrots, disturbed by the engine noise, exploded from one of the bushy emergents.

"We're at the road!" the radio operator gasped. "They're not far behind us. How far out are the choppers?"

"Not far now," Rocky said soothingly. I'm sure he didn't fool them for a moment.

"I'm going down to take a look," I said, no plan in mind.

Rolling the aircraft inverted, I pulled back the throttles to keep the airspeed from building up and eased the stick in my lap. The aircraft came level about a hundred feet off the ground, flying directly down the road. I glanced under the tree line on either side of the red dirt road and saw no ground fire, so I concentrated on trying to spot the team. Suddenly, they were there, and then I was by them, climbing sharply back to altitude.

"Take a look at it, Rock. I'll watch from up here."

He immediately put his aircraft in a near-vertical dive, leveling just above the road and flying down it slowly. He waggled his wings as he passed the team, then hauled the aircraft quickly back to altitude.

"Boss," he said. "Are you thinking what I'm thinking?"

"Hell, that road's as good as our airstrip back at Quan Loi and it's just about as wide. Are you willing to try it? It could get hairy if they catch us."

"Yeah," he said, "and that team's dog meat if we don't and they know it."

"OK, hero. Let me talk to the team. Let's go back to their frequency."

"Bluebird, this is Pretzel 01. Here's the situation. The choppers are at least twenty minutes out, and I'm afraid if we wait for them the little folks are going to have the road so covered that it's going to be a hell of an extraction. But that road looks smooth and straight enough for us to get these airplanes down there and off again. Are you willing to try it?"

"Hell, yes!" he answered immediately. "Just tell us what to do."

"Well, you all were in these same planes a few nights ago so you know what the cargo bay is like. The only difference is that we put the doors back on them. Now, the door handle is on the right side back there as you look forward, and once you're in, the last man is going to have to shut the door before we can take off."

I wasn't really sure about that but I didn't want to play test pilot on this trip.

I continued: "Make sure that one of the Americans is the last man onto the airplane so he can do that. Leave all your gear that isn't classified because we're not going to have room for any damned souvenirs. We'll try to come to a stop pretty close to your position, but if you do have to chase us down just make sure you don't come toward the aircraft from the front. We don't need anybody walking into the props. Tell your indigs about that. As soon as you're aboard, rap the floor with your rifle butt two or three times. Real hard. The pilot will flash the jump light two or three times, and then hang on 'cause he'll be hitting the throttles right away for takeoff. The other plane is going to be strafing the woods about seventy-five meters back from the road while I make the first landing. Then, I'll do the same for him. Just hold on and don't worry about it because there's probably going to be some wild gyrations taking place. Then, back to home plate after the other ship is up. Any questions?"

"I've got it," he said. "But let's do it right now. We can hear them coming through the woods."

"Got any questions, Rocky?" I asked over the interplane frequency.

"Just let me know when to start shooting."

"Any time, amigo."

I powered back and dropped the landing gear and some flaps as I lined up with the road. I tried to forget everything except making the airplane touch down just where I wanted it. The ground came up quickly but I didn't lift the nose into a flare as I would have done for a normal landing; instead I let the sturdy aircraft bang straight ahead onto the road in the manner of a carrier landing. I needed to get the wheels on the ground quickly so I could pull the throttles back into reverse range for added braking. I did it so well that I had to add power to speed up my taxi toward the team's position.

"I think the road's smoother than our runway," I transmitted to Rocky. I heard explosions and looked to my left in time to see him pull out of a rocket run. He seemed to be shooting close to the road but I guessed that was just my new perspective.

Three figures burst from the jungle, the single American towering over the other two. As I drew abreast of them they scrambled for the rear of the aircraft and I felt bumping and shifting as they clambered aboard. Three distinct bumps. I hoped they'd been able to shut the door properly. I flicked the jump light twice and immediately began to move the throttles forward. With the extra weight the aircraft accelerated like a sick chicken. Glancing down I double-checked that I had full nose-down trim this time; I didn't need another fight like I'd had the other night.

Looking up I saw several figures run into the road well ahead of me. Automatically, I squeezed the gun trigger on the stick. Nothing happened. Swearing, I took my hand from the throttles, quickly threw the proper arming selectors, and squeezed the trigger again. This time a satisfying burst of gunfire chewed up the road behind the figures firing at me. They turned and scampered off the road.

This time the aft center of gravity worked well for me, allowing the nose to pop off the ground when I released the forward stick pressure I had been holding. We were almost a hundred feet in the air when we passed the tiny men at the jungle's edge. I looked away from them; I really didn't want to see them shooting at me. Then we were over the trees and I could see the other aircraft starting his approach.

"Land short, Rocky," I called over the team net. "There are people about half a mile past the team's position. I'll try to take 'em out and stay out of your way."

"Rog," was his terse reply.

I could see the three remaining team members backing from the tree line to the road. They looked as if they were firing, but I had to look away to concentrate on my own strafe. I made as gentle a turn as I could in consideration of my three passengers trapped in the dark cargo bay, but even so I had to pull the aircraft around quickly in order to be of some use to Rocky. Flicking the arming panel switches to "salvo," I nosed the aircraft toward the area where I'd seen the NVA. As the altitude passed 400 feet I punched the button on the stick and watched the seven rockets wing toward the ground, then punched it twice more in rapid succession. I didn't really care whether I hit the NVA or not, I just wanted them to keep their heads down for the next few moments.

"Here we go!" radioed Rocky. And then, "We're taking fire from both sides of the road."

I watched in helpless silence. By the time I could get into position to suppress the fire it would be all over, one way or the other. They'd either be off and out of it, or they'd be dead. The bird stayed on the ground for a long time, then lifted and, as it gained airspeed, started a hard climb over the trees. As he turned toward the border I cut him off in the turn and snuggled into a close formation position on his right wing. He rolled into level flight.

"I'll look you over," I said, then eased the throttles back to slide behind and look at his fuselage and tail. "You've got about a dozen holes, most of them in the tail. You're in pretty good shape. Want to do me?"

I watched as he moved smoothly clockwise around my aircraft before settling into position by the right wing.

"You've only got three or four holes but they're all right through the cargo bay. We'd better alert the meat wagon in case they hit some of your people."

I was consumed with dread when we touched down at Quan Loi. Maybe I'd been hauling back a load of corpses. We'd contacted and diverted the helicopter team on the flight back, then radioed ahead for medical assistance.

I taxied quickly into the revetment after landing and shut the engines down immediately. A crowd gathered at the aft end of the aircraft, out of my sight, as I struggled to release myself from my harness. As I crawled to the ground I saw all three of my passengers on their feet and gesturing wildly with their arms, telling their audience about how close the AK rounds had come to them. I was so relieved I thought my knees were going to give way. I wobbled over to a jeep and sank into it sidesaddle. Rocky joined me there. I solemnly shook his hand.

"That was damned good work you did, my friend," I told him.

"Aw, shucks, coach. It weren't nothing."

The team walked over to us and each member shook our hands. The Khmers also made little bowing motions to each of us. The team leader cleared his throat.

"There is no doubt in my mind that you two saved our asses," he said. "I just want you to know that if there is ever anything I can do for you, name it. I mean it. Any time, any place."

"Forget it, Sarge, it was a pleasure doing business with you."

"Buy me a beer tonight and we'll call it even," Rocky told him with a grin.

"You've sure got that!" he said, grinning back, and walked toward the truck.

"Let's go get some chow," I said. "It's been a long morning."

The end came almost too quickly. One day I was flying combat missions and the next I was packing to leave for Bien Hoa, where I would spend my final two days in-country with the required processing. The party the previous night had been one of the great ones. I began to get maudlin late in the evening and had to be reminded by the others that the whole year had been bullshit and not to forget it. In a way I suppose it was. I couldn't see anything that I'd changed by spending another year of my life in South Vietnam. Maybe I knew myself a little better, but there had to be a more pleasant way to do that. Certainly, I didn't feel that I had helped the Vietnamese. Perhaps I'd helped some of them stay alive a little longer, but I'd sure been instrumental in the destruction of more than I'd saved.

At the Bien Hoa processing center, the sergeant tried to figure out how many and what kinds of awards I'd be receiving at my new duty station.

"Jeez, Major. They've got you in for the Silver Star, two Distinguished

Flying Crosses, twenty Air Medals, two Vietnamese Gallantry Crosses, and a whole shitpot full of other stuff. You're going to look like a frigging general when you put all that on.''

"Yeah, I'm a regular Steve Canyon. Let's do this as quickly as we can, OK?"

"You bet, sir."

I watched him finishing up the form I'd hand-carry back to the States, and thought how ironic it was that governments could get men to do things for tiny pieces of metal and ribbon that it would be impossible to get them to do for money. Not an original thought, I was sure.

Turning in my weapons at Supply was the strangest feeling yet. For only brief moments of the past year had I not felt the weight of the .38 Special swinging on my hip. It felt oddly unbalanced to walk without it. My K-Bar knife was already en route to the U.S. in the bottom of my footlocker. I wasn't about to give that old companion of a night on the Cambodian jungle floor to anyone who didn't appreciate it. In its place I turned in a rusty old air force survival knife.

And then it was over. Nothing else to do until wake-up at 0500 the next morning. My flight wouldn't be leaving until 1000, but there are some inviolable rules in military travel, the primary one being that troops must be required to hang around long enough to be completely pissed off by takeoff time.

I wandered back to the O-Club and found that I was already looking forward to the air-conditioned sleep I'd have that night. Toying with a beer, I listened halfheartedly to the raucous conversation of a group of newly arrived FACs, still awaiting their duty assignments. Jesus, had it really been a year since I'd been sitting there like that? I started to join the conversation, then thought better of it. They'd ask a lot of questions that I probably didn't have answers to. Better to let them find out for themselves. I couldn't recall anyone giving me a piece of advice that was worth a damn, or that made a bit of difference one way or the other. Take that back. Steve had told me that if I ever went down, to act like a tree. He'd been right. OK, make that 99 percent of the advice I'd received hadn't been worth a damn.

I'd expected to be on an emotional high at this point. Instead I felt flat, almost bored with the idea of going home. Now I was going to be like everyone else, nothing special. I went to bed as soon as the sun was down.

The next morning as I packed my B-4 bag, I suddenly thought of my wedding band, still hanging on my dog-tag chain around my neck along with the GI can opener. I took the ring from the chain and looked at it closely before slipping it onto my finger. It was tarnished almost completely green from the humidity and sweat of the last twelve months. I tried to brighten it with a piece of toilet paper but with little success. It slid over the second joint of my finger as if it belonged to someone else. I stared at it, puzzled for a moment, then really looked at myself in the mirror.

The face staring back was long and gaunt, the ears protruding more than I remembered. The body under the ill-fitting khaki uniform looked as if all the spare flesh had been burned from it, leaving behind not a trim-looking beachboy but rather a worn-down farmer, burned a deep brown by the sun. A white band across my forehead and eyes showed the outline of my helmet visor. Red dirt was so embedded in the skin pores that it made an exotic coloration, more Indian than Scandinavian. The picture was completed by one of nature's beauty marks, in this case a tropical ulcer, tastefully located on my neck by the right ear. Jesus, would Mary Ann even want me back?

Things moved rapidly once the inbound Pan Am jetliner set down. The fresh troops were herded from its innards and returnees almost jogged up the ramp to fill the still-warm seats.

Five hours later we were in Tokyo, landing for fuel. We disembarked, and the expected one hour on the ground turned to three. Finally, an announcement told the weary troops to reboard. The next leg would take us straight across to the States.

I hung back and let everyone go before me, since I was sitting in the forward section. As I finally climbed the stairway, an aircraft in front of us started its engines and as the pilot advanced his power to taxi, the jet blast blew tiny cinders over me. I reached up with both hands to brush them away, and on the downstroke my wedding band flew from my skinny finger and rolled in front of the aircraft. I stared at it, then feeling other eyes on me, turned to see the flight attendant looking at me sympathetically.

"Do you want to try to find it?" she asked. "We could ask the captain if he could delay the engine start. I don't know if he'd do it but we could try."

I gazed in the direction the ring had taken under the nose of the aircraft.

"To hell with it. Let's go home."